To Hear the Word

1,2,5,6

To Hear
the Word

Invitation
to Serious Study
of the Bible

by
MILTON P. BROWN

MERCER

ISBN 0-86554-251-1 (cloth)
ISBN 0-86554-252-X (paper)

The paper used in the publication meets
the minimum requirements of American National Standard
for Information Sciences—Permanence of Paper
for Printed Library Materials, ANSI Z39.48-1984.

Library of Congress Cataloging-in-Publication Data

Brown, Milton P.
To hear the Word.

Includes indexes.
1. Bible—Textbooks. I. Title.
BS605.2.B76   1987   220.6′1   86-31082
ISBN 0-86554-251-1 (alk. paper)
ISBN 0-86554-252-X (pbk. : alk. paper)

Contents

A NOTE TO THE READER

Those accustomed to seeing B.C. and A.D. ("before the Christian era" or "before Christ" and "in the year of the Lord" or during the Christian era) as era designations will note that the common-era designations are employed in this book, namely, BCE and CE (before the common era and [during] the common era).

Preface

This book has come together as the product of many years' experience (and no little trial and error) in trying to teach college students how to study the Bible. In fact, in some sense those students have become my partners over the years in the sifting of material and final formation of a course in "Introduction to the Bible," and I gratefully acknowledge their contributions—largely unwitting—to the present volume. Student response both in class and out has been an invaluable guide in the selection of topics treated and in finding the appropriate level of discussion.

My debt to my own mentors and to others who have written introductions will be obvious to the reader who endures to the end, and the footnotes and "suggestions for further reading" indicate something of the extent of that debt. But beyond particular literary reference I owe much to my colleagues in the Religion Department of Rhodes College (formerly Southwestern at Memphis), from whom I am constantly learning and whose support in this project has been most encouraging. To the president and the dean of Rhodes College and to the Faculty Development Committee I am especially grateful for the financial assistance and research grants in support of this venture.

For the patience and technical advice of Mercer University Press, I am also thankful. But most of all, I have to look back in admiration and gratitude to my most faithful reader and merciless critic, my wife Anne, without whose prodding this book might not have been finished.

Milton P. Brown

Introduction

Of making many books there is no end, and much study is a weariness of the flesh.

Ecclesiastes 12:12bc, RSV

This quotation from "the Preacher" has proved to be a favorite with many generations of students, some of whom no doubt subscribed to its sentiments long before they read it in the the Bible. And yet here is another book to add to their bibliography, still another cause for weariness, they might say. Why? As if the Bible itself were not long enough or hard enough to understand, do we really need more books *about* it?

That is a fair question, deserving a fair answer. But to treat it as seriously as it ought to be treated, we need to deal with both its general and its particular aspects—first, why the seemingly endless list of books about the Bible? and, second, why *this* one in particular?

To raise the general question is in effect to ask, "What *is* the Bible, that it should have been (and continues to be) the focus of such attention?" What is there about this book that so many other books are written about it? The answer, it may be suggested, lies in a set of circumstances and characteristics that we may divide, for the sake of convenience, into three categories.

1. For many people, the Bible is *sacred literature*—that is, Scripture. The contents of it, whether all or some part, have for centuries served Jews, Christians, and Muslims as a source of religious and ethical direction. Its value as authoritative Scripture to these continuing communities of faith is a primary consideration in any attempt to explain its distinctive appeal as the subject of "endless" books. While it is conceivable that some parts of biblical literature *might* have survived the ages on their literary merits alone, apart from any canonical status,[1] the best historical evidence indicates how

---

[1] By "canonical status" I mean the position of honor and authority given to the books as normative, sacred Scripture for the community. The meaning of *canon* as applied to the Bible is discussed in ch. 2.

very important the role of religious bodies has been at virtually every phase of the Bible's formation. Most of the books of the Bible (if not all) were (a) composed by members of a religious body—whether Jews or Christians; (b) collected and preserved and copied by the community; and (c) read, studied, and otherwise used by the community and by its heirs over the centuries. While it is not wrong to think of the Bible as one of the world's "classics"—along with Homer's epics, for example—it would be a mistake to assume that its status rests on exactly the same grounds as that of other ancient classics. Again, what sets the Bible apart and makes it the perennial object of attention that it is, is its place of honor as the fount of wisdom and the medium of inspiration for certain communities of believers.

But how does this account for the "endless" list of books *about* the Bible? It is easy enough to explain in this way why the Bible itself is the "all-time best seller," as the Bible societies and publishers keep reminding us, and why there are so many new versions and translations printed. But what about all those *other* books? Why the plethora of commentaries, concordances, handbooks, introductions, and surveys—*ad infinitum?*

2. The Bible is *ancient literature,* the product of a people and a culture far removed from our own. As such, it demands interpretation in order to be understood in every new time and place where is is read. The Bible is *not* self-explanatory, even to the community of faith for whom it is Scripture. In fact, it is very largely out of that community's desire to understand and make newly relevant to its own day the Bible's message that most of those other books have been written. Hence the plethora of various exegetical aids—dictionaries, concordances, and commentaries of all shapes and sizes.[2] These are nothing new; the demand for such aids in interpreting the biblical texts, in trying to find their meaning and relate it to the needs of the ongoing community, was implicit from the beginning, as later chapters will make clear. But through the ages, first among the Jews and then among Christians, the attempt to live by the teachings of that ancient (and

---

[2]"Exegetical"—from *exegesis* (Greek ἐξήγησις), "a leading out"—is a term embracing basic methods of finding out what an ancient writer meant by the words he used. Dictionaries of the Bible (for example, the new Harper's edition prepared by Paul Achtemeier, et al.) explain the most important words and phrases. Concordances list (usually) *all* the words and where they are found in the text. Commentaries provide a running explication of the text, usually book by book (even verse by verse), and vary as to degree of technicality and amount of detail.

increasingly alien) Book in an ever-changing historical situation has necessitated the continual scholarly inquiry into its meaning, which is represented by the countless volumes written about it.

3. The Bible, moreover, has had a powerful influence on the social history of Western civilization, shaping the minds, mores, arts and political institutions of at least half of the world's inhabitants. Far beyond the confines of synagogue and church, the impact of biblical ideas on the "secular" world of Europe, then of the Western Hemisphere, was such as to leave indelible impressions on the intellectual legacy that is ours today. Many groups and movements in history have claimed some portion or passage of the Bible as incentive or sanction for their programs, for good or ill, and often with no regard for the traditional communities of faith. Kings were crowned and uncrowned, laws made and repealed, wars were fought, and national boundaries were drawn—all by people who were consciously or unconsciously motivated by principles derived (or thought to be derived) from the Bible. And especially for the "founding fathers" of the American colonies it was a formative force, not only in justifying the War of Independence but also in molding concepts of political and economic justice that still operate in our public lives today.

In short, while in the strictest sense it may be said that the Bible belongs to those communities for whom it is Scripture, in a wider sense it is fair to say that it has been adopted, appropriated, and to a great extent absorbed into the larger culture of which most of us are a part. And to that extent the Bible has been and continues to be a matter for study among nonbelievers and agnostics as well as among believers. For its value as a dominant and pervasive influence on human history—to say nothing of the particular arts and letters—the Bible enjoys a place in the curriculum of many public schools, colleges, and state universities. And rightly so, for there are those who would insist that no education is complete without some attempt to understand one's cultural roots, the ideological sources of one's own heritage.

In view of the Bible's place in history, then, it is not surprising that "outsiders" as well as "insiders" (people identified with some body of believers) have made notable contributions to that endless list of writings. It seems that the Bible has provoked a wide range of reaction among its readers—almost everything from the sharp cynicism of a Friedrich Nietzsche to the sympathetic appreciation of a Mohandas Gandhi. But whether hostile or friendly, the reaction of many illustrious "outsiders" has become a part of an ongoing dialogue involving people of various religions or philosophical persuasions, all of which testifies that the Bible touches the nerve centers of human life and raises questions that are of concern to the world at large, not just to Jews and Christians.

Now to address the second, more particular, question: why *this* book? Another quotation from the Preacher (Ecclesiastes) comes to mind at this point.

> What has been is what will be,
> and what has been done is what will be done;
> and there is nothing new under the sun.   (Eccl. 1:9)

In one sense, perhaps, the world-weary sage was right, and maybe writers of books *do* tend to repeat ''what has been done'' already, so that ''nothing new'' remains to be said. It is true, of course, that one way we learn is through repetition. In the sciences the repetition of experiments, under various controlled conditions, is indispensable. In fact, in almost any discipline advances are made, not by ignoring ''what has been done'' but rather by demonstrating its value and building upon it, or showing up its weakness and finding something better.

In any case, few writers seem to be deterred by the thought that what they have to say somebody, somewhere, at some time has said before—much less those of us who have taught many generations of students and know there is always a possibility of fresh insight or of new ways of dealing with old material, however often it has been discussed. New generations raise new questions about the Bible, as about anything else, and sometimes the old answers no longer satisfy. Moreover, scholarship in biblical studies has not stood still; if anything, it has tended to run ahead of most of the questioners, especially those adults whose last serious attempt to read the Bible was in a children's Sunday School class. But in the past fifty years changes in approach and developments within the discipline have been so drastic or so rapid as to create tensions within the membership of certain denominations and, in some instances, even divisions. Discoveries in the sands of Egypt, the caves of Qumran, and the archives of ancient Ebla—to name but a few[3]—have greatly illuminated and broadened the historical setting of the Bible, enriching and correcting our earlier

---

[3]See ch. 5 for a more complete account of recent discoveries and their significance for interpretation of the Bible.

picture of the people who produced it. Over the past century remarkable gains have been made in amassing valuable manuscripts of the text, unknown to translators of the King James Version, serving now to remove scores of previous perplexities and resulting in vastly improved translations. Because of these and other such developments in the study of the Bible, the danger is not that there is nothing new to say about it; the danger is rather that the benefits of recent scholarship may somehow be confined within the scholars' halls of ivy or encased in such technical jargon that the nonspecialist or layperson has little chance of enjoying them.

This book is devoted to an effort to make those benefits available to people who are not Bible "scholars," but who are seriously interested in reading the Bible with understanding and appreciation. Much of what this book contains can be found elsewhere, often in much more complete treatments, and many of these sources will be listed in the suggestions for further reading listed at the end of each chapter. If there is any claim of originality to be made, it will lie in the attempt to summarize in (mostly) nontechnical language what the scholars have to say in their various fields of expertise, and to bring under one cover matters usually treated in many separate volumes. Whatever may be lost in brevity, it is hoped, may be gained in convenience.

To use this book to best advantage readers will need to refer to the Bible itself at virtually every turn. This book is not designed to introduce (in the usual sense of that word) every book of the Bible nor will it replace the standard commentaries; readers will do well to make use of such aids as the occasion demands. At the opening of each chapter there is a list of sample passages that are especially relevant or exemplify somehow the topic of that chapter, and a careful reading of those passages will be essential. Use of the Revised Standard Version, the Bible ordinarily cited in this book, is recommended.[4] In connection with the chapter (4) on the English Bible, it will be appropriate to compare readings from other versions, like the New English Bible or The Jerusalem Bible, as well as the time-honored King James Version.

This book is an attempt to prepare readers (and would-be readers) of the Bible for what they find there by way of a few "prolegomena"—to use a scholarly word for things one ought to read or know beforehand. It rests

---

[4]Especially useful is *The New Oxford Annotated Bible with Apocrypha,* ed. H. G. May and B. M. Metzger (New York: Oxford University Press, 1977).

on the assumption, often confirmed by experience, that careful explanation of certain matters *in advance* of detailed or in-depth study will be re-
warding in terms of better understanding what the Bible contains and of
greater appreciation of its meaning in specific places. If it means standing
at a distance, at first, from encounters with particular texts, it is only in
order to gain perspective and to see the whole forest before examining the
several trees. This approach can sometimes do much to reduce the misconceptions that beset those whose acquaintance with the Bible is at best
secondhand, and perhaps to remove some common misgivings about the
value and direction of biblical scholarship today. Our prolegomena will take
into account many ways in which the study of the Bible has changed in
recent times, calling attention to questions that seriously disturb some people, questions for which we may not have any simple answers to offer. The
aim in such cases is to present as objectively as possible what has changed
and explain how and why, leaving the reader some foundation for reaching
his or her own conclusions. No doubt this author's own point of view will
sometimes become obvious, but an honest effort has been made to minimize its intrusion, and the intention of the book is to describe and inform,
not to convert or indoctrinate.

Relevant Passages in the Bible*

(in the order of their appearance in chapter 1)

Joshua 24	**Ruth**
Exodus 15	**Malachi**
Judges 4-5, 14-15	**1 Chronicles 28-29**
1 Samuel 4-6	**Ezra 5-7**
2 Samuel 9-11	**Ecclesiastes 1-4**
Genesis 1-3, 37, 39-50	**Daniel 1-2, 7**
Amos 1-7	**Galatians**
Isaiah 5-7	**Mark 1-8, 14-16**
Deuteronomy 12-15, 26	**Acts 6-15**
Habakkuk 1-2	**Revelation 4-10**
Jeremiah 7-10, 36	**John 1-4, 18-21**
Psalm 137	**1 John**
Isaiah 40-46	**2 Peter**
Haggai	

---

*See also the chronological list, showing the relative dates of all the books, at the close of ch. 1.

Chapter 1

How the Bible
Came to Be

There was a time when there was no such thing as the Bible. This simple statement may seem too obvious to mention, but it does come as a surprise to many people to realize that the *Holy Bible* has a history and a beginning, just as any other book or books. The Bible has been so much a part of our common heritage in Western Civilization generally that it is easy to assume that it is one of those things we have had with us always; given its special status as God's Word for Christians, it is at least understandable if some of us never stop to ask about the Bible's origins in time. It is understandable, but unfortunate still, because the story of how it came to be, or why there *is* a Bible, is not only a fascinating story but also something very important to the proper appreciation of the Bible's meaning.

Our word "bible" comes from the Greek phrase *ta biblia* (τὰ βίβλια), which means "the books." This term was first applied to parts of the Jewish Scriptures around the year 100 Before the Common Era (BCE),[1] and was used by the Christian author of 2 Clement (about 150 CE) to refer to what Christians now call the Old Testament.[2] But what was "bible" to

---

[1] See the so-called "Letter to Aristeas" in R. H. Charles, *The Apocrypha and Pseudepigrapha of the Old Testament*, (Oxford: Clarendon Press, 1913) 94-122.

[2] 2 Clement 14:2. By the mid-second century the collection of books held to be sacred by Palestinian Jews would have included approximately the same number of books as are now included in the Jewish Tanak (or *Torah, Nebi'im, and Kethuvim*); see ch. 2 for further particulars.

the latter was a somewhat larger collection of books than what was "bible" to the former, and neither one meant what a Christian of three centuries later would mean by that term. In other words, the Bible came into being and *grew* into its present form (or forms) over a considerable period of time; in fact, the Bible (as we know it now) has existed for a shorter time than it took to grow up! The process by which this growth took place is the subject of the first two chapters of this book.

In this chapter the focus is on that part of the process that we may call "composition"—the origin of the books, their variety, and their historical setting. In the next chapter the focus will be on "canonization" or the process by which those books achieved their special status as sacred or Holy Scripture. In a sense, it is true, these are but two aspects of a single line of development, and my separation of them is to that extent artificial. On the other hand, for the sake of simpler explanation and less risk of confusion, it seems preferable to consider them in sequence. Thus, also, I may give proper emphasis to one recurring pattern in the picture—that, in general, "canonization" or recognition of a given book as authoritative Scripture occurs only after that book has been read and has served the believing community for some time.

But now what can be said of the composition, the very earliest "publication" of the writings that now make up our Bible? "Publication" in ancient times was, of course, nothing like our modern, highly mechanized technique, but we use the term simply to refer to the appearance in *public* of a document or some part of it. And we have to understand that the "public" we have in view, when we speak of the contents of the Bible, is in the first instance the covenant people of Yahweh (יהוה), God of Israel, and later the people known as the Jews. The earliest authors of the books were members of that particular people, participants in that unique religious cult, and whatever they wrote, they did so in the interest of their nation and their God. This fact is basic to all else that can be said of their books.

At the outset it should also be said that our attempt to reconstruct the way those ancient documents came into being, or to identify the historical setting of them, is based on long and complex investigation by many scholars, too many to mention at this stage.[3] Many of the statements we are about to make rest on the kind of studies we will discuss later on; many

---

[3]The reader may find it helpful to consult the suggestions for further reading at the end of chs. 1 and 5, in which these scholarly findings are more fully explained.

are made, in fact, as inferences from a reading of evidence that is in itself ambiguous or capable of variant interpretations. In short, it should be obvious that we are dealing with a very obscure development, where direct testimony is often lacking, and about which even one's best inferences must be tentative and open to revision. But, of course, that is the character of historical reconstruction.

Before 1000 BCE. Those who have made thorough investigations in the literature of the Old Testament, where the oldest books are to be found, agree that most of Israel's earliest "records" were carried in the corporate memory and transmitted by word of mouth. This was so among the ancients generally. Although writing was an art developed by the Sumerians, as well as others, long before the days of Abraham, its use was restricted in most ancient societies to a privileged few, mainly to scribes especially trained for the task and, often, retained for service to rulers of state. Ordinary folk managed very well without the ability to read and write, because they were preoccupied with the more mundane business of survival, and if any bit of news or any piece of family "history" was important enough to remember or repeat to their children, they did so, building up over the generations a body of folk tradition.[4] This oral tradition was kept fresh and continually polished by repetition, whether a tale of a tribal ancestor told about the campfire of shepherds, or perhaps a listing of "rights and duties" for the parties sealing a covenant. Often, as is the case of Israel's patriarchal stories (of Abraham, Isaac, and Jacob), tales of past heroes and their covenant with their God would become a part of the cultus, a part of regular celebrations in which such stories were recited in order to inspire the descendants of those heroes to emulate their faith and courage. Gradually, what may have started as mere tribal lore was transformed, by extension to others and by incorporation into the cultus, into a kind of "affirmation of faith."[5]

It is reasonable to assume that over the years some details would drop out of the stories of the ancestors, and others would be drawn in as occa-

---

[4]"Tradition" means simply what is handed down from one generation to the next, and use of the word to refer to biblical material is not by any means to prejudge the "truth" of it, nor to call into question the inspiration of such material. Readers are requested to await later discussion (ch. 6) on the matter of inspiration.

[5]See a clear instance of such a "creedal affirmation" in Deuteronomy 26:5-11, where the offering of "first fruits" (probably at a harvest festival) is the occasion for gratefully recalling god's acts of deliverance and care from Jacob through the settlement in "this land."

sion demanded, but the conservatism of cultic usage would assure the basic stability of the tradition. Indeed, as the very form of certain stories now shows, what was remembered and repeated was only what served the purposes of the community of faith. There was no "history" in the sense of research, like that of Herodotus or Thucydides among the Greeks, but what took shape among the tribes of Israel in this period was a rich assortment of testimonies to the faith of the fathers, at first only loosely joined together by connection to a particular holy place, or perhaps by association with a certain ancestral name, like Abram or Jacob. Scholars have conjectured that Joshua's covenant-renewal ceremony (Joshua 24) at Shechem gives us a good example of the kind of occasion we must imagine: having called the tribes (perhaps tribal representatives) together, Joshua recites at length the story of Yahweh's covenant with his people Israel, then solemnly charges the congregation, including some who had never before identified themselves with the Lord,[6] to dedicate (or rededicate) themselves wholly to this god, forsaking all others. The people swore an oath of loyalty, and we are told that Joshua "wrote these words in the book of the law of God."[7] We can no longer say what book that was, or what form it took, but the writer of the book of Joshua (composed centuries later) lets us know here, as he does elsewhere, that he is citing an ancient source.

The writers or editors of later times made no secret that they were using and citing older sources. Sometimes they named the source; other times they did not. Two examples of sources mentioned by name are the "Book of Wars of the Lord" (cited in Numbers 21:14-15) and the "Book of Jashar" (quoted in Joshua 10:12-13 and 1 Kings 8:12-13). Neither of these books has survived intact, and like the lost "Book of the Chronicles of the Kings of Israel"—cited frequently in 1 and 2 Kings—they are known to us only by name.[8]

---

[6]See especially Joshua 24:14b. The case of Shechem was probably not unique, but may reflect a rather general procedure whereby Israel's covenant with the Lord was extended to their Canaanite (but distantly related?) neighbors. Modern English Bibles most often use the name, "the Lord," for the Hebrew יהוה, as did the ancient Jews, who did not vocalize the name of their God.

[7]Joshua 24:26a. In the view of many literary critics the notion that Joshua wrote some formal document at that time is anachronistic—a reading back of later practice into earlier times—and, though not impossible, is not very probable.

[8]These "Chronicles" are not to be confused with the books by that name in the Bible, books evidently composed much later than those of Samuel and Kings.

Though no datable documents have come down to us from the times of tribal confederation, we have good reason to suspect that numerous pieces of poetry, found embedded in later books, actually originated very early—some, possibly, at the scene of the action described. Investigation shows that, on the whole, tradition in poetic form, especially song-form, has the greatest durability. Bits of lore in rhythmic meter are more easily remembered and more accurately preserved in oral transmission than the same lore handed on in prose narrative. One possible example of this is the Song of Miriam (Exodus 15:21), as she led the women in their dance to celebrate their safe passage through the Sea of Reeds.[9]

> Sing to the Lord,
>   for he has triumphed gloriously;
> the horse and his rider
>   he has thrown into the sea.

The careful reader of Exodus 15 will notice another quotation of this verse (only slightly altered) in Exodus 15:1, but here the song has been expanded (probably by a lyricist of some years later) and attributed to Moses, not Miriam. It is a clear illustration of the way such bits of tradition tend to develop or grow through incorporation with ever new experiences of "the mighty acts of God."

Another instance of early poetry set into later narrative is the Song of Deborah, found in Judges 5:2-30. This fine poem, celebrating the victory of certain tribes of Israel over the Canaanites at Taanach, captures at least three different moods, each one so "true to life" as to have sprung from the hearts of actual participants in the drama described. First, it declares the exultation of a people fresh from a marvelous victory, praising the Lord, who raised up Deborah and Barak as leaders; then it tells of the various kinds of responses the tribes made to the call to arms, very pointedly castigating those who stayed home and warmly commending those who risked their lives in the common cause. Finally, with rare sensitivity and a sympathy for the enemy unexpected in "war songs," it describes the anxious waiting and wondering of the Canaanite commander's mother, as she peers out the window in hopes of her son's return, which never comes. Apparently, the original song ended with that moving scene (at verse 30), but a

---

[9]"Sea of Reeds" is a more accurate translation of the Hebrew; the familiar "Red Sea" comes from the Greek (Septuagint) translation, which dates to about 250 BCE.

later editor evidently did not appreciate that ending and therefore added
lines to give the poem a decidedly miltant thrust.

> So perish all thine enemies, O Lord!
> But thy friends be like the sun
> as he rises in his might.

Also among the poetic pieces which reflect a premonarchical setting
are certain wise sayings, proverbs, and even riddles scattered through the
narratives of later books. Such may be the case with the lines in Genesis
2:23, where God has made woman from the rib of the man.

> Then the man said,
> This at last is bone of my bones
> and flesh of my flesh;
> she shall be called woman (*'ishshah*),
> because she was taken out of man (*'ish*).

This might well be a fragment of a longer poem; in any case, its rhythm
and parallelism[10] are characteristics of Hebrew poetry, and the closing play
on words of similar sound (technically, *assonance)* is a rather common device of the sages. These "puns"—as we sometimes call them—figured
prominently as ancient teaching devices, not too far removed in aim from
that of our "Mother Goose" rhymes and modern reading books.

While the book of Proverbs, as it stands, was compiled long after the
time of Solomon, with whom it is traditionally linked, scholars now find
reason to think that one section of the book (22:17-24:22) might be even
older than Solomon, perhaps dating to a time closer to Moses.[11] It is certainly true that what we call "Wisdom" (the literary genre and the philosophical outlook) can now be traced back in Egyptian and Babylonian
writings to at least 2000 BCE. Unfortunately we have no written Hebrew
examples from before 1000 BCE; on the other hand, the Old Testament itself mentions the presence in Israel of wise men *and* wise women as early
as the time of David. In fact, on two occasions they figure prominently in

---

[10]Parallelism of members (the full name of this feature) refers to the common practice
of repeating the thought of one line by slightly changed wording in the second (or third),
or of stating a thought positively in one line and negatively in the second.

[11]This section seems to follow closely the Egyptian Wisdom of Amen-emope; cf. J. B.
Pritchard, ed., *Ancient Near Eastern Texts Relating to the Old Testament,* 2nd ed. (Princeton: Princeton University Press, 1956) 421-25.

the story, and command the respect of no less a person than the king himself.[12] In the earlier instance it is a "wise woman" of Tekoa, whom Joab summoned and engaged to intercede with King David on behalf of Absalom, begging him to have his son recalled from exile. Later, when Absalom's rebellion is underway, the wise counselor Ahithophel defects and offers his service to the young rebel, and in 2 Samuel 16:23 we read, "Now in those days the counsel which Ahithophel gave was as if one consulted the oracle of God; so was all the counsel of Ahithophel esteemed, both by David and by Absalom." But when the advice of the wise man is rejected in favor of Hushai's, he is devastated, goes home, "sets[s] his house in order" and hangs himself (2 Samuel 17:23).

Riddles are associated, in our minds, with childhood games, and therefore it may seem strange that among the ancients they had a higher status. In Greek legend the riddle sometimes appears as a serious test of a person's wisdom, as in the most famous instance of Oedipus, who solved the riddle of the Sphinx and thereby earned the gratitude of the city of Thebes, even becoming king of that city. So in the lore of Israel and her neighbors riddles become a favorite device of the sage and teacher, serving to challenge the wit and imagination of their students, and providing another memorable form for passing along stories of tribal heroes. Such is the case of Samson, in Judges 14:10-20, who propounded a riddle that apparently he expected to dumbfound his wedding party. If it did, they were to pay for the "festal garments," but if they solved the riddle within seven days, Samson himself would have to pay the bill. The riddle: "Out of the eater came something to eat; out of the strong came something sweet" (Judges 14:14). For three days the wedding attendants were baffled, but secretly threatening the bride—whose persistent and tearful pressure wore down Samson's resistance—they learned the answer just in time to win the wager. Samson's violent revenge then led to the blood feud with the Philistines and eventually his own tragic death.

In summary, the period before 1000 BCE (about the time of the united kingdom under David) has left us no datable documents, but we have reason to think that many of the songs, fragments of poetry, and tales of heroes like Samson, now embedded in later narratives and books, originated in that period. But if the written remains of Israel's earliest history seem scarce, we have to recall that the ancients generally, and Israelite elders in

---

[12]See 2 Samuel 14:1-3 and chs. 15-17.

particular, had neither the same cause nor the same opportunity to preserve the traditions of their fathers in *writing* as did their descendants. Ancestral and tribal lore was carried in the *memory,* perpetuated by repetition in cultic celebrations, and passed on by word of mouth from generation to generation. True, we can only infer from the writings of a later period the main themes contained in that oral tradition, but even so the emergent picture is one that is amazingly clear despite its remoteness in time and the circumstances of its transmission.

From 1000 to ca. 800 BCE. Scholarly estimates for the entrance of Israelite tribes into Canaan vary according to the interpretation of the books of Joshua and Judges, two somewhat different accounts, both from the seventh-century Deuteronomic Historian.[13] But there is general agreement that somewhere between 1200 and 1100 BCE several (if not all) of the "twelve tribes" had occupied territory in Canaan as well as Transjordan, and formed a loosely knit confederation, "the sons of Israel."[14] As noted in my remarks about the Song of Deborah, unity and cooperation among these more or less autonomous tribes could not be taken for granted, and we have reason to suppose that the primary bond of unity in those days was the common religious allegiance, their "covenant with Yahweh," which they celebrated in annual (if not more frequent) cultic ceremonies. Already, we can imagine, such festival occasions included the recitation of those formative "works of the Lord," especially the sequence of events of the exodus from Egypt, and perhaps the solemn reaffirmation of certain covenant laws—for example, the Decalogue (Ten Commandments) of Moses. Though still, as far as we know, unwritten, such traditions served to pull the several tribes together and to lay the foundations for future development both as a cultic community and as a nation.

Then, in the eleventh-century BCE came a dramatic turn of events. An aggressive band of "sea peoples," the Pelasti, gained a foothold in Southwest Canaan and began relentless incursions into the hilly midsection of

---

[13]"Deuteronomic Historian" (often cited as DH) refers to the anonymous editor, or editors, who compiled materials that make up the four Hebrew books (six in English) called "Former Prophets"—Joshua, Judges, Samuel, Kings. The term "Deuteronomic" is appled to this work in recognition of certain features (of style and outlook) resembling the book of Deuteronomy.

[14]It is not certain just when the phrase "sons of Israel" became the common designation for the confederation, but the earliest reference outside the Bible, an inscription on the Merneptah Stele (an Egyptian monument), dates to ca. 1220 BCE.

that land, where the tribes of Israel were. This forms the backdrop for the story of Samson, and a bit later, the setting of stories of Eli and Samuel (1 Samuel 1-3). Better known to us as "Philistines," these people threatened to swallow up the whole land for a time, and just how close they came to success may be indicated in the fact that later ages would refer to it as "Palestine"—the land of the Pelasti!

The danger to Israel was critical, and it demanded drastic measures. Israel's response was to select one leader, a "prince," who could command the respect of all the tribes and forge them into a unified front to withstand the Philistine menace. This man of the hour, Israel's first monarch, was Saul. Anointed by Samuel, Saul rose to the occasion and managed to turn back the enemy, at least in a few early engagements. Thus, about 1020 BCE, Israel was launched on its experiment with kingship and all the benefits and perils that attended it.

David succeeded Saul and brought Israel to the status of a Middle Eastern state. His son Solomon further centralized national authority at Jerusalem, where he also built a fine temple to house Israel's most significant cultic object, the ark of the covenant. A time of relative peace and prosperity brought an unparalleled opportunity for the collection and compilation of Israel's traditions, and at the same time an occasion for some observers of Israel's changing fortunes to raise questions about the meaning of it all.

On careful analysis of material in the later Deuteronomic History—the books of Joshua, Judges, Samuel, and Kings—scholars have isolated a few blocks of narrative that show signs of having been composed during, or perhaps just after, the Solomonic era. Three, in particular, stand out: (1) the story of the ark in 1 Samuel 4-6; (2) the story of Saul's rise to power in 1 Sam. 9:1-10:16; 11; 13; and (3) the account of David's reign, often called the Succession Narrative or Court History, in 2 Sam. 9-20 and 1 Kings 1-2. They were not necessarily composed by the same writer, for each has its distinctive point of view and its own "moral." But all three seem to reflect views very close to the times of which they write, and at least one was meant to raise a warning, or call for moral reassessment, on the state of things in Israel. Even at this early stage of the development of Israel's sacred literature it is obvious that a "prophetic" element was operating to shape not only the course of Israel's future but the formulation of its past history as well. History, from that prophetic viewpoint, could never be merely an accumulation of past deeds or *bruta facta*,[15] but rather an ongoing dialogue between tradition and the crisis at hand. At each crossroad in its career Israel recalled the past in order to reread it in the light of a new challenge or fresh promise.[16]

The Court History of David is a prime example not only of the art of storytelling but also of that "prophetic" kind of history, in which the God of Sinai still thunders forth his commandments, even to kings and to the sons of kings in all their regal splendor. 2 Samuel 9-20 tells the story of King David's reign from its heyday through years of crisis and decline, and it portrays the character of David as only an intimate could. The writer's identity is unknown, but his skill and sensitivity are remarkable. He has captured for all time a very human picture of one whose fame continued to swell with the passing years and, in some circles, even reached a point of fantastic idealization.[17] It is a picture of David that neither flatters nor demeans him, but simply allows the reader to see both greatness and weakness, both "saint" and "sinner," in his complex character.

With a straightforward, matter-of-fact style the writer tells how King David, at the peak of his power, coveted Bathsheba, wife of his neighbor and faithful officer Uriah. He wanted her, made inquiry who she was, and then promptly ordered her to come and share his bed. Uriah was away from home, fighting in Israel's front lines, and when Bathsheba told David (months later) that she had become pregnant, David again acted with cool efficiency. He summoned Uriah home from the war, so that he could sleep with his wife and take credit for the pregnancy. But much to the king's dismay that stratagem failed, because Uriah staunchly refused to break the ban on sexual activity he (and his fellow soldiers) had assumed. So David,

---

[15]The Latin for "brute facts" became a kind of byword among certain nineteenth-century historians, who supposed that the aim of modern research into the past was simply to amass all the objective facts about it, ideally stripped of all elements of "interpretation"— a supposition that has been more recently repudiated by the majority of historians. Cf. R. G. Collingwood, *The Idea of History* (London: Oxford University Press, 1946).

[16]This "re-collection" of the past is precisely what we find in the book of Deuteronomy, where Moses is represented as demanding of the people "this day" (the time of the writer) a new affirmation of their commitment to the covenant, as if they were actually "there" with Moses in Moab.

[17]Compare 1 Chronicles 18-29, which covers the same period of David's reign as the Court History but omits all reference to David's adultery, or to the chain of events which followed, but enlarges his contribution to the cultic life, even giving David credit for planning Solomon's temple.

now not so cool but still efficient, devised another scheme to cover himself and avoid scandal: he wrote a letter to Joab, his commander in the field, and sent it by the hand of Uriah himself—"Set Uriah in the forefront of the hardest fighting, and then draw back from him, that he may be struck down and die" (2 Samuel 11:15).

The scheme achieved its objective, and after the usual period of mourning, David added Bathsheba to his harem. Then follows what must be regarded as one of the jewels of biblical literature, a scene at once artlessly simple in narrative style and powerful in its dramatic intensity. "The Lord sent Nathan to David"—the court prophet, telling the king his story of the rich man who stole from the poor man his one pet lamb and served it to his guest for dinner. David, assuming that Nathan had brought this case before him for judicial opinion, pronounced emphatically, "The man who has done this deserves to die." Then, without explanation (but with abundant moral courage), Nathan said to David, "You are the man!" (2 Samuel 12:7a). The parable hit home, and David acknowledged his guilt.

The sequel shows in vivid detail the unfolding of divine judgement on David and his household. Though David's personal confession was accepted, and his sin "put away," Nathan promised David, "the sword shall never depart from your house [hold]." And it never did. Like a tragic curse it was felt in the death of the child that Bathsheba bore, in the rape of Tamar, the vengeance of Absalom against his brother Amnon, and in the alienation and revolt of Absalom, which virtually broke David's heart. Without distracting commentary or moralizing, our Court Historian lets the story make its own point, and alongside the later tradition of a perpetual Davidic dynasty,[18] it stands in the record as a solemn prophetic warning against the arrogance of those in high places, who despise the Lord's covenant and set themselves above God's law.

If we assume that these stories of early kingship were composed during the reign of Solomon (ca. 961-922 BCE), it must have been about the same time or shortly thereafter that one of the major sources of Israel's premonarchic history began to take shape. This is the material found mainly in the books of Genesis, Exodus, and Numbers, and attributed by scholars to "the Yahwist"—an anonymous editor so designated because of his preference

---

[18]See 2 Samuel 7, especially verses 18ff., which probably reflects the belief of a later age (perhaps of the Deuteronomic Historian) that God had promised David a dynasty (the meaning of "house" in verses 16 and 27) of kings without end; cf. Psalm 89:1-4 and 132:11-12.

of the sacred name יהוה (AV: Jehovah; RSV: LORD) for God.[19] In the scholarly discussions of the past two centuries, resulting in a widespread consensus that the material of Genesis through Numbers is composite, the product of various sources, this earliest stratum of material came to be labeled "J" (For *Jahve,* the German spelling of Yahweh).[20] Coincidentally, many scholars argue that its place of origin was probably the southern kingdom of *Judah,* rather than the northern Israel, so that the "J" may be doubly appropriate.

But far more important than the label is the work itself, for we have here the foundational stage in the development of the Torah, or Law, which reached its present form only around 500 BCE. If the scholarly hypothesis be correct, it was the Yahwist who set in motion a centuries-long process of compilation and revision that finally produced the Pentateuch.[21] This is *not* to say that the Yahwist created *de novo;* it is understood that his work was largely that of a collector and compiler of many, originally separate selections of oral tradition, stemming from people and events as much as seven or eight centuries earlier than his own day. Even so, it was no mean achievement to weave together those bits and pieces into one continuous story, starting with the creation of Adam and Eve and tracing their descendants through Shem, son of Noah, to the patriarchs Abram, Isaac, and Jacob, and finally to the climax of his story, the marvelous exodus from Egypt.[22]

Even to summarize the Yahwistic Epic here would run beyond our purpose in this chapter. Let it suffice to refer to two samples of the Yahwist's work, which will demonstrate both the nature of his material and the distinctiveness of his style. The first selection will be a sample from the ac-

---

[19]The earliest Hebrew manuscripts, written in consonants only, used the four letters יהוה—YHWH, the *tetragrammaton* to spell this name, regarded by the Jews as sacred and unutterable; in reading aloud they substituted the word *'adonai* (Lord), and because medieval manuscripts inserted the vowels of that word into YHWH many translators began to render the name as "Jehovah."

[20]German was the language of the pioneering scholars who formulated the basic hypothesis.

[21]"Pentateuch" comes from a Greek word meaning "fivefold," and has become a convenient scholarly label for the first five books of the Old Testament, the books designated *Torah* (Law or teaching) by the Jews.

[22]Obviously, the story contained in the Torah goes well beyond the exodus, but this involves material judged to be compiled by other, later editors, and will be considered later.

count of "primeval history," contained in Genesis 2-11, and the second from the story of Joseph in Genesis 37, 39-50. One will afford the reader a chance to compare "J" with "P" or the Priestly editor, who about 500 BCE supplemented parts of the Yahwist's story; the other will allow us to see how "J" compares with "E" or the Elohist, the editor from the northern kingdom (Israel) whose work was done about a century later and often parallels "J".[23]

One outstanding feature of the Yahwist's work was to set the patriarchal stories (of Abram and others) into a frame that embraced all mankind; the beginnings of Israel's covenant with God are thus to be seen as Yahweh's election or singling out of a chosen people from the rest of humanity. To emphasize the pivotal importance of Abram's call, and the redemptive grace of God expressed therein, the Yahwist retreats in time to describe "pre-Abramic" humanity and so pushes his starting point back to the Garden of Eden. But the careful reader will notice that the "history" recited in Genesis 2-11 is not so much a matter of fixed, datable events as it is a story of human life, universal in its appeal, timeless in its appraisal of human dignity and misery. Whoever he was, the Yahwist was remarkable for his breadth of vision and for his insight into the nature of the human predicament.

Protagonist in the story, which begins at Genesis 2:4b,[24] is "the LORD God." This double reference (Hebrew: *Yahweh 'elohim*) is a peculiar fea-

DIAGRAM OF THE PENTATEUCHAL SOURCES

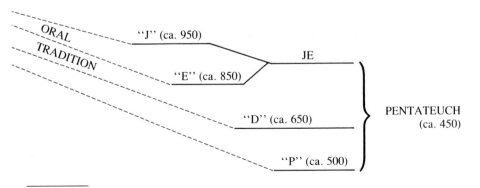

---

[23]For a graphic aid to understanding the supposed relationship of the main sources to each other, refer to the diagram on this page.

[24]Genesis 1:1-2:4a (the "a" means the first half-verse) belongs to the work of the Priestly ("P") editor, and although it stands first in order this account of Creation was composed centuries later than "J".

ture of Genesis 2-3 and one other text, Exodus 9:30. But use of the sacred name from the very beginning sets "J" apart from the stories of "E" and "P," who show that the sacred name was revealed later, to Moses (cf. Exod. 3:13-15, 6:2-3). Also distinctive is the Yahwist's preoccupation with humankind and their earthly habitat; whereas the Priestly account (chapter 1) gives an elaborate description of the steps taken to order the heavens, to separate land and seas, and so on; "J" focuses quickly on the creation of 'adham ("mankind") from 'adhamah ("ground" or "earth"). As we might put it, Man is an "earthling," but for the Hebrew writer this was more than just a pun: it was a way of indicating the intimate bond between God's good earth and the creature designed to till its soil and keep it (cf. Gen. 2:15). Far from being demeaning, the story would maintain that it was indeed an instance of mankind's dignity and of God's purpose for Adam to be the Gardener of the earth that sustained all creatures.

The Yahwist makes clear the Man's bond with his Creator, also, by telling that God "breathed into his nostrils the breath of life." Unlike the "P" account, where humankind appear only after the sea creatures and animals of the land, "J" says that Man came first, and God let Man assign names to the other creatures, made because "it was not good that the man should be alone" (2:18). On the other hand, "P" says of Man (male and female) that they were created "in the image of God," and so—though in a different idiom—both accounts testify to the very special status of Man in the divine scheme of things, and to the tremendous responsibility that imposes.[25]

Throughout Genesis 2-11 it is characteristic of the Yahwist to portray the deity in very humanlike language—technically, *anthropomorphic* when it describes God's "breathing" or "walking in the garden," and *anthropopathic* when it tells of God's anger, repentance, or other emotional states. This feature certainly stands out in the "J" account of Creation, again contrasting sharply with that of "P," where the work of creation is performed by *fiat*, by the mere utterance of God (*'elohim*): "let there be. . . . " And the Priestly references to deity are characterized by a sense of reserve, and attributes of power and majesty, in keeping with a more sophisticated stage of Israel's theology.

---

[25]This estimate of human dignity stands in sharpest contrast with the description of Man's role in the Babylonian account known as *'Enuma 'elish*, where human beings are created, as a kind of afterthought, from the blood of one of Marduk's enemies, in order to be slaves to the gods.

But sophistication is not necessarily an adequate measure of meaning. With all its poetic naiveté, the Yahwist's message is a profound one. In the Priestly account there is nothing at all to match the penetrating analysis of temptation and sin that we find in Genesis 3. Here in all its vivid hues the root of human disorder and misery lies exposed: God's gardener has rebelled; Adam and Eve, arrogating to themselves "knowledge" reserved for God alone, have broken faith and sundered the bond between themselves and their Creator. The "expulsion" from Eden is not so much a spatial dislocation as it is a symbol of that irrevocable step that Everyman (and "Adam" is in that sense everyman) takes, wherever it may be, when he decides to take control of his own destiny, to be his own master, to assume the role of God. And the "curse" that is pronounced on humankind is not so much an arbitrary cancellation of former rights and privileges as it is a dramatic recognition of sin's inevitable consequences, the ugly reality that human rebellion against God invariably produces in this world.

Our second sample of the Yahwistic Epic is found in Genesis 37, 39-50: the story of Joseph.[26] Whereas in the stories of Creation the demarcation between "J" and "P" is very plain to see, because the Priestly editor simply placed his account in front of the Yahwist's with no attempt to weave the two together, in the story of Joseph it is an altogether different matter. Here the two sources—in this case, "J" and "E"—have been combined, and so artfully interwoven that the casual reader will scarcely distinguish one from the other. But on careful scrutiny the differences do appear.

"J"	"E"
1. Joseph's father is "Israel."	The father's name is "Jacob."
2. Judah intercedes for Joseph.	Reuben's role is emphasized.
3. Ishmaelites buy Joseph.	Midianites take Joseph.
4. Joseph rises to prominence in prison.	Joseph interprets dreams but is forgotten.

Throughout the story, especially through chapter 40, the alternation of *Yahweh* and *'elohim* coincides with these data and thus serves to confirm the basic distinction. It would appear that the main story line, that Joseph provoked his brothers to plot against him, was taken as a slave to Egypt,

---

[26]Genesis 38 obviously interrupts the flow of the Joseph Story, but it probably belongs to the Yahwist's collection, too, and serves here to fill the gap between Joseph's departure from Canaan and his fortunes in the land of Egypt.

and wondrously rose to political power years later, was followed by both
"J" and "E," but that variations in details crept into the story perhaps as
a natural result of the division of the kingdom after Solomon's death. It is
not surprising that during a century or more of division and often overt
hostility between North (Israel) and South (mainly Judah), much of their
common tradition would be colored by the partisan interests of those who
preserved and transmitted it. What is remarkable is that the editor who
combined the two versions was so evenhanded; rather than eliminate one
in favor of the other (as a modern editor might do), he preserved them both
in a carefully woven conflation.[27]

What stands out in "J," however, is more than distinctive language
and a certain partisan pride in the role of his ancestor Judah, who not only
kept his brothers from killing Joseph (Gen. 37:26-27) but later gave his
father a personal guarantee of Benjamin's safety (Gen. 43:8-10). The
Yahwist shows here, as in the "primeval history," a notable sensitivity to
human emotions and a flair for their dramatic portrayal, even in the midst
of such far-reaching events as make up the framework of his history.
Against the backdrop of world famine and the threat of economic disaster
the Yahwist finds a way to paint the very subtle lines of father Jacob's ag-
onizing decision to let Benjamin (Joseph's only full brother, son of his beloved Rachel) go with the others to Egypt. It is also the Yahwist who stresses
Joseph's own inner struggle, torn between love and lingering resentment
of his brothers as he devises a test of their loyalty and their change of heart.
So lifelike are the characters in "J" that the reader almost forgets the larger
scope of the epic as a whole, and the pattern of slavery to freedom (or sin
and redemption) that those personal characters dramatize. But as one views
the sweep of the Yahwist's work in Genesis, it seems clear that some such
concept has guided the work from start to finish, and indeed, in a sense,
the story of Joseph serves *both* to explain historically how so many "sons
of Israel" came to reside in Egypt *and* to prefigure, in Joseph's own career, the more amazing instance of divine compassion and redemption
wrought in the exodus of his descendants centuries later.

On the work of the Elohist ("E") we must linger a little, if only to draw
out some implications of what has already been told, since this work rep-

---

[27]Apparently in only a few spots did the editor of Genesis deem it necessary to make
harmonizing touches—for example, in 37:28b, where he tried to smoothe over the dis-
crepancy between "Midianites" and "Ishmaelites" by having the former sell Joseph to the
latter, who then transport Joseph to Egypt; cf. Genesis 37:25, 27, 36, 39:1.

resents (along with the Court Historian and the Yahwist) the third great contribution of the period 1000 to 800 BCE. Scholars generally agree that what can now be identified as ''E'' probably took shape about the middle of the ninth century, and reflects the Northern (Israelite) version of sacred tradition. Some scholars also maintain that the scope of the Elohist's work was once much larger than what now remains, since many parts were lost or perhaps obscured over centuries of redaction.[28] On the other hand, it is likely that the Elohist never meant to parallel the whole of the Yahwistic Epic; he began not with the Creation or ''primeval history,'' but rather with Abram and Sarai, and traces of his work appear intermittently through the rest of Genesis, Exodus, and Numbers.

Among the many distinctive marks of ''E''—aside from his preference for 'elohim to refer to God before the time of Moses—there is also a preference for ''Horeb'' instead of Sinai, as the name of the sacred mountain, and for ''Amorites'' where ''J'' spoke of Canaanites. The Elohist tends to be less anthropomorphic than ''J'' in portraying the deity, often introducing angels into the story as mediators between God and human beings, and stressing the importance of dreams as vehicles of divine communication.[29] He lacks the subtlety and sensitivity of the Yahwist, on the whole, and is much more given to moralizing or otherwise explaining, where ''J'' simply tells the story and lets the action speak for itself.

This tendency to moralize and ''to preach'' becomes understandable, and even appropriate in the light of the ninth-century developments in Israel. In fact, many other features of ''E'' may also be accounted for, when we consider the character of religion and morality prevalent at the time of its collection or composition. It was a time of social transition in Israel, when a predominantly pastoral economy gave way increasingly to the agrarian, and people whose fathers had been seminomadic shepherds were learning how to settle down and be farmers. The whole pattern of life was changing, and even the ancestral religion, with ethical precepts formulated for life in the desert, seemed to some people inappropriate for life in the walled cities like Samaria. But on top of all that, new Israelite farmers had learned their agriculture at the hands of the resident experts, the Canaan-

---

[28]See, for example E. A. Speiser, *Genesis,* Anchor Bible 1 (Garden City NY: Doubleday, 1964) xxx-xxxiv.

[29]So in the ''E'' account of Joseph's imprisonment; see also Genesis 20 (the story of Abraham and Sarah in Gerar) and Genesis 28:10-22 (Jacob at Bethel).

ites, and included in the course would be all necessary directions for gaining the favor of the *ba'alim* ("lords" of the land) and their divine consorts,
the local manifestations of the Canaanite god and goddess of fertility. In
sum, it was very much the situation so well depicted in the Elijah Cycle (1
Kings 17-21, especially). The faith of the fathers was indeed in peril, not
just because of the aggressive zeal of individual queens like Sidonian Jezebel, who threatened to destroy all the prophets of Yahweh, but primarily
because of the widespread (and largely unwitting) acceptance by the people of *both* Yahweh *and* Ba'al, or—as Elijah's accusation put it—their
"hopping" back and forth between the two.[30] Hence the prophet's demand for a showdown, to determine by the ordeal of fire which one was
really God (*'el*).[31]

At stake in this time of syncretism was much more than a simple choice
of names for God, and more than a matter of keeping the First Commandment. At bottom it was a question of what (or who) God is, a matter of
crucial importance to Israel then, as to us today. Is the power "that makes
the world go 'round" to be identified with the fructifying forces at work
in the rain, the seed and the soil—imagined by the ancients as male and
female elements to be brought together through ritual acts of sexual union?
Or is the Sovereign somehow apart from, even superior to, those powerful
forces, and thus to be reckoned rather as One whose works transcend the
natural cycles and whose worship requires of men trust and obedience? Not
even the marvelous victory of Yahwism at Mt. Carmel could settle that
question once and for all; in a sense it was the question that set the agenda
for Israel's prophets for centuries to come.

The Elohist, too, in his own way responded to that religious crisis. By
recalling the ancient traditions and expounding upon them he, too, set before the people the awesome question and called for decision. If he mor-
alized some of the familiar stories, it was the better to bring out what was
most distinctive about the faith of the fathers—that "fear of God"[32] which

---

[30]The New English Bible modernizes the challenge: "How long will you sit on the
fence?" (1 Kings 18-21); RSV is more literal with "How long will you go limping with
two different opinions?" "Limping" translates a Hebrew word (also used of the prophets
of Ba'al in 18:26) meaning "To leap, skip, or limp."

[31]*El* is another Hebrew word for god or mighty one, also used in the myths of ba'alism
for the father of Ba'al; it is interesting that the very name of the prophet Elijah is a compound meaning "my god is Yah [short form of Yahweh]."

[32]This phrase indicates the Elohist's "most prominent theme" according to H. W. Wolff
("The Elohistic Fragments in the Pentateuch," *Interpretation* 26 [1972]: 158-73.)

could never be confused with ba'alism or any other -ism. The hand of the Elohist can be seen very clearly in the closing episode of the story of Joseph (Gen. 50: 15-21), where the brothers, fearing Joseph's reprisals on them after the death of their father, beg Joseph's forgiveness; his reply is worth quoting in full.

> Fear not, for am I in the place of God? As for you, you meant evil against me; but God meant it for good, to bring it about that many people should be kept alive, as they are today. So do not fear; I will provide for you and your little ones.

The words are remarkable not only as a demonstration of Joseph's magnanimous pardon, but also as a mark of the Elohist's faith in God as the Mover and Fashioner of human destiny, as the One who provides the grain in seasons of plenty and withholds it in times of famine, but more than that the One who overrules the "evil" that people would do, in order to bring about good. Truly a magnificent concept of history and a stinging rebuke of the insipid syncretism that threatened to dilute religious fervor and morality in the ninth century.

From the eventful period 1000 to 800 BCE may have come a few other, and smaller, portions of the Hebrew Bible. For example, some scholars would assign to this period some of the earliest Psalms, whether actually composed by David or not,[33] and another collection of wise sayings to be collected later and become a part of Proverbs. But by far the greater, both in volume and in long-range consequence, are those texts we have already surveyed: (1) the Court History (and kindred materials) in Samuel and Kings; (2) the Yahwistic Epic from Judah; and (3) the Elohistic parallels from Israel.

From 800 to ca. 600 BCE. Already by the mid-ninth century the aggressive Mesopotamian power, Assyria, had cast a threatening shadow over the smaller states of Syria, Israel, and Judah. For about two centuries Assyrian dominance in the Near East, and its hot-and-cold rivalry with Egypt, provided the backdrop for developments within both Israel and Judah. By

---

[33]The caption "A psalm of David," which appears in the superscription of many Psalms is taken by some scholars to indicate dedication *to* David or, in some instances, Psalms belonging to a royal collection. In any case, the superscriptions were probably later than the Psalms themselves and should not be taken as reliable evidence of the date of composition. See B. W. Anderson, *Out of the Depths: The Psalms Speak for Us Today* (Philadelphia: Westminster Press, 1970) 14-17.

721 BCE, in fact, the Assyrians had overrun both Syria and Israel, leaving only little Judah to carry on the heritage of the Covenant. Thousands of Israelites were carried into exile and scattered, some to intermarry with Mesopotamians and eventually to lose their identity, some perhaps to keep alive their faith in Yahweh and their hope of someday returning home. The Assyrians also uprooted other subjects and resettled them in what had been Israelite territory, and over the years the mingling of Israelite and foreigner gave rise to a people of a peculiar religious mixture, later to be known as Samaritans.[34] Almost all that survived of Israel's sacred traditions has come down to us through the literature of Judah, and owes its existence to the prophets and priests of that Southern kingdom.

Of the prophets who were active in the North during the Assyrian crisis only two books and one other name (Jonah ben Amittai) have come down to us. The book that we know today as "Jonah" borrows the name of that prophet,[35] who was active in the reign of Jeroboam II, but is itself a composition of postexilic times. The two books that contain the oracles, or preaching, of prophets to Israel are those of *Amos* and *Hosea*, the earliest of the so-called literary prophets. "Literary" is often used to indicate those whose oracles were collected and made into separate books, as opposed to those (like Elijah and Elisha) about whom we are told in the ("historical") books of Samuel and Kings. But the term may be misleading if taken to mean that the prophets themselves were "literary men" in any modern sense of the word. The prophets were primarily *speakers,* not writers, and it is likely that their sayings were recorded in writing some while after they were said, perhaps by disciples or other followers and sympathizers. Most of the books in the collection of "the prophets"[36] show clearly the signs

---

[34]The Samaritans figure most prominently in the story of the Restoration, after the Babylonian Exile, as told in Ezra and Nehemiah; still later, probably in the third century BCE, they established their cultic center on Mount Gerizim (near ancient Shechem, modern Nablus), breaking with the Jews and holding only the Pentateuch to be sacred Scripture.

[35]2 Kings 14:25 tells us only that Jonah was from Gath-hepher and that he spoke to King Jeroboam about restoring "the border of Israel." There is no mention of his being sent to Nineveh, as was the character in the book of Jonah.

[36]As will be seen in chapter 2, Hebrew Bibles have three main sections—*Torah (Law) Nebi'im* (Prophets), and *Kethuvim* (Writings)—and further divide the "Former Prophets" (Joshua, Judges, Samuel, Kings) and the "Latter Prophets" (Isaiah, Jeremiah, Ezekiel, Book of Twelve). The "Book of Twelve" corresponds to our English list of "minor prophets."

of editorial handling, often with obvious clues to a time of composition later than that of the prophet himself. But, allowing for some editorial additions, we may safely assign the bulk of Amos and Hosea to the late eighth century.

The preaching of Amos, a Judean shepherd and "dresser" of fig trees,[37] came about 750 BCE, a decade or so before that of Hosea. As Amos put it, the Lord "took [him] from following the flock" and sent him northward to Bethel, Samaria, and possibly other prominent cities of Israel, where he announced the approach of "the Day of the Lord." but, contrary to popular expectation, this would be for Israel a day of Judgment, a time of darkness and doom. The oracles of Amos blasted the "first families," the royalty of Israel, and other supposedly responsible people for their exploitation of the poor and needy. Luxury-loving men, goaded on by spoiled wives, accumulated more and more wealth, but were less and less concerned about the attendant suffering of the masses. Never were religious celebrations more popular or offerings more extravagant; but never were they more hollow or offensive to Yahweh! Away with your vain oblations, Amos said; rather "let justice roll down like water, and righteousness like an everflowing stream" (Amos 5:24).

In such scathing words of denunciation Amos held before the people the prospect of certain retribution, a picture of almost total disaster for the nation. Readers today can only dimly imagine how scandalous, how outrageous, Amos' words must have seemed to his original hearers, riding a tide of economic prosperity and national optimism as they were. But whether Amos was able to shake the prevailing mood of complacency or not, the next ten or fifteen years proved enough to dash any false optimism that Israel may have had. The Assyrians, aroused from a period of dormancy, were again asserting themselves and coveting lands to the west. Moreover, with the death of Jeroboam II Israel's political instability became obvious to all; torn between those who favored appeasement of Assyria and those who favored alliance with Egypt and resistance to Assyria,

---

[37]Amos 7:14. Though the RSV translates "sycamore trees," the Hebrew term refers to something other than the sycamore known on this continent; it was a tree that bore a kind of fig, which would ripen properly only after a "dresser" had punctured the fruit to remove any infestation.

the nation suffered under a rapid turnover of kings, four of whom were removed by assassination.[38]

In the midst of this turmoil appeared the prophet Hosea. Unlike Amos
he was a native of the Northern kingdom, and his task was not so much to
warn of coming danger as to offer a word of theological interpretation for
the danger already at hand. His message to Israel contained some of the
same complaints as Amos had lodged, but for Hosea the widespread im-
morality and social injustice were symptoms of an even deeper malady—
Israel no longer "knew" her God. Israel's failure was like that of a marriage gone sour, for lack of "steadfast love."[39] Indeed, the figure of marriage and divorce is one of the characteristic features of Hosea. And it seems
that the prophet's own personal experience with his wife Gomer became a
living parable (Hosea 1-3) of the rampant "infidelity" of Israel, leading
to an inevitable separation (captivity and exile) of the unfaithful nation.
Yahweh must put away the harlot people, just as Hosea put away Gomer.
And yet—and here Hosea addresses the theological dilemma—beyond
Judgment lies a new beginning, a new exodus, a second honeymoon. Just
as Hosea redeems and takes Gomer back, so Yahweh (whose "steadfast
love" had never wavered) would one day restore his people Israel. The
door of disaster, through which they must go away now, would appear from
the other side to be a "door of hope" (Hos. 2:15; cf. 11:8-11).

The disaster was not long in coming. Following an abortive effort on
the part of Israel and Syria to form a coalition of Western states to meet
the Assyrian threat, Israel declined rapidly, and Tilglath-pileser III moved
against them. A puppet ruler, Hoshea, remained on the throne for a few
years, but finally rebelled, bringing on armed invasion and the sack of Samaria under Sargon II of Assyria.

The Southern kingdom, Judah, did not remain unscathed in all this. In
fact, that it survived this crisis and managed to stay politically alive for
another century and a half is truly a wonder, even in secular history. To
the eyes of prophetic faith, as expressed in biblical history, it was surely

---

[38]2 Kings 15-16 tells the sad tale; Zechariah, Shallum, Pekahiah all fell within a twelve-
year period.

[39]The Hebrew word חסד, also translated "mercy" or "kindness," almost defies any
one-word translation; its primary significance in Hosea is that all-important covenant loyalty, without which neither human marriage nor the God-man relationship could endure;
see Hosea 4:1, 6:6.

an act of God's mercy. Syria and Israel had tried to compel Judah to join their coalition (ca. 735 BCE), threatening to invade and remove King Ahaz bodily, if necessary. It is here we find one of the earliest reports of the activity of the prophet Isaiah (Isa. 7); meeting the king of Judah as he frantically inspected Jerusalem's water supply—no doubt expecting a military siege—Isaiah counseled the king not to panic, but to trust in Yahweh to confound the coalition: "Thus says the Lord God: It shall not stand" (Isa. 7:7a; cf. 2 Kings 10:1-20). But the terrified Ahaz rejected the word of the prophet, choosing to put his trust in the Assyrian emperor, who of course responded by smashing the Syro-Israelite forces and, as already mentioned, eventually overrunning both of those "smoldering stumps of firebrands." But the price that Ahaz paid for his protection was virtual subjugation of Judah, imposing upon her people years of severe economic burdens and an equally costly toll in moral and spiritual integrity. Much of Isaiah 1-8 reflects the prophet's protest against the faithlessness of such policies and the failure of nerve in the house of David.

Only with the death of Ahaz and the accession of Hezekiah (ca. 715 BCE) was there a brief respite for Judah. Hezekiah was a reformer, apparently a much more devout Yahwist than his father, and it is likely that the poems of Isaiah 9:2-7 and 11:1-9 capture current expressions of renewed hope in Judah for a new Davidic kingdom and the attendant Age of Peace. The Assyrians were preoccupied for a time with internal disorders, encouraging the subject states to dream of release from their bondage. Many of Isaiah's oracles seem to be directed against involvement in such plotting, and it may be that on at least one occasion, when neighboring states conspired against Assyria, Hezekiah heeded the prophetic warning and stayed out of it. Later, however, prompted by the promises of Egyptian aid, Judah did join the rebels, causing Isaiah to decry the "covenant with death" (Isa. 28:14-22; 30:1-5). And true to his word, Judah suffered the consequences, feeling "the rod of (God's) anger" in a devastating invasion and siege by the Assyrian Sennacherib.[40]

During the same hectic period another Southern prophet raised his voice to condemn "those who devise wickedness . . . because it is in the power of their hand"—confiscating the fields and houses of their debtors, bribing judges and "skinning" the powerless. This was Micah of Moreshah,

---

[40]Isaiah 10:5-11. The annals of Sennacherib, recovered in recent times, refer to his capture of forty-six walled cities and having Hezekiah "caged like a bird" in Jerusalem.

another of the so-called minor prophets, whose oracles were included in the Book of the Twelve. Whereas Isaiah's work was in Jerusalem and often in the presence of royalty, Micah seems to espouse the cause of the rural peasant-farmer, and his figures of speech (like those of Amos) are drawn from life in the open country. Yet, like Isaiah, he knew where policy was made and where standards were set, and some of his sharpest words were aimed at the political and religious leaders in Jerusalem: "'because of you Zion shall be plowed as a field; Jerusalem shall become a heap of ruins'" (see Mic. 3:9-12).

The siege of Sennacherib was marvelously lifted, and Jerusalem was for that moment spared. Thus the seventh century BCE opened with rejoicing and high hopes in Judah, but it proved to be a century of rapid change both in the international scene and within the nation's political and religious fortunes. Hezekiah was succeeded on the throne by Manasseh, whose long reign was regarded by the Deuteronomic Historian as a standing invitation to religious disaster. With his policy of appeasement Manasseh curried Assyrian favor by openly encouraging the worship of Assyrian gods, and whatever reforms Hezekiah had achieved for Yahwism were certainly lost. The prophets of Yahweh were apparently silenced by order of the king,[41] so that it is no coincidence that we have in the extant prophetic literature not a single name to represent the first half of that fateful century.

During that period, while Yahwism was virtually pushed ''underground,'' it is very likely that our present book of Deuteronomy had its origin. Precisely what form and how much of the book existed then are questions still debated, but many scholars are convinced that ''the book of the law'' discovered (ca. 621 BCE) when workmen were repairing the temple at Jerusalem (2 Kings 22-23) was the nucleus of our Deuteronomy.[42] The scroll had presumably gone unnoticed for years, perhaps due to devout priests who kept it hidden because of their fear of Manasseh. Some scholars think that it may even be traced back to northern sources, which Israelite refugees from the Assyrians brought into Judah at the fall of Sa-

---

[41]2 Kings 21:16 is usually so interpreted; cf. the full account of Manasseh's ''abominations'' in 21:2-15.

[42]The book as we have it probably went through at least three ''editions.'' But close correspondence between Josiah's reforms (see 2 Kings 22-23) and the admonitions of Deuteronomy (especially Deuteronomy 12-26) strongly suggests Josiah's dependence on a ''first edition'' of the book.

maria. In any case, when it came to light, the book caused wide consternation among the king's counselors and eventually became the basis for King Josiah's sweeping reforms. More will be said in the next chapter about the significance of the book, and we must be content here to register the fact of its discovery and one very important inference—namely, that it brings to light the first evidence of another major stratum in the composition of Torah or Pentateuch, the Deuteronomic or "D" Source. The same editor—or, better, school of editors—is thought to have retouched and supplemented "J" and "E" (possible already combined), thus leaving on parts of Exodus and a few places in Numbers the marks of a distinctive outlook and style of writing.

To mention only a few of these distinctive marks, the outlook of "D" is characterized by a conscious effort to make the past relevant to the present (the editor's own day). Touchstone of Israel's covenant obligation was the Decalogue given to Moses at Horeb, repeated in Deuteronomy 5:6-21 with slightly modified language, but in Deuteronomy Moses is presented as virtually "contemporary" with the readers, calling on *them* to "hearken to the voice of the Lord" or to heed "the ordinances of the Lord, the God of thy fathers." Repeatedly readers are urged to decide between "blessing" (or "life") and "cursing" (or "death"), and there is no neutral ground. Likewise, the theology of history in the work of "D" shows this same *either-or* character: obedience to God brings blessing (success, prosperity, life) but disobedience brings cursing (failure, suffering, death). For the Deuteronomic school it was a critical time, demanding nothing short of the absolute and total commitment expressed in Deuteronomy 6:4: "Hear, O Israel, the Lord our God is One Lord; and you shall love the Lord your God with all your heart, and with all your soul and with all your might."

From the latter half of the seventh century, probably in the early years of Josiah's reign, come three short prophetic books which mark the end of the long "eclipse" of Yahwism: Habakkuk, Zephaniah, and Nahum. The first—Habakkuk—comments upon the emergence in Mesopotamia of "the Chaldeans" (neo-Babylonians), who appear to be appointed by Yahweh to punish Judah for her sins. Habakkuk, however, raises the question: how can the God of righteousness use as agent of retribution a people "more wicked" than their victims (Hab. 1:12-13)? Recognizing that God's ways do not necessarily conform to the rules of human justice, Habakkuk goes on to pronounce a series of "woes" upon Judah and calls on the people to "live on faithfulness."[43]

The danger foreseen by the prophet began to materialize after the death of the Assyrian Emperor Ashurbanipal, when subject nations like the Medes and Chaldeans began to rebel. The city of Nineveh fell before that combination of rebels ca. 612 BCE, and by 605 the Babylonians had established themselves as new masters of the Middle East.

The book of Zephaniah may reflect a slightly earlier decade, because one of the main concerns of the prophet is widespread apathy (Zeph. 1:12), and Nineveh apparently still stands (2:13). But Zephaniah, like Amos in his warning to Israel, speaks of a "Day of the Lord" that will bring judgment on many nations as well as Judah. It will be a terrible "day of (God's) wrath," which only the humble and lowly will survive (Zeph. 2:3; 3:12-13).

Nahum's burden is concentrated almost exclusively on the downfall of Nineveh. With vivid imagery and almost brutal intensity the prophet exults in the vengeance of the Lord on the Assyrians: "Woe to the bloody city, all full of lies and booty" (Nah. 3:1). Whatever else the message holds, it rings with deep-seated conviction that those who live by the sword will by the sword perish, and that Yahweh has remembered the atrocities committed on his people in ages past.

One more prophet has to be included among the representatives of this period, and though some parts of the book named for him actually stem from times after 600 BCE, most of his own career belongs to the last quarter of the seventh century. This was Jeremiah of Anathoth, witness to the waning years of Judah's national existence, and bearer of the Word of Yahweh to at least three of its last kings. That message contained a penetrating critique of the nation's spiritual disorder, a malady (according to Jeremiah) requiring a far more radical treatment than Josiah's reforms of the cult. Moreover, Jeremiah pronounced as futile the efforts to forestall the advance of the Babylonians, because it was by God's own will that the great Nebuchadrezzar had come to power. Such counsel, tantamount to treason in the ears of the king, inevitably led to suppressive reaction, even public ridicule and imprisonment for Jeremiah. Unable to gain a personal hearing before Jehoiakim Jeremiah dictated oracles of the Lord to his faith-

---

[43]Habakkuk 2:4b, where the RSV reads "the righteous shall live by his faith," but indicates in footnote the more accurate translation used here.

ful scribe Baruch and had them delivered to the king, who listened as the scroll was read aloud, but with cold contempt carved it to pieces and burned it (see Jer. 36). Later, however Jeremiah repeated what he had recited to Baruch, adding even more (Jer. 36:32), producing thus a "second edition, enlarged" of the prophet's book. This rare report gives us an unusual glimpse into the process by which the words of the prophet, though scorned and rejected by some, were preserved for posterity through the careful recording of a scribe.

To sum up, from the crucial years 800 to 600 BCE came the beginnings of the Latter Prophets—in particular, oracles of Amos and Hosea in the North, of Micah and Isaiah in the South (all middle and late eighth century); then the nucleus of Deuteronomy (probably early seventh century), later to be revised and extended, along with the Deuteronomic ("D") editing of "JE," brought the formation of Torah one step nearer completion. Finally, adding to the prophetic corpus, were the three short books of Habbakkuk, Zephaniah, and Nahum (mid-seventh century), and the beginnings of the greater collection to be known as Jeremiah.

From 600 to ca. 400 BCE. The decline of Judah followed hard upon that of Assyria. Shortly after the fall of Nineveh (612 BCE), King Josiah of Judah led his troops northward to cut off an Egyptian army that was meant to aid the remnant of Assyrians against the Chaldeans; at Megiddo Josiah lost the battle and his own life. Jehoahaz, heir to the throne, was replaced after three months by Jehoiakim, whose rebellion (ca. 599 BCE) brought the forces of Nebuchadrezzar against Judah. Jehoiakim, who had despised the words of Jeremiah, died before the Chaldeans arrived, so that his son Jehoiachin had the humiliation of surrendering. In 597 BCE thousands of captives, including the king, were marched off into Babylonia, the first of three deportations marking the beginning of the Exile.

One of those captives was the priest Ezekiel, whose activity as a prophet of Yahweh extended over a period of some twenty years. The book that goes by his name, like those of the other "major" prophets, shows signs of an editorial hand, supplying much of the narrative material, but within its very carefully organized contents one can still detect the marks of this highly original priest-prophet. Ezekiel's labors among the exiles at "the river Chebar" began some years before the second invasion of Judah (ca. 586 BCE) and the devastation of the temple at Jerusalem, and the burden of his visions and oracles then was to affirm the certain coming of that divine judgment against the false hopes of many people, both exiles and those left in the land. In a characteristic vision Ezekiel saw the throne-chariot of the Lord—Yahweh had wheels! The glory of God was not to be confined to his house in Jerusalem, but appeared to follow his people and reside with them even in Babylonia. No doubt it was through this kind of prophecy that many of the defeated Judeans managed to hold on to faith and hope, when the fatal blow came and the temple was destroyed.

From the period of the Exile have come many poems and songs lamenting the dreadful fall of Jerusalem: much of the book of Lamentations was composed at the time or shortly thereafter, though not by Jeremiah, as was once believed. "How lonely sits the city that was full of people! How like a widow has she become. . . . She weeps bitterly in the night, tears on her cheeks; among all her lovers she has none to comfort her" (Lam. 1:1a, 2ab). So runs the mournful theme of this book, one of the *megilloth* (or rolls) in the Writings, and still recited or chanted by Jews in observance of the fall of the temple on the Ninth of Ab.[44]

The classic example of exilic psalms—at least, of those now included in the canonical book of Psalms—is Psalm 137. It is perhaps our most direct testimony to the profound grief of the people who were actually marched away into Babylonia, there to have every casual reference to their homeland become a painful reminder of all they had lost.

> By the waters of Babylon, there we sat down and wept, when we remembered Zion. On the willows there we hung up our lyres. For there our captors required of us songs, and our tormentors mirth, saying "Sing us one of the songs of Zion!"
>
> How shall we sing the Lord's song in a foreign land? If I forget you, O Jerusalem, let my right hand wither! Let my tongue cleave to the roof of my mouth, if I do not remember you, if I do not set Jerusalem above my highest joy!   (Ps. 137:1-6, RSV)

The last section of this psalm (verses 7-9) contains a prayer for divine vengeance against both the Babylonians and the Edomites. With bitter resentment the psalmist recalls how those Eastern neighbors, the nation said to be descended from Jacob's brother Esau, had encouraged the Babylonians to destroy Jerusalem in 586. Apparently the book of Obadiah, "the shortest book in the Old Testament," alludes to the same unbrotherly spirit

---

[44]The Jewish month of Ab coincides roughly with our August. The annual observance features lamentation at the Western Wall (the remains of Herod's temple) in Jerusalem.

on the part of the Edomites, promising in the name of the Lord severe punishment upon them. Obadiah's very detailed indictment of Edom's treachery (especially verses 11-14) suggests a date not long after the actual events.

Another prophetic voice to be heard by those in exile is one without a personal name; this anonymous poet, apparently active about the middle of the sixth century, sounded a new note of hope and encouragement, and his lyrical style befits his message of coming release for the exiles. The scholarly label assigned to his work, found in Isaiah 40-55, is "Deutero-Isaiah" (or "Second Isaiah"). The poet-prophet proclaimed a "new exodus" in which Yahweh will make a highway through the desert and lead his people back to their homeland. A remarkably innovative theologian, Second Isaiah combined the themes of Creation and Redemption, and saw the hand of Israel's God in the call of Cyrus the Persian prince, who was destined to grant relief to the captive Jews. As never before in the prophetic books, foreign gods and idols are ridiculed unmercifully in light of a truly monotheistic faith in Yahweh, God of the whole earth. In a series of poems that refer to "the servant of the Lord" he projected the image of one—whether individual or group—whose mission was to give God's teaching to the nations, despite opposition, and even to suffer vicariously for sins.[45] In so many respects Deutero-Isaiah marks a new level of theological insight among the prophets.

The Babylonian ruler, Nebuchadrezzar, died in 562, and shortly thereafter his empire began to show how much it had depended on his strong hand. For about seven years there was an open power struggle among contenders for the throne, finally ending with Nabonidus in shaky control and more often away in his residence at Teima than in Babylon. Meanwhile, the Persian Cyrus seized control of Media and eventually conquered the kingdom of Lydia (in Asia Minor). By this time the Babylonians, thoroughly disillusioned with Nabonidus, offered little resistance to Cyrus; in fact, priestly conspirators in Babylon actually opened the gates to welcome him in 539. Cyrus lost no time in making himself master of the whole empire. He also quickly showed himself to be "an enlightened despot" by adopting a policy of humane treatment for subject nations, and in 538 BCE

---

[45]These poems, often called "Servant Songs," are found in Isaiah 42:1-4; 49:1-6; 50:4-11; and 52:13-53:12. The question of the servant's identity (if there was one particular figure in the poet's mind) is notoriously difficult; not without reason early Christians found in Jesus the fulfillment of this "suffering servant of the Lord"; cf. Acts 8:26-35.

he issued the edict that allowed the exiled Jews to return, if they wished, to their homeland (see 2 Chron. 36:22-23, Ezra 1:1-4).

Response among the Jewish exiles was not unanimously enthusiastic, because some of them had settled down, raised families, and engaged in business pursuits that they were reluctant to give up; others were too old or infirm to pack up and make the long journey back; still others, no doubt, simply preferred the certainty of a life they had known for years to the uncertainty of an unknown future in Judea. At any rate, the returnees were few in number, and the period of the Restoration[46] got off to a slow start; the story is told in part by the books of postexilic prophets such as Haggai, Zechariah, and Malachi, and in part by the later work known as Ezra-Nehemiah.[47]

Haggai and Zechariah 1-8 clearly belong to the end of the sixth century; their oracles are carefully dated in the years 520 to 518 BCE. Both prophets were concerned with problems faced by the people of Jerusalem in the governorship of Zerubbabel. Haggai, seeing that economic distress was widespread—crops were meager, wages did not cover expenses— called on the people to adjust their priorities, to "put first things first." Build the house of the Lord, he said, and let other things fall into line. For many years only the foundation of the temple had been restored; under the urging of Haggai, apparently the work was resumed and (ca. 516) completed. Meanwhile, Zechariah's oracles took the form of reported visions, most of which had to do with the coming age of peace and prosperity. Implicit in both of these prophetic works is an expectation, possibly encouraged by current political instability in Persia, that the Lord was about to restore kingship to his people through his "servant the Branch"—probably a messianic title, alluding to Zerubbabel, a descendant of David.[48]

The short book we call "Malachi" provides no clue as to the author's identity; in fact, the title (which is Hebrew for "my messenger") may have

---

[46]This is a common designation for the period, roughly 538 to 400; an alternative label, "the Persian period," would extend the time to 333, when the Macedonians under Alexander took over the territory.

[47]Ezra-Nehemiah comprises one scroll in the Hebrew Writings, and is thought to be composed after 400 BCE either by the author of our 1 and 2 Chronicles or one from the same "school" of record keepers.

[48]See Zechariah 3:8, 6:9-14, where the original wording may have included the name of Zerubbabel, which could have been removed later to avoid giving offense to Persian overlords.

been supplied by an editor from the reference in 3:1—"Behold, I send my messenger to prepare the way before me, and . . . he is coming, says the Lord of hosts." And unlike Haggai and Zechariah, Malachi gives little indication of a specific date for his work, but some of his concerns suggest a time somewhere in the mid-fifth century. Problems in the cult had arisen over improper offerings, careless priests, and negligence in tithing; abuse of divorce laws and "faithless" treatment of wives "cover the Lord's altar with tears."[49] Against all those who are thus heedless of the Lord's covenant Malachi promised the coming day of judgment, reminding us of the great preexilic prophets in this respect.

Readers of the English Bible find that Malachi is the very last book of the Old Testament. In the Hebrew Bible, while it is the last of the "Book of the Twelve," the whole collection of Prophets stands between the Torah (Law) and the Writings, so that our books 1 and 2 Chronicles come last of all. But in neither case was the arrangement of the books based on chronological consideration. Alert readers may indeed be wondering where in the sequence Joel belongs, or the last part of Isaiah (56-66), or Zechariah 9-14. The best answer is that all these are "of uncertain date," because there is a rather wide range of opinion among the experts, from sixth to fourth centuries BCE. Each book, or section, needs to be treated separately and judged by its own lights, but because this would take me beyond my purpose here, I must be content simply to count these among the postexilic writings to which we cannot assign a definite date of composition.

With somewhat more confidence we can include in this period the completion of the Deuteronomic History, which drew on very old tribal traditions, some written sources no longer extant, and probably other records unknown to us, to extend the story of the covenant people down to the last days of Judah. This is the story that we now read in Joshua, Judges, Samuel, and Kings. Another product of the "Deuteronomic" school,[50] this work apparently achieved its final form early in the exilic period. True to the moral and theological outlook that marked the earlier literary efforts,

---

[49]See Malachi 2:13-16, on the question of divorce; chs. 1 and 3 primarily deal with the cultic matters.

[50]While certain common features of style and outlook justify speaking of all the works— Deuteronomy itself, the "D" stratum elsewhere in the Pentateuch, and Joshua through Kings—as "Deuteronomic," scholars often differentiate among two or three "editors" and prefer to think of a "school" of writers or compilers possibly extending over many generations.

our Deuteronomic Historian *de*scribes in order to *pre*scribe—the ups and downs of Israel's history become dramatic illustration of the rule that faithful obedience brings its rewards and apostasy or disobedience its punishment.

The experience of national disaster and exile was the occasion not only for drawing lessons from the more immediate past, but also for the reappraisal of more ancient traditions, even of those most fundamental to Israel's faith and practice. Here, most likely in the time of Restoration, the literary results of such reappraisal took the form of a new, "enlarged edition" of the To-rah—what scholars ascribe to the Priestly ("P") writer or writers.[51] Gathering the ancient sources (whether oral or written)—we assume that he had at least "JE" and "D"—the Priestly writer set this material into the arrangement and form that we know now as the Pentateuch.

As with the earlier sources, "P" contributed materially as well as editorially to the formation of Torah, and scholars generally agree that most of the material in Exodus 25-31 and 35-40, Leviticus, and Numbers 1-10 derives from "P". As I have already noted, the very first story of the Bible (Gen. 1:1-2:4a) comes from the Priestly writer, and serves to introduce some of the distinctive features of his language and style, as well as his most prominent interests. There, for example, we detect the somewhat stilted, formulaic repetition of phrases—"and God said, Let there be . . . and there was . . ." and "there was evening and there was morning. . . ." "P" prefers *Elohim* in referring to deity, but sometimes in stories of the Patriarchs he uses the ancient name El Shaddai,[52] and waits to introduce the name *Yahweh* in the story of Moses.[53] In keeping with a priestly interest in the cultus, the "P" account of Creation is framed in the six days of God's work and is obviously a theological justification for observance of the seventh day as *Sabbath*—a day of rest. In many other places "P" shows a similar concern to authenticate cultic rites and institutions by tracing their origins to the very earliest times, just as he finds in the figure of Aaron, Moses' brother, the prototype of the later Levitical priesthood. Likewise, in the case of the many, sometimes lengthy, genealogies (the "begats")

---

[51]As in the case of "D," it is better to think of a "school" of priestly scribes than of one individual who was responsible for the whole. In any case it should be stressed that this relatively late composition includes much that is obviously of very ancient origin, though not in the earlier J, E, and D.

[52]This is the name translated in the RSV as "God Almighty"—as in Genesis 17:1—perhaps to be more literally rendered "mighty one of the mountains."

[53]See Exodus 6:2-3, which obviously disagrees with the Yahwist's notion in Genesis 4:26 (when "men began to call on the name of the LORD").

for which the Priestly source is noted, there is usually very practical motivation—namely, to legitimate family lines and to ground claims of kinship among the later generations of "the sons of Israel"—a matter of utmost importance for returning Judeans after the Exile, many of whom would have had nothing more than the family name on which to base their claims on property.

The tendency to schematize, seen in the six-day sequence of Genesis 1, extends also into the priestly arrangement of patriarchal narratives, whereby human history moves in stages from one "covenant" to another—from that with Man (Adam), to one with Noah, to that with Abraham, to one with Moses.[54] All in all, one misses in "P" that interest in flesh-and-blood personalities that characterized the Yahwist Epic and finds instead a preoccupation with stereotypes and with the formalizing of relations between God and cultic community. And yet, in terms of its broad theological scope and the rigor of its moral ideals, the work of "P" stands as a monument to the inspiration and intellectual vitality of those postexilic leaders who composed it. Not only did it serve its own day as a rallying call for recommitment to God and the cult, but it became in time to come *Torah*, the "teaching," the all-sufficient revelation of God's Will to mankind, on which Judaism was founded and lives to this day.

The turmoil and suffering of the Exile may have been the occasion for yet another literary achievement of the highest quality: the book of Job. Though the scholars are far from unanimous as to date or place of origin, the questions addressed in Job strongly suggest a time when the old, traditional answers were being challenged, when the meaning of faith and the goodness of God needed especially to be examined. The name of Job (along with Noah and Daniel) was mentioned in Ezekiel 14:14 and 20, as an example of a righteous man, and there is no doubt that he had long before figured as a hero of ancient wisdom; it could be that the prose sections (Job 1-2, 42:7-17) of our present book represent the epic of Job in a form much earlier than the one we have. The bulk of our book is the long, three-cycle dialogue in poetic form, in which Job defends his integrity and answers the charges of his "three friends." Their position is essentially that Job is suffering because he has sinned against God and therefore needs to confess

---

[54]Each covenant seems to support new ethical requirements and to be accompanied by a "sign" like the sabbath, the rainbow, and so on; cf. B. W. Anderson, *Understanding the Old Testament*, 3rd ed. (Englewood Cliffs NJ: Prentice Hall, 1975) 433-35.

his guilt. Job denies—vehemently, and sometimes arrogantly—that accusation or explanation of his condition. In short, the all-too-pat "solution" to the problem raised by "innocent suffering" comes in for severe testing by the poet in the moving and eloquent book of Job.

As for other instances of the growing body of Wisdom writings, it is likely that by 600 BCE or shortly thereafter the collection of wise sayings had been expanded to include "proverbs of Solomon which the men of Hezekiah . . . copied."[55] The proverbs, by their very nature, are timeless and exceedingly difficult to assign specific dates, as are most of the songs that were to become our book of Psalms. But a reasonable assumption, supported by external evidence, is that both collections—Proverbs and the Psalter—continued to grow well into the Restoration, possible reaching their final form only about the fourth century BCE.

Two more books remain to be set within this period (before 400), Ruth and Jonah. Ruth is a beautiful story of family devotion, set in the time of the Judges (hence its location in our English Bibles). And the book of Jonah, while counted now among the "minor prophets," is also best regarded as a story or allegory, although its name comes from a real person of the eighth century.[56] Different as the two books are, they probably were composed to address essentially the same situation. In the middle of the fifth century, as already noted, questions arose over the matter of marriage and divorce; many Jews returned from exile with foreign wives, and perhaps others contracted such mixed marriages after returning. Apparently, in the interest of cultic purity and the desire to avoid the mistakes of the past, Nehemiah (and, later, Ezra) called for faithful Jews to put away their non-Jewish wives. It was, in short, a time when the walls—both of Jerusalem and of Judaism—were a high priority, and the prevailing mood was one of exclusivism.

The story of Ruth, a Moabitess, and her Israelite mother-in-law, Naomi, seems to reflect a certain negative reaction to the prevailing mood. Very subtly, yet very frankly, it tells of the love and loyalty of one foreign wife—even a widow—to her mother-in-law and to her religion. Dutifully Ruth marries Boaz, the next-of-kin, to secure property rights for Naomi

---

[55]According to the caption at Proverbs 25:1, heading a subcollection that extends through 29:27. If "men of Hezekiah" means scribes of that king of Judah (ca. 715-687 BCE), then it would, of course, belong to a period contemporary with Isaiah and Micah.

[56]Jonah ben Amittai, mentioned in 2 Kings 14:25; see n. 38.

and to raise up heirs to her dead husband. The "punchline"—so unobtrusive that it is often missed—lies in the closing genealogical note about the son born of that *mixed marriage:* he would in time become the grandfather of none other than David, the king of Israel (Ruth 4:17-22).

The story of Jonah is not so subtle; in fact it drives home its point with a vengeance. Jonah, the prophet of the Lord, was called to go the city of Nineveh, capital of the Assyrians (and here the symbol of pagan wickedness), and "cry against it."[57] But the exclusivist Jonah would have no part of it; he boarded a ship bound for "Tarshish" (the opposite direction from Nineveh), avoiding his mission by escape from "the presence of Yahweh." His failure to become God's missionary to foreigners endangered the ship and its crew, and Jonah had to be thrown overboard to calm the angry sea. There he was swallowed by "a great fish" (not a whale) and vomited out, so that he might finally fulfill his mission. Still reluctant, Jonah went part way into the great city, and preached a *part* of his message—that the city was doomed! He left out all prospect of repentance, but the foreigners repented anyway—much to the dismay of Jonah, who wished that he could die. The parabolic character of all this should be clear: like Jonah, the Jews had been swallowed up in exile, then released to witness to the God of all peoples (cf. Second Isaiah's "light to the nations"), but still held back and valued their wilting vines more than whole cities of people who "know not their right from their left" (see Jon. 4:9-11). It is hard to imagine a more penetrating indictment of the fifth-century policy of exclusivism.

From the years 600 to 400, then, we have a tremendous burst of literary output, especially remarkable in view of the social upheaval that came with the fall of Jerusalem and its aftermath. Perhaps, after all, the more crucial the times, the more need there is for the preservation in writing of sacred traditions, and visual reminders for future generations of lessons to be learned from crises of the moment. It was no doubt some such need that encouraged not only new documentation but the collection and editing of older works, the books of the prophets in particular. Words of warning that had gone largely unheeded in their own times now began to win new respect and to prompt a chastened, wiser generation to take their lessons to heart. So the oracles of Jeremiah were gathered, and along with Baruch's

---

[57]Jonah 1:2. Implicit in the phrase, of course, was a call to repentance, as was true of most prophetic warnings, even when not expressly stated.

memoirs made into a book; likewise the rest of the Latter Prophets, as they were later to be called. During this span of two centuries, to recapitulate, there came into being the book of Ezekiel; the work of Deutero-Isaiah; certain psalms, additions to Proverbs, and the book of Lamentations; Obadiah, Haggai, Zechariah 1-8, and Malachi; completion of the Deuteronomic History; the Priestly edition of Torah; the book of Job; the book of Ruth; and the book of Jonah. In sum, all the Pentateuch (or Torah), and most— if not all—the Prophets (according to the Hebrew divisions) existed by 400 BCE, and the few remaining parts of the Old Testament, books composed after that date, all belong to the third division of the Jewish Canon, the Writings.

After 400 BCE. Reconstruction of the history of Judea in the late fifth to early fourth centuries is extremely difficult, partly because of some disarray in the primary source, Ezra-Nehemiah.[58] Modern efforts to untangle and rearrange the sequence of events leave certain questions, but on the whole it seems best to follow their consensus and to set the work of Ezra a few years *later* than that of Nehemiah. Both—one the governor of Judea under the Persian Artaxerxes I, the other the priestly scribe who taught Judeans the Torah—apparently left ''memoirs'' or first-person records of events (roughly 450 to 425 BCE), which were later gathered by the Chronicler, presumably the same writer (or school?) who composed our 1 and 2 Chronicles, and were used along with other documents to extend the history of Judea at least a century after the events of Ezra's day, a circumstance that would surely explain his confusion over the sequence of certain events.

Chronicles—one book, not two, in the Hebrew Bible—obviously borrowed heavily from earlier sources; in the parts which parallel Samuel and Kings[59] the wording is often verbatim, and yet the Chronicler felt free to omit or to provide additional data to suit his own purposes. His orientation was definitely that of the religious cult, and his concern to highlight the role of priests and Levites is such as to suggest that he was himself a member of the temple staff. Passing over in silence the unsavory affair of David and Bathsheba, the Chronicler emphasizes David's contributions to worship and makes him virtually ''high priest'' even without a temple! Of a

---

[58]It is mainly a matter of inserting Ezra's career a bit too soon; Ezra 7-8 probably should come after Nehemiah 7.

[59]From 1 Chronicles 10 through the end of 2 Chronicles.

later king, Uzziah of Judah, the Chronicler expands on his source (2 Kings) to reinterpret the reason for his leprosy and to provide entirely new information about Uzziah's interest in agriculture and engines of war (see 2 Chron. 26:6-15). Chronicles is an interesting reappraisal of the past in the light of the needs and dominant concerns of a restored community that found its focal center in its temple and cult.

As already noted, Ezra-Nehemiah was written as a sequel or supplement to Chronicles, presumably not long afterward. Without exact parallel in the Old Testament, it provides very valuable historical data for the Restoration, even allowing for the aforementioned disorder in chronology, and our understanding of other books like Ruth, Jonah, and Malachi (among others) now depends heavily on that data.

One thing to be learned from the Chronicler's work is especially helpful in assessing later stages in collection and composition as well—namely, the growing preoccupation among the Jews of Judea with their cultic life, and with worship at the temple in particular. During the fourth century BCE, as we infer from the Chronicler's work, reorganization and regulation of the priests and Levites took place, bringing new order and regimen to cultic affairs. The calendar of annual, monthly, and daily observances was set, and with it the importance of proper offerings at the proper times. Interest in ''the liturgy'' (as we might say today) was high, and it was a most appropriate time for the collection of psalms and hymns (old and new) into one book—''the hymnbook of the second temple''[60] Although the final five-part arrangement may have come some time later, it is likely that the contents of our canonical Psalter expanded little, if at all, after 300 BCE. It is very likely that most of the superscriptions, especially those giving musical captions,[61] were added at this time. In short, the process that began early in the monarchical era—indeed even earlier if we count the Song of Miriam or that of Deborah—reached its consummation centuries later in this rich treasury of praise, lament, and thanksgiving that we call the Psalms.

---

[60]This designation is applied to the Psalms by many scholars, not always with the same connotation; it should not be interpreted to mean that all 150 (151 in the Greek) were composed for use in temple worship. ''Second temple'' refers to the one rebuilt ca. 520-516 BCE .

[61]Aside from obvious references ''to the choirmaster'' and to guilds of temple singers (Sons of Asaph, or of Korah), some superscriptions apparently indicate the melody or tempo—''the Hind of the Dawn'' (Ps. 22) or ''Lilies'' (Pss. 69, 80).

The other anthology of poetry, the book of Proverbs, may also have reached completion about this time, receiving a new beginning (chapters 1-9) and perhaps the supplements now in chapters 30-31. The name of Solomon had by this time become a traditional signature for Wisdom literature in general, just as the name of David had been for the psalms, and Moses had been for the Pentateuch. So even relatively recent products of the Wisdom movement, where actual authors were unknown, tended to be regarded as "Solomonic." Thus, as a matter of course, Proverbs 1-9 were included along with much older sayings as "the proverbs of Solomon," and by an easy extension of the same notion a collection of love poems, the Song of Songs, came also to be "Solomon's." Some scholars would date this collection as a whole in the third century BCE, although certain themes and allusions reflect a possibly older origin for parts of it. In any case, the Song was probably intended as celebration of human love and marriage, and any other supposed religious meaning has to be derived from an allegorical interpretation.

Somewhat more guardedly, but with the same effect, Solomonic authorship was assigned to another book, known in Hebrew as *Qoheleth*.[62] This very "unorthodox" book, a mixture of prose and poetry, is better known to us as Ecclesiastes. Like most of the Wisdom material it defies assignment of a precise date, but its language, style, and outlook all suggest a time after 300 BCE. The anonymous "Preacher" sets forth his pessimistic philosophy ("all is vanity") in striking contrast to what we might regard as the mainstream of biblical faith and thought; not even in the book of Job was there such an expression of despair over the injustice or meaninglessness of life. Only the addition at the end (Eccles. 12:9-14), probably by an editor, relieves somewhat the somber mood of futility by advising readers to "fear God, and keep his commandments."

In the arrangement of the Hebrew Bible, a subdivision of the Writings came to be known as "the rolls" (*ha-megilloth*), five books that were especially associated with various festivals and fasts of the Jews. Four of them we have already mentioned: Song of Solomon, Lamentations, Ruth, and Ecclesiastes; the last, and apparently most popular of the five, was Esther. In this book the story is told of a beautiful woman, the Jewess Esther, who

---

[62]A word derived from the same root as *qahal* ("an assembly"), this came to be translated *ekklesiastes* in Greek versions (from the Greek for "assembly," which Christians later adopted as a word for "church").

became queen to the Persian King Ahasuerus—better known in history by his Greek name Xerxes.[63] Informed by her kinsman Mordecai that a powerful officer of the court has planned a pogrom against all Jews, Esther dares to incur the king's wrath by approaching the throne uninvited, but gains his attention and cleverly turns the tables against her enemy and saves her people from disaster. The very day that had been set for slaughter of the Jews then became a day of celebration—the feast of Purim—that is still observed in Judaism, usually in early March. The book, best regarded as a "festal legend" (designed to justify the celebration), seems to have circulated among Jews of the Dispersion[64] in the early third century, and was known in Alexandria (Egypt) in expanded form in Greek about 200 BCE.

While I will say more in the next chapter about books that were known and read in Greek, but failed to become a part of the Hebrew Bible, it should be noted in passing that after about 300 BCE the collection of sacred books in Alexandrian synagogues included a number of such books, like the expanded Esther. Translation into Greek for the benefit of Jews who no longer read the Hebrew eventually produced what is known as the Septuagint, embracing "additional" books such as Tobit, Judith, Wisdom of Solomon, and the Wisdom of ben Sirach,[65] alongside the older books of the Law and the Prophets. Although Jewish tradition said that "prophecy ceased with Ezra," it is clear that the Greek Period (ca. 333-150 BCE) was one of continued literary activity both in Judea and in the Dispersion.

Only one other Old Testament book remains to be accounted for: the book of Daniel. Like Ruth and Jonah, the book is named for its hero, not its author, and, also like them, Daniel has its setting in an age past. Daniel is represented, at the outset, as one of four young Judean exiles who are being primed by Nebuchadrezzar for service to the state. The first half of

---

[63]Xerxes I (485-464) is probably the king represented here. The same Hebrew form of the name is used in Ezra 4:6 and Daniel 9:1. For the best historical data on Xerxes, see the *Histories* of Herodotus, 3-7.

[64]"Dispersion" and the alternate term *Diaspora* are commonly used to refer to the scattering of Jews outside Palestine and to the resultant set of conditions and customs, some of which deeply affected the development of Judaism in the centuries just prior to, and coincident with, the rise of Christianity.

[65]These are only a few examples; for the full list see the Oxford Annotated RSV or other versions that contain the *Apocrypha*—the label assigned by Protestants (after the Reformation) to the group of books found in the Vulgate (based on the Septuagint) but not in the Hebrew Canon.

the book consists primarily of stories showing how these young men remain steadfast in their devotion to the God of Israel, even at the risk of their lives. God reveals to Daniel what the king dreamed, just in time to save the whole profession of magicians and soothsayers; punished for refusing to bow down to the king's idolatrous image, the three friends of Daniel are thrown into a fiery furnace, only to be protected by an angel from on high. The second half of the book has Daniel himself seeing visions, full of strange, symbolic figures, no doubt meant to baffle the outsider (or enemy to the faith) but to convey to the faithful a message of comfort and hope.

Most scholars have recognized these elements as classic marks of the literary genre called "apocalyptic."[66] Special revelation by means of visions, often concerning the coming of Judgment Day and the end of the present Age and replete with angelic beings to interpret to the seer the mystifying images he has seen—these are some of the dominant features of a series of books (*apocalypses*) from this late period, apparently reaching a peak of popularity among Jews just prior to the time of Jesus. Many of the books now known to us as "Pseudepigrapha"[67]—largely from the first century BCE and the first century CE—are of this genre, as is 2 Esdras (4 Ezra) in the Apocrypha, and in the New Testament the book of Revelation.

Apocalypticism, as the movement that produced these books is called, seems to be grounded in Old Testament Prophecy, but in many ways it moved beyond that ground and developed a tradition all its own. It took the earlier prophetic oracles, expecially those that seemed to have fallen short of fulfillment, and reinterpreted them in the light of recent events. Reinterpretation in most cases meant finding a hidden message, a meaning other than the literal or most obvious, a practice reinforced by situations of oppression and persecution of the faithful, where cryptic language was used to thwart would-be censors. Thus the book of Daniel is best under-

---

[66]This adjective, like the noun *apocalypsis,* comes from the Greek verb "to reveal." Of course, some of the distinguishing marks of this kind of writing can be traced back to Ezekiel or even to Isaiah 24-27, as well as to Zechariah 1-8.

[67]The word is from the Greek, literally "false writings," in recognition of their pseudonymous character—i.e., naming as authors such famous heroes of the past as "the twelve patriarchs," Moses, Enoch, Ezra, etc. Cf. R. H. Charles, *The Apocrypha and Pseudepigrapha of the Old Testament in English,* 2 vols. (Oxford: Clarendon Press, 1913), or the more recent edition of J. H. Charlesworth, *The Old Testament Pseudepigrapha* (Garden City NJ: Doubleday, 1983).

stood as a prime example of apocalyptic writing, intended for the encouragement of "the saints of the Most High" in their conflict with the Syrian ruler Antiochus IV Epiphanes (176-164 BCE). Drawing perhaps on older tales of the folk hero Daniel,[68] the anonymous writer recast Jeremiah's reference to a seventy-year exile (Jer. 25:11-12, 29:10) into a prophecy to be fulfilled in "seventy weeks of years" or 490 years (Daniel 9:2, 24-27). But throughout the author was preoccupied with the threat posed by the Seleucid regime in its blatant attempts to force Hellenistic culture on subject Jews. That regime is characterized as the kingdom of iron (or iron mixed with clay) in one place, as the "fourth beast" in another, and Antiochus himself appears in the little horn with "a mouth speaking great things."[69] Behind the allusion to "the abomination that makes desolate" (Dan. 11:31, 12:11) lies the heathen altar that Antiochus ordered to be set up in the temple precinct. It was a desperate time for the hard-pressed Jews, and the writer of Daniel gave no cheap comfort; setting these trials in the larger, cosmic plan of world history, he called for his troubled people to look for relief at last in the Kingdom that shall crush all earthly kingdoms, and in that King whose dominion is everlasting.

In summary, after 400 BCE came the work of the Chronicler, including our 1 and 2 Chronicles, Ezra, and Nehemiah; final compilation of the Psalms and Proverbs; the book of Ecclesiastes; Song of Songs; Esther; and Daniel. Thus it appears that by about 150 BCE the writings that were to become the Jewish Tanak, or the Christian Old Testament, were all known among the Jews, both in Judea and in Dispersion. It remains to speak of one further stage in the story of the Bible's composition, the development of Christianity and the writings destined to become the New Testament. My sketch of the contents of the Old Testament has taken us from tribal songs and stories of the second millennium BCE to court records, psalms and proverbs of the monarchical period, to the books of the prophets and down to the postexilic compilations and books of the second century BCE— a long story, covering a span of about twelve centuries. The final stage

---

[68]Recall Ezekiel's earlier mention of Daniel; references to a certain "Dan'el" also appear in Canaanite records from Ras Shamra, which would suggest a very ancient figure, but possibly not to be identified with the hero of the book.

[69]See Daniel 2 for the sequence of four kingdoms, ch. 7 for the four beasts; in both cases the reference is apparently to Babylonia, Media, Persia, and the Macedonian (Ptolemies and Seleucids) kingdom. The "little horn" is said to come from the fourth beast (Dan. 7:7-8).

covers only about one century—roughly 50-150—but lends itself to sub-division along these commonly accepted lines: (A) the "Apostolic Period" (to ca. 65 BCE); (B) the "Subapostolic Period" (after 65 CE).

The Apostolic Period. It may seem strange, but the first parts of the New Testament to be composed were *not* the Gospels, although they now stand first in order of arrangement. That, of course, is a reasonable order, since they tell of the ministry and teachings of Jesus of Nazareth, his death and resurrection, without which there would have been no Christian Church and no literary products thereof. But as far as we can now ascertain, the first written expressions of the Christian movement that we have are the letters of the Apostle Paul, and none of the four Gospels appeared before ca. 65 CE, about the time of Paul's death.[70]

As with many of the crucial, formative events in Old Testament times, the first communication of the message—the "good news" of Christ—was made by word of mouth. Like the old prophets, the first Christians were speakers, not writers, and for many years after the pivotal events of Passover in 29 CE,[71] they were apparently content with this oral testimony. So it was not until the Pharisaic opponent of the movement, Saul of Tarsus, was dramatically converted (Acts 9:1-19) that we have written documentation of any sort. And what we have from him are nine or ten letters, written to various Christian churches or individuals.[72] Paul, as he is best known in the New Testament, traveled as a missionary—an "Apostle to the Gentiles"—and founded (or helped to found) many new churches in the regions of Asia (Minor), Galatia, Pontus, Phrygia, and parts of Greece and Macedonia. Most of his letters were addressed to people in those places, and were intended to encourage, to give pastoral support, to correct misunderstandings, or to admonish, according to the particular need of the moment. In keeping with the custom of the day, Paul made use of an *amanuensis* or scribe, some of whom are mentioned by name in the let-

---

[70]Specific dates for Paul's life and career are at best tentative, and the question of how and when he died is notoriously difficult: Acts leaves it open, and later writings of the church (for example, 1 Clement 5) refer obliquely to Paul's martyrdom, which we presume took place under the Roman Emperor Nero.

[71]Again, exact dates for Jesus' ministry are problematic, but the best "educated guess" is 27-29 CE, and the time of Paul's call is probably four or five years later.

[72]The traditional count is thirteen (fourteen, if Hebrews is included), but modern research leads scholars to suspect that some of those—especially Ephesians, 1 and 2 Timothy, Titus—are pseudonymous and later than 65 CE.

ters,[73] dictating his message and, usually, adding in his own hand a closing greeting and identifying mark. It seems clear that Paul looked on these letters as simply an extension of his ministry to people for whom he cared deeply, and though some of them he meant to have read aloud in a church assembly, or perhaps passed along to another group, he probably never dreamed that the letters would one day be collected, copied and handed on to future generations as "Scripture." But more of that subject in the next chapter.

This is not the place, either, to treat the question of Pauline chronology or to try to assign dates to all the letters. Let it suffice here to suggest a relative order of composition, drawn from a fairly wide consensus of modern scholars. Two short letters to the Thessalonians (the church at Thessalonica) are probably the earliest of our collection; next comes the Corinthian correspondence (1 and 2 Corinthians), which indicates that Paul wrote other letters besides those which survived in the New Testament.[74] Then follow Galatians—although there are some scholars who would put it before 1 Thessalonians—and the letter to the Romans, including the "postscript" (chapter 16) which may originally have been part of another letter. The "Prison Epistles" (all supposedly written from jail)—Philippians, Colossians, Philemon—would come next; a fourth epistle, Ephesians, is traditionally counted in this group, but for reasons that will be explained later, there are serious questions about its authorship and date. Thus we have nine letters presumed to be authentic, actually dictated and sent by Paul in the years 50 to 65.

Two other epistles that might *possibly* come from the same period are those we know as 1 Peter and James, two of the seven called "Catholic (or General) Epistles." Though there are strong objections to counting them as authentic letters of the apostles Peter and James,[75] a good case can be

---

[73]For example, Tertius in Romans 16:22; the inclusion of Timothy in the greeting of certain letters may suggest that he served in this way, although he was not a professional scribe (cf. 2 Cor. 1:1; Col. 1:1).

[74]See 1 Corinthians 5:9, a clear allusion to a letter now lost, or perhaps represented (according to some scholars) by 2 Corinthians 6:14-7:1, which seems out of place there. Many scholars argue that 2 Corinthians is really a combination of two originally separate letters, and that chs. 10-13 could be the "severe letter" mentioned in 2 Corinthians 2:3 and 6:8-12.

[75]Full discussion of the criteria for judging authenticity is reserved for a later chapter; objections to that of 1 Peter are partly matters of language and style, partly the difficulty

made for dating both in the decade of the 60s. 1 Peter makes reference to coming "trials" and "the fiery ordeal" by which Christians will be tested—possibly alluding to the kind of persecution already underway in Nero's Rome.[76] James, which is more like a sermon or a group of ethical admonitions than a real letter, also mentions the need for steadfastness in the face of testing, but on the whole it lacks any sure sign of its date or place of origin. Its discussion of "faith and works" (James 2:14-26) seems to presuppose an understanding (or misunderstanding?) of Paul's teaching on that score, and therefore argues for a date in the late 50s, at the earliest.

Before turning to the later, more prolific period, I should make it clear that in the development of Christian literature—as it was in the Old Testament—late compositions often depend on very early sources, oral and possibly even written. Absence of any written gospels before 65 CE does not mean that nothing at all of Jesus' life and teachings had assumed a set form by that time. Ancient sources testify to the circulation of certain *logia* or collections of Jesus' sayings,[77] no longer extant, but very probably a major fund of information for our gospel writers. Modern investigations have also probed into the period of oral transmission and enhanced our understanding of certain formative forces at work within the community of faith, whereby units of tradition like the Passion Narrative (the story of Jesus' arrest, trial and execution) were molded very early into their basic form by the repeated use of them in preaching and teaching. Thus we have every reason to suppose that what Luke tells us of his own efforts (Luke 1:1-4) was true of the others as well—they had and used reliable sources from earlier days.

The Subapostolic Period. Lest the use of the label "subapostolic" be misunderstood, let me make clear that it is not meant to disparage or dis-

---

of fitting its contents (especially references to persecution) into known historical data. As for James, although tradition has assigned it to James the Lord's brother (cf. Gal. 1:19; Acts 15:13ff.), there is hardly any internal evidence to support a positive identification of the author.

[76]An early tradition said that the apostle Peter died a martyr under the persecution of Nero (64/65 CE); the letter, of course, is addressed to Christians in the East (cf. 1 Pet. 1:1), where we suppose the first concentrated attack on the church came under the reign of Domitian (81-96 CE). Therefore some scholars assign 1 Peter to this later time.

[77]The fourth-century historian, Eusebius (*Historia Ecclesiastica* III.39.16), quotes the second-century bishop Papias as saying that Matthew composed such *logia* "in the Hebrew language." Some scholars prefer to think of these *logia* as Old Testament quotations used by Christian preachers to show how Jesus fulfilled the Scriptures (as, in fact, Matthew does in about eleven places).

count the value of the writings about to be described. It is a modern term of convenience, and admittedly somewhat arbitrary, to draw a line between what might roughly be defined as "first-generation" Christian authors and "second (or third?) generation" writers. I will keep separate the question of apostolic *authority* that eventually became attached to writings on *both* sides of the line, and stick for the moment to the matter of composition.

On the basis of both external and internal evidence, modern study of the four gospels leads us to suppose that the first three stand in a very close literary relationship to each other, whereas the fourth—John—stands quite apart, by itself. The question of just how Matthew, Mark, and Luke are related is known as "The Synoptic Problem"—the term "synoptic" pointing to a common viewpoint.[78] They share not only much the same material but tell their story in much the same order and often in the very same words; and yet each of the three is distinctive and in some ways unique.

Not to become involved prematurely in the somewhat complex analysis used by scholars to "solve" the Synoptic Problem, let it suffice here to state the widely held conclusion: (1) that the Gospel of Mark was the first to be written (ca. 65-70 CE); (2) that both Matthew and Luke made use of Mark's work in composing their own; and (3) that there was another source (besides Mark) shared by Matthew and Luke—designated "Q" and consisting (apparently) of some 250 verses, mostly sayings.[79] The relationship, based on this two-source theory, can be diagrammed in this way:

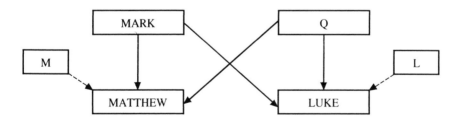

---

[78]"Syn-optic" is from the Greek "seen together [in common]." Thus Matthew, Mark, and Luke are often called "Synoptic Gospels."

[79]"Q" stands for the German word *Quelle* ("source"), and is used to designate material common to Matthew and Luke but *not* in Mark; as a source it is hypothetical, of course, like "J" or "E" in the Pentateuch—there is no surviving document corresponding to "Q."

The symbols "M" and "L" would indicate the relatively small amount of material peculiar to—that is, found *only* in—Matthew and Luke respectively.

Attempts to identify the individual authors with apostles or other figures known to be associated with them seem to derive from the second century, after the fourfold collection became the accepted "Gospel."[80] Originally, they were anonymous writings, each one achieving "success" at first in its own place of origin, then circulating in a wider circle, until (perhaps ca. 140-150 CE) someone had the good sense to bring the four together. At any rate, the name of Mark came to be linked with the one said to be composed in or near Rome, since it was supposed that Simon Peter had gone there to preach, and that John Mark served as his "interpreter," later to record in his book some of the things he had heard.[81]

Early tradition is less specific about the date or place of origin for Matthew and Luke, and even yet the scholars disagree as to which of the two was composed first. Somehow the name of Matthew, one of the twelve apostles (often identified as a "tax collector"),[82] was associated with the gospel that circulated around Syrian Antioch, and the name of Luke, physician and companion of the Apostle Paul, with the other, thought to have been a favorite in Caesarea Maritima. Both probably arose within the years 80 to 90.

Within the next five years, it may be assumed, the sequel to Luke—what we know as the Acts of the Apostles (or simply Acts)—was composed, tracing the development of the Christian Church and its missionary outreach from its beginnings in Jerusalem, to efforts in surrounding areas and eventually to the capital of the Empire. By this time (ca. 95) it is likely that the anonymous Epistle to the Hebrews had appeared, an impressive homily designed to show the superiority of God's revelation in Christ over

---

[80]That the fourfold set was once considered a single unit is suggested by some of the earliest manuscripts, where the heading *to euangelion* ("the gospel") appears as a heading for the whole group. By mid-second century there were probably other books about Jesus that were not deemed acceptable to the main body of Christians.

[81]Such is the tradition reported by Papias, according to Eusebius (*H.E.* III.39). Mark is generally identified with the person mentioned in the Acts of the Apostles (see Acts 12:22, 25) and 1 Peter 5:13.

[82]Compare Matthew 9:9-13 with Mark 2:13-17 and Luke 5:27-32; in the latter two his name is given as "Levi." But in Luke's lists (6:14-16 and in Acts 1:13) he is "Matthew."

any that had gone before, and to exhort Christians not to "backslide" or slacken in the pilgrimage on which they had set out.

Next came the Apocalypse of John, or Revelation, according to those who find the reign of Domitian the most likely occasion, or provocation, for the book. There are some scholars who prefer to put it back in the years after Nero's death (the late 60s), but on the whole its strange allusions are best explained by a setting in the tenth decade. "John"—not necessarily identified with the apostle of that name—was exiled to the Isle of Patmos (off the coast of Asia) and addressed his words to a beleaguered people, apparently already in peril of their lives, and called on them (in effect) to stand fast in the Faith, even as the writer of Daniel had in earlier times, in esoteric images depicting the certain Victory of God over the beastly forces of the Devil. John's visions of divine retribution for "the blood of the martyrs" might baffle the hosts of "Babylon" (code name for Rome) but would inspire courageous endurance in those being tested for their Christian witness.[83]

Just as in the Old Testament the present arrangement of the books does not correspond with the order of their composition, so also in the New: the book of Revelation stands last in the table of contents, but was not the last to be written. Modern studies have consistently assigned later dates to six other documents, and not so consistently to another four—or ten in all. Let us deal first with the questionable four, since they are still judged by some reputable scholars to belong to the Apostolic Period—namely, Ephesians, 1 and 2 Timothy, and Titus.

All four of these, of course, claim Paul as their author. Only in recent centuries has their Pauline authorship (or "authenticity") been challenged, and this on the basis of mainly linguistic criteria. Study of the style and vocabulary of these epistles raised questions because of the large proportion of words and phrases in them, *not* characteristic of Paul's other letters, and some not found elsewhere in the whole New Testament. Many terms, though used elsewhere by Paul, were found to be used in Ephesians and the Pastoral Epistles with very different meanings. In the case of Ephe-

---

[83]Domitian (81-96 CE), who claimed such titles as *dominus et deus* (lord and god), is said to have encouraged the "worship" of *Dea Roma* as a test of political loyalty among subjects in Asia. It may be about this time that burning incense on a pagan altar and cursing Christ became the requisite signs of such "loyalty"—and the sticking point for devout Christians.

sians there was also the oddity that in the oldest manuscript the words "in Ephesus" (1:1) were missing from the salutation, and in fact the highly formal, impersonal tone was not at all what one would expect of Paul, writing to people with whom he had lived for three years (see Acts 19-20; 1 Cor. 15:32).

Such research has been carried out in the light of a better understanding of the ancient use of *pseudonyms* in literature. This will be more fully treated in a later chapter; now it is enough to acknowledge that pseudonymous writing was widely known in the Graeco-Roman world as well as in certain circles of the Jews, and it is very likely that one or more of Paul's followers adopted the practice to extend that apostle's authority beyond the grave and over problems and issues of later years. The object was not to deceive the readers but to deal with the questions of a new day "as Paul would"—in very much the same spirit as the writer of apocalypses adopted the name of an honored hero of the past. Thus our Epistle to the Ephesians, though making extensive use of Paul's real letters,[84] was probably intended as an encyclical (to be sent round to many churches) calling for a greater show of unity among Christians who had in fact owed so much to the work of Paul. The best guess as to a date for Ephesians, would be in the 90s.

The problem of the Pastorals (1, 2 Timothy, Titus) is made somewhat more complex by (1) the difficulty of fitting them into Paul's lifetime— they virtually demand, if authentic, a date after 65 CE; and (2) scattered personal references, some so intimate as to be inconceivable as pure invention by a writer other than Paul himself. The latter feature has led some scholars to seek a solution in terms of authentic "fragments," perhaps scraps and notes by Paul, which were collected after his death and later used by the unknown author. In any case, on many grounds, the Pastoral Epistles in their present form are best understood as pseudonymous works, intended to give sage counsel, from the old master himself to young pastors of a growing, more highly organized church. Qualifications for the offices of "elder" and "bishop," eligibility for financial aid as widows, and a preoccupation with "false teachings" and how to avoid them dominate these letters, and suggest the concerns of a time decades later than Paul, very possibly ca. 100 or shortly thereafter.

---

[84]Excessive "self-quotation" from the known letters of Paul is one of the stylistic peculiarities of Ephesians; some allusions to all nine can be found, but dependence on Colossians seems the heaviest.

As for the final six books of the New Testament, by our reckoning the Fourth Gospel (John) probably came next, early in the second century. A long-standing tradition, traceable to Irenaeus (late second century), linked this gospel to John the disciple (one of the Twelve) at Ephesus, but upon close examination Irenaeus's testimony seems to be founded less on hard evidence than on the common identification of the "beloved disciple" (John 13:23-25; 19:26; 20:2; 21:20) with John ben (son of) Zebedee.[85] But without discounting the possibility that the disciple John was one source of material in the gospel, modern scholars have generally agreed that it reflects a circle of thought quite distant (in more ways than one) from that of the Synoptic Gospels, a circle much more attuned to Hellenistic thought than to that of Galilean Jews. The Fourth Gospel is a magnificent reinterpretation of the Christ event for a church that is increasingly Gentile, already separated from Judaism, and witnessing to people better acquainted with Dionysus than with Daniel, or with Stoicism more than Mosaic Torah. Not content simply to retell what the earlier gospels told, the writer reproduced "the good news" of Christ in terms meant to communicate with the world as he knew it; thus the figure of Jesus himself seems transformed in the many "I am" sayings and the "signs" that replace the synoptic parables and miracle stories.[86] Surely, this work deserves its popularity down through the centuries; a work of art and a model of creative theology for all time, it has an appeal perhaps unmatched by any other gospel.

The remaining five books, while clearly later than those already named, defy efforts to pin down precisely either dates or places of origin. All five— along with 1 Peter and James—came to be regarded as "Catholic Epistles," presumably marking their more *general* destinations as compared to those of the Pauline letters. They are named 2 Peter; 1, 2, and 3 John; and Jude.

In chronological sequence, the Johannine Epistles (as the three by "John" are known) probably came before 2 Peter or Jude, and perhaps not

---

[85]Eusebius, *H.E.* III.23, quoting from Irenaeus's work, *Against Heresies* II, III. For thorough examination of the ancient tradition by a modern scholar, see C. K. Barrett, *The Gospel According to St. John* (New York: Macmillan, 1955) 83-119.

[86]Compare, for example, John 6:35 (bread of life), 8:12 (light of the world), 10:11, 14 (good shepherd), 11:25 (the resurrection and the life), and so on. Though some of the "signs" reported in John rest on events common to the Synoptics, John seems to press beyond "what happened?" to "what does this mean?"—as if to make explicit the contemporary redemptive value.

long after the Gospel of John, with which they have some affinities of idea and expression. The three epistles apparently came from one writer, although the only self-designation used is "the elder" and that only in 2 and 3 John. In fact, 1 John lacks the usual salutation and seems more like a homily or formal treatise than a real letter. A concern common to all three, however, was the threat of false teachers—"liars" and "deceivers"—and the mischief they were causing in certain quarters. In 1 John, where we have the fullest account, it would appear that the heresy in question was a form of Gnosticism, or Docetism, denying that Christ had "come in the flesh."[87] Here, as in the Pastoral Epistles, we see Christians in the process of refining the tenets of their faith, alert to the subtle but highly significant influence of the Hellenistic thought-world in which they now had to live and work.

The danger of "false prophets" or teachers of heresy is also a dominant concern in 2 Peter and Jude, which seem to have a literary connection. Much of the language of 2 Peter 2:1-8 parallels Jude 4-16, and many scholars think that Jude was known and quoted by the pseudonymous writer of 2 Peter. That writer also refers to "all" the letters of Paul, suggesting that he had access to a known collection, and further that Paul's letters were by that time virtually regarded as "Scripture."[88] Against scoffers who taunt Christians about the apparent delay of "the Second Coming," he gives the now famous reminder "that with the Lord one day is as a thousand years, and a thousand years as one day" (2 Pet. 3:8).

In Jude the opponents of the "faith which was once for all delivered to the saints" (1:3) were charged with licentiousness and defiance of godly authority—things which were predicted by "the apostles of our Lord" (implying that Jude excludes himself) and even condemned by Enoch (quoting from the pseudepigraphal book of that name, 1:9). Jude is thus a very short but vigorous appeal to the faithful to separate themselves from the ungodly, "keep (themselves) in the love of God," and "wait for the mercy of our Lord Jesus Christ unto eternal life" (Jude 21). No doubt such

---

[87]See especially 1 John 4:1-6, and cf. John 1:14 ("the word became flesh"), which may have been a direct and intentional repudiation of Docetism—so called because it maintained that Jesus only seemed (Greek *dokein*) human. "Gnosticism" designates a wider range of theosophical notions, in which the emphasis was on salvation by knowledge (Greek *gnosis*), based on a rigidly dualistic view of the world (spirit vs. matter).

[88]2 Peter 3:15-16. The implications of this for the question of the canonization of such writings will be discussed later.

timeless advice commended Jude not only to the churches of his own time and place but also to an ever widening audience in the years to follow.

So by about 150 CE the several documents that make up the New Testament had been written. As far as the story of the *composition* of the Bible is concerned, we have finished our journey, a very long journey through time, and one (as the reader can now agree) very much *in* time—a process involved inextricably with events of history, with nations in birth and in death, and with the countless hosts of people *to* whom and *for* whom, as well as *by* whom, the books were composed. To understand and appreciate this very human and historical dimension to the story of the Bible is but a step—but a tremendously important step—toward the final objective of this book.

But because this is all, so far, only one dimension, let me go on to add another and consider the equally important process by which "the books" became Scripture or Sacred Canon.

Chronology of Biblical Literature
showing approximate dates of composition

BEFORE 1000 BCE—period of oral tradition: no datable documents, although some songs and fragments of poetry now embedded in Old Testament narrative probably originated in this period. Ancestral, tribal lore carried in memory and perpetuated in cultic celebrations.

1000 to 800 BCE—gathering of Israel's "national traditions":
"J" or the work of the Yahwist (probably from Judah) ca. 950;
"E" or the work of the Elohist (probably from Israel) ca. 850;
"Court History" (Succession Narrative) in 2 Samuel 9-20, 1 Kings 1-2, late tenth-century (Solomon's reign?);
Parts of Proverbs; perhaps "Book of Jashar,"
"Book of the Wars of Yahweh," other books now lost.

800 to 600 BCE—period of Assyrian domination:
Prophetic oracles of Amos, Hosea, Isaiah (mostly 1-39), Micah—
all from latter half of eighth century;
Nucleus of Deuteronomy, and "D" (Deuteronomic) edition of Torah;
Cultic hymns and songs (now in Pss.), other proverbs, perhaps some law codes;
Oracles of Habakkuk, Zephaniah, Nahum; early oracles of Jeremiah (?).

600 to 400 BCE—decline, fall of Judah, the Exile:
"DH" or Deuteronomic History,
extending the record from Joshua through Kings;
Lamentations, some psalms, Obadiah, most of Ezekiel;
Completion of Jeremiah; most of Isaiah 40-55 (called Deutero-Isaiah);
The book of Job (?); the work of "P" or the Priestly editors of Torah;
Haggai, Zechariah, Malachi; perhaps Ruth, Jonah.

AFTER 400 BCE—Persian period to Greek and Maccabean times:
Work of the Chronicler (1-2 Chron., Ezra, Neh.);
Completion of the Book of the Twelve (perhaps Joel, Zech. 9-14);
Ecclesiastes, Song of Solomon, Esther, perhaps additions to Isaiah (56-66);
Completion of the Psalms and Proverbs (adding 1-9);
Daniel, ca. 160 BCE.
[Others: Tobit, Judith, additions to Esther and Daniel, 1-2 Maccabees, Wisdom of Solomon, Baruch, Wisdom of Sirach, possibly more.]

CHRISTIAN WRITINGS (eventually forming "New Testament")—
ca. 50 to 150 CE:
"Apostolic" period (to ca. 65 CE): Epistles of Paul,
possibly James, 1 Peter, Hebrews (?);
"Subapostolic" (after 65): Gospels (Mark, Matt., Luke), Acts of the Apostles, Revelation to John, Gospel of John; Paulinist Epistles (Eph., 1-2 Tim., Titus); Johannine Epistles, Jude, 2 Peter.
[Others: 1 Clement, Letters of Ignatius, *Didache* —in "Apostolic Fathers."]

For Further Reading

Anderson, B. W. *Understanding the Old Testament.* Fourth edition. Englewood Cliffs NJ: Prentice-Hall, 1986. Especially 18-52.

Bewer, Julius A. *The Literature of the Old Testament,* Third edition revised by E. G. Kraeling. New York/London: Columbia University Press, 1962.

Ehrlich, Ernst L. *A Concise History of Israel.* Trans. James Barr. Harper Torchbook. New York: Harper and Row, 1965.

Kee, H. C., F. W. Young, and K. Froehlich. *Understanding the New Testament.* Third edition. Englewood Cliffs NJ: Prentice-Hall, 1973. Especially 37-93, 231-312.

Kelly, Balmer. ''The History of the People of God.'' In *Introduction to the Bible.* The Layman's Bible Commentary 1. B. H. Kelly, ed. Richmond: John Knox Press, 1959.

Meek, T. J. *Hebrew Origins.* Harper Torchbook. New York: Harper and Brothers, 1960.

Scott, E. F. *The Literature of the New Testament.* New York: Columbia University Press, 1936.

Relevant Passages in the Bible

2 Kings 22-23
Exodus 20-23
Deuteronomy 5-6
Jeremiah 29-31
Nehemiah 8
(cf. Ezra 7)

Esther (cf. additions
  in the Apocrypha)
1 Corinthians 1-3
2 Peter 3
Revelation 1-3

Samples from the OT Apocrypha:
Tobit; Susanna (one of the additions to Daniel); **2 Esdras 9:26-14:48;
Sirach** (or **Ecclesiasticus**) prologue and 44-50.

Chapter 2

How the Bible
Came to Be Scripture

The term "Bible" comes from a Greek expression meaning "the books." In the light of what can be discovered about their composition, and especially in view of *other* books that were known and read by ancient Jews and Christians, we are compelled to ask, "Why *the* books?" On what grounds were *these* particular documents regarded as special, distinctive, set apart from all others? And how, or when, did they achieve that status?

These are a few of that cluster of questions that scholars classify under the title "Canon" or (if they mean the process) "canonization." The root of these words can be traced back to a Semitic word meaning a reed or cane; the word appears, for example, in Ezekiel 42:16-19 in reference to a measuring device, a kind of yardstick. The Greek equivalent (*kanōn*) in time acquired figurative meanings, just as our word "standard" can mean a gauge of excellence (or other things) as well as an upright pole. Applied to a group of books, then, "canon" has come to denote those books (and those alone) that provide a *standard* of some sort and are regarded as *authoritative* or normative for a certain community.

There are, of course, different canons for different communities. In some cases it may be true to say that having and living by a particular canon of Scripture is what really *defines community* —that is, insofar as it sets up norms of faith and practice to which those who "belong" are bound. In other words, wherever a certain book or group of books functions as the ultimate authority for a people in explaining who they are (and, therefore, what they must do, and so on), it is proper to speak of such literature as a Canon, as Scripture, as Bible. Not that the way canon functions is the same in every community; for Hindus, who cherish the Vedas and Upanishads as Scripture, canon may not play the same role as it does in Judaism with its Tanak or in Islam with its Quran. But, obvious differences aside, many of the world's great religions share in some sense the character of being *scriptural* communities of faith, in appealing to "the books" of their sacred past to sustain and guide their faith.

(A) Tanak: the Canon of the Jews and the Christian "Old Testament"

Readers who were careful to check the footnotes of chapter 1 will already be introduced to the term "Tanak"—an acrostic formed by the initial letters of the Hebrew subtitles, *T* orah, *N* ebi'im, and *K* ethubim, made pronounceable by the arbitrary insertion of the vowels. This has become in recent times a widely accepted designation of the whole Hebrew Bible, the books that comprise the Canon of the Jews. In modern editions they are usually listed in this way.

TORAH (Teaching, Law)	NEBI'IM (Prophets)		KETHUBIM (Writings)[1]
Genesis	"former"	Joshua	"books" Psalms
Exodus		Judges	Proverbs
Leviticus		Samuel[2]	Job
Numbers		Kings	"rolls" Song of Songs
Deuteronomy	"latter"	Isaiah	Ruth
		Jeremiah	Lamentations
		Ezekiel	Ecclesiastes
		The Twelve[3]	Esther
			"others" Daniel
			Chronicles
			Ezra
			Nehemiah

Christian readers of the Bible in English are accustomed to a longer list (thirty-nine titles) and a different arrangement, counting Joshua through

---

[1] I have chosen to transliterate the Hebrew letter *beth* as a "b" in both *Nebi'im* and *Kethubim*, although the phonetically proper "v" is often used instead.

[2] Samuel, Kings, and Chronicles were one book each in Hebrew, but were divided when the Greek translations proved too long for one scroll. Parchment scrolls rarely exceeded thirty feet in length, but some papyrus scrolls might be a few feet longer.

[3] The twelve so-called "minor prophets"—Hosea through Malachi—were all on one scroll in Hebrew, a matter of convenience primarily, and in no way derogatory of their individual importance.

Kings (plus Ruth, Chronicles, Ezra, and Nehemiah) as "historical books," and including Daniel among the Prophets. Since most Hebrew texts do not separate the books of Samuel, Kings, or Chronicles into two parts, and lump the so-called "minor prophets" into one book, and Ezra-Nehemiah likewise, they have a total of twenty-four books. This figure seems to agree with the count of the first-century writer of 2 Esdras (4 Ezra),[4] and probably represents the full extent of the Bible for Palestinian Jews of 100 CE.

But Jews had migrated and settled in many places long before the Christian era, and wherever they went they took their books and established synagogues. One of the largest colonies of Jews in the Diaspora was in Alexandria, where (ca. 250-150 BCE) Jewish scribes produced a Greek Bible—later known as the Septuagint—that eventually became the favorite version of many Christians as well as Greek-speaking Jews.[5]

But the Septuagint included seven or eight books not found in the Hebrew Bible, plus expanded versions of Esther and Daniel. This relatively small variation between the Palestinian (Hebrew) Bible and the Alexandrian (Greek) collection was to have far-reaching implications in the centuries ahead. In itself, as a witness to the process of canonization in or about 150 BCE, it simply testifies to a certain latitude regarding the form and content of Jewish Scripture. At least, as yet, there were apparently no very rigid restrictions being imposed. By about 100 CE, however, conditions had changed, and the variations between the Hebrew Bible and the LXX became a focal point of debate among Jewish rabbis. But beyond that dispute, to which I shall return, lies the genesis of another, and to this day one of the differences that separate Roman Catholic and Protestant Christians.

I refer to the difference between the Roman Catholic Canon and that of Protestants. The Catholic Bible[6] is longer; while it contains the same

---

[4]2 Esdras 14:19-22, 37-48. 2 Esdras, an apocryphal book, is also listed in the Latin Vulgate as 4 Ezra, where it is part of the appendix to the New Testament.

[5]"Septuagint" is from the Latin *septuaginta* (seventy), a name derived from the legend (cf. "Letter of Aristeas," in R. H. Charles, *The Apocrypha and Pseudepigrapha of the Old Testament in English*, 2 vols. [Oxford: Clarendon Press, 1913] 94-122) that seventy (or seventy-two) scribes had worked in pairs to produce copies of the translation, all of which were miraculously the same. Hence, also, the abbreviation often used to designate this ancient version: LXX.

[6]See, for example, the Revised Standard Version, Catholic Edition (New York: Thomas Nelson and Sons, 1965), or the *New American Bible* (Paterson NJ: St. Anthony Guild Press, 1970).

twenty-seven books of the New Testament, it includes in the Old Testament books that Protestants have traditionally relegated to "the Apocrypha." The explanation, put very briefly, starts with the Septuagint, which the scholar Jerome used in making his Latin translation ca. 400 CE. This work (later to be known as the Vulgate) originally contained Jerome's prefatory notes marking the books not found in the Hebrew, but somehow in subsequent editions (hand-copied, of course) these notes were omitted and the distinction Jerome had made was soon forgotten—not that Jerome had any notion of advocating the shorter collection or of dismissing the "additional" books, since these were already by his day well-established parts of the Christian Canon. But in effect, gradual acceptance of the Latin Vulgate as *the* approved Bible of the Western Church meant the adoption of the Alexandrian collection as its Old Testament.

Then came Martin Luther and the Protestant revolt in the sixteenth century, with its insistence that Scripture should supersede Tradition as the basis for determining God's Word for the church. "Scripture" for the Reformers meant a return to the original languages, which in turn called into question not only the accuracy of the Latin translation but also the authority of those books of the Old Testament not supported by the Hebrew Bible. Luther's own German translation included some of these books but grouped them together (between the Old and New Testaments, as some English Bibles still do) with this caption: "Apocrypha, books which are not held equal to the Holy Scriptures but nonetheless are useful and good to read." So Protestants, in effect, rejected the Greek Old Testament in favor of the Hebrew, and assigned a lesser value to its Apocrypha.

In reaction, Roman Catholics at the Council of Trent (1546) reaffirmed their traditional, Vulgate-based canon; however, a few years later the Pope designated as "deutero-canonical" the books listed by Luther as Apocrypha, except for the Prayer of Manasseh and 1 and 2 Esdras (3 and 4 Ezra), which were placed in an appendix following Revelation. Thus the church acknowledged that such books were *later* entering the canon than the rest, but were not at all inferior as authoritative Scripture.

It would take us far afield to try to describe the deutero-canonical (apocryphal) books here, but it seems appropriate to commend them to the modern reader, whatever his or her religious affiliation may be. As even Martin Luther said, those books are "useful and good to read." We do not contend that they are all equally useful nor that their theological quality runs consistently high. In fact, they are as varied in quality as they are in literary genre—containing examples of the novel (Tobit, Judith), narrative history (1 Maccabees), wisdom or didactic epigram (Ecclesiasticus, Wisdom of Solomon), apocalyptic (2 Esdras), and even a prototype of the "detective story" (Susanna, Bel and the Dragon—additions to Daniel). But on the whole they often serve to fill in gaps or throw new light on the course of biblical history, and to enrich our understanding of Jewish piety in the years just prior to the time of Jesus.[7]

THE LINEAGE OF "OLD TESTAMENT APOCRYPHA"

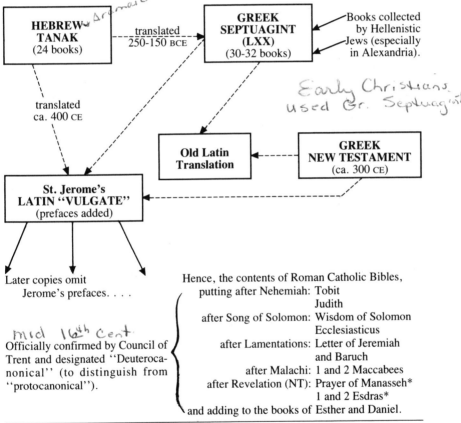

HEBREW TANAK (24 books)

Aramaic

translated 250-150 BCE

GREEK SEPTUAGINT (LXX) (30-32 books)

Books collected by Hellenistic Jews (especially in Alexandria).

Early Christians used Gr. Septuagint

translated ca. 400 CE

Old Latin Translation

GREEK NEW TESTAMENT (ca. 300 CE)

St. Jerome's LATIN "VULGATE" (prefaces added)

Later copies omit Jerome's prefaces. . . .

mid 16th Cent.
Officially confirmed by Council of Trent and designated "Deuterocanonical" (to distinguish from "protocanonical").

Hence, the contents of Roman Catholic Bibles, putting after Nehemiah: Tobit
Judith
after Song of Solomon: Wisdom of Solomon
Ecclesiasticus
after Lamentations: Letter of Jeremiah and Baruch
after Malachi: 1 and 2 Maccabees
after Revelation (NT): Prayer of Manasseh*
1 and 2 Esdras*
and adding to the books of Esther and Daniel.

*These were set apart by the Council of Trent (1546) as "apocryphal" and simply appended to the Catholic Bible.

Protestant Reform. — return to orig. lang.

[7]For an excellent introduction to the Old Testament Apocrypha, see that of Bruce Metzger, either bound with the Revised Standard Version (Oxford Annotated, 1957) or printed separately by Oxford University Press, 1965.

Still other books, we now know, were read by Jews of the Dispersion, and many of these survived without enjoying a place in the Alexandrian or Palestinian Canon. As noted before, books now called *Pseudepigrapha* had wide circulation, some even in Palestine, as discoveries at Qumran show. In short, the evidence suggests no rigidly fixed definition of Scripture had been established before the time of Jesus. In fact, the first signs of anything like an official review of the matter came from the period following the First Jewish Revolt (67-70 CE), when many rabbis and other refugees from Jerusalem engaged in debate over certain individual books. Even among Palestinian Jews there was not complete unanimity about Song of Songs and Ecclesiastes, for instance. To some, these books "defiled the hands"—an expression that occurs in rabbinical literature—apparently meaning that the books were sacred, or holy, and therefore before (or after?) handling them one must ceremonially wash.[8] But to others the Song was no more or less than erotic love poetry, and Ecclesiastes the murmuring of a world-weary cynic. Such disputes continued, perhaps to the end of the first century, so that it is virtually impossible to name a specific date or point to a single decision after which the Jewish Tanak was complete.

Two facts, however, seem to emerge from the reports of that period: first, we have to do with a *gradual process* rather than one official act; second, the process of canonization involved *both* a tacit, perhaps unconscious acceptance, *and* a conscious rejection, on the part of the faithful community. Whatever may be said about divine inspiration—and I intend to deal with this later—what finally came to be regarded as Scripture by the Jews was, in some sense, the result of human deliberation and conscious choice. Not that all the books underwent the same kind of screening; not that they all had to pass some official "board of review" to receive the seal of approval, for about many of the books—older ones especially— there seemed to be no question, just silent consent and tacit acceptance. But for others, there were questions, and the need for sifting, leaving along the way a residue of documents, leftovers still cherished by some, perhaps revered by a few, but failing (for whatever reason) to gain the hold on hearts and minds that others books did.

So far we have been looking at the outcome, the latter end, of the gradual process. Now we need to engage in another effort of reconstruction, somewhat parallel to that given in chapter 1, in order to trace some of the

---

[8]In the codification of laws known as the *Mishnah*, see *Yadayim* 3:5.

earlier stages of that process we call canonization. Here we have even less solid evidence from the ancients, and many more gaps to be filled by inference (and educated guesses!). The writers and editors of the books could hardly foresee the distant end-result, and at the time of composition were not themselves conscious of creating sacred Scripture, in the sense that word has for us. It is not surprising, then, that they left us in their books no direct and explicit answers to the modern questions we have raised about the growth of the canon.

We must therefore be content with the indirect and implicit, with the hints and allusions we find in the Bible, and from them try to isolate at least a few milestones along the way. One such milestone appears in the story told in 2 Kings 22-23. A certain "book of the law" was found in the Jerusalem temple in the course of repairs on the building; various officials examined the book and with obvious consternation passed it on to King Josiah, who consulted Huldah the prophetess. She confirmed Josiah's worst fears, finding in the book a message of divine judgment, an indictment of the nation for its sins. The story goes on to tell how the pious king then set in motion sweeping reforms in the religious affairs of Judah—centralizing worship at Jerusalem, closing many "high places," and reorganizing the priestly orders.

The evidence is convincing that "the book of the law" is to be identified with an early edition of our Deuteronomy.[9] What concerns us here, however, is that Josiah's reforms seem to have been prompted (or, at least, given greater urgency) by the words written in that particular book. Whatever the exact form or extent of the book, it functioned at that moment in Judah as *the Word of God*, as *Scripture*. It served in that time of crisis as *Canon*.

The element of crisis, of national danger, should be especially noted; it may indeed be an important factor at every stage in the process. Here it certainly had much to do with Josiah's anxiety and the promptness of his response to the book's discovery. The Northern kingdom, Israel, had already been swallowed up by Assyria, and now (ca. 621 BCE) after enduring nearly a century of subjugation to that power, Judah was being led by her young king to sever relations and stand on her own feet. It was a time fraught with danger. Any overt act of rejecting Assyrian cults or gods—as implied in Josiah's re-

---

[9]Careful examination of 2 Kings 23 shows about thirty points of correspondence with the commandments recorded in Deuteronomy (especially 11-26).

forms—could be interpreted as political rebellion and would invite possible retaliation. On the other hand, there were signs of weakness in Assyria and the stirring of rebellion among the Medes and Chaldeans, so that the time seemed ripe for Judah to assert itself and cast off its bondage.

While it may be too much to claim that the discovery of the book tipped the scales toward a bid for independence, it is fair to say that the book provided Josiah precisely the kind of *authority* he needed to undergird what he did. Yes, the discovery was timely, but more than that, the book (assuming it to be the nucleus of Deuteronomy) called the community back to its roots, setting Judah at the feet of Moses, as it were, and demanding nothing short of total and unqualified obedience to *torah*. Apparently it was not enough that a few lonely preachers like Jeremiah were already demanding in God's name the same repentance; these prophets were as yet "without honor" and the only voice that could command the respect of the nation, it would seem, was that of the great lawgiver Moses.[10]

Many questions about Josiah's "book of the law" remain unanswered— for example, why it had gone unnoticed in the temple, and for how long? Was it hidden there during Manasseh's persecution of Yahwistic patriots, or was it simply a casualty of time and negligent librarians? We do not have data enough to answer these questions. But if our assumptions about the book's identity be correct, a more significant question might be, why was this the first indication (in the biblical record) of such a written law book? Where were the earlier stories of Moses assumed to be in "J" and "E"? An argument from silence is always risky, and the story in 2 Kings does not compel us to deny the existence in 621 BCE of other written *toroth* (collections of laws like the Decalogue and Covenant Code, Exodus 20-23), whose authority for the covenant people of God had been recognized for centuries. In fact, Deuteronomy itself was directly dependent on such earlier materials; that it was *this* book that caught Josiah's attention, rather than older documents, may be due primarily to the very emphatic *way* it presented the ancient tradition—restating the old, familiar story in terms appropriate to the contemporary crisis, in terms of the choice between obedience ("life") and ("death"). Like the good

---

[10]Curiously enough, 2 Kings makes no reference to prophets known to be active in this period and (later) included in "The Latter Prophets." On the other hand, it does give brief notice of Isaiah's activity in the time of King Hezekiah (2 Kings 19-20), perhaps an indication of the temporal distance between a prophet's work and the recognition accorded him— in this case, about a century.

sermon it is, Deuteronomy made the past relevant to Judah's present situation, and King Josiah had the good sense to know a good sermon when he heard (or read) it.

Implicit in the episode, as told in 2 Kings 22:8-20, is the recognition on the part of prophet, priest, and king that the book authentically reflected Israel's most sacred heritage. This in itself leads me to presume an already existing body of tradition—whether oral, written, or a mixture—against which the religious leaders could measure the newly discovered book. Thus the age of the *scroll*, the actual copy, did not figure in their deliberations; what mattered was its contents and their faithfulness to well established, long-standing religious teaching. This is why we cannot claim to find in the story "the beginning" of canonization, but only an early milestone in that process, testifying to a dynamic principle already at work but at this point becoming visible in history.

To resume the story and look for another milestone, I must review the sad sequence of events that marked Judah's fall to the Babylonians and the period of Exile (586-538 BCE). Despite the bold reforms of Josiah, that young king died at the hands of Egyptians at Megiddo, and after a few years of inept rule by his sons, the mighty Nebuchadrezzar carried off Jehoiachin and thousands of Judah's leading citizens as captives.

During the years of the Exile the deported people from Judah, far from being enslaved or incarcerated, were granted lands to till, given jobs to do, and generally allowed to maintain a fairly autonomous community life. Many, it seems, followed the advice of the prophet Jeremiah (29:1-9) and continued to live, build, plant, marry and pray in the pattern of old, even though some (according to Ps. 137) only wept when they remembered Zion, unable to sing "the Lord's song in a foreign land." In short, it was a time when the religious faith of Yahweh's people was severely tested. Being without Temple and familiar cultic ritual, they were compelled to turn to whatever store of sacred tradition had survived, and no doubt this meant gathering the oracles of preexilic prophets into books, and perhaps the first arrangement of even older sources, such as we ascribe to "P."

Of all this, of course we can only surmise on the basis of what eventually took place, once the faithful were allowed to return and rebuild Jerusalem. For the milestone we have in mind actually comes from the Restoration; the record of it is found in the story, told in Ezra 7 and Nehemiah 8, of the efforts of Ezra—a "scribe skilled in the law of Moses"—to engage the restored community in a program of reading and study of the *torah.* As already indicated, the writer known as the Chronicler was many years removed from the events of Ezra's day, and we suspect that he tended to idealize the achievements of Ezra, giving impetus to some of the legends we find in the apocryphal literature.[11] Yet, allowing for that tendency, we have no reason to deny the underlying fact, to which the later records testify, that the priestly scribe was responsible for initiating an educational program for the people of Jerusalem, and that its aim was to interpret "the book of the law." Again, as in the case of Josiah's book, there is nothing in the story to specify what form it took or how much of the Pentateuch it contained. Scholarly speculation has ranged from one part (such as the Levitical Code) or one whole book (like Deut.) to the whole of our present Pentateuch. Allusions to the contents of it are too few and too vague, unfortunately, to allow for a positive identification.

The story told in Ezra-Nehemiah would suggest that the book—whatever its name—was virtually unknown to Ezra's audience at the Water Gate. We are told that handpicked associates and Levites were engaged to assist Ezra in his task, which seems to have involved both interpretation of the words (perhaps, as we would say, *exegesis*) and exposition of their meaning in terms of ethical and ritual requirements. That actual *translation* was involved is entirely possible, and very likely, if the book (as we assume) was written in Hebrew and most of the people by that time used Aramaic.[12] The story may supply important evidence at this point that by 400 BCE the use of Hebrew was already limited to a scholarly few, and that Aramaic had virtually replaced it as the spoken language of ordinary people. This was surely *one* reason—if not the only one—that Ezra's book was unknown to the masses. It was not so much the substance of the book, as it was the language, that was strange to them.

Even so, I cannot discount the real possibility that to many Judeans, only recently returned from Exile, even the substance was strange. Some

---

[11]Cf. 2 Esdras; for example, in 14:19-48, the law had been "burned," and Ezra was commanded to take five scribes and dictate to them, for forty days and nights, until ninety-four books were written—twenty-four to be made public and the rest to remain for "the wise" only.

[12]Aramaic and Hebrew belong to the same "Semitic" family of languages but were sufficiently different to be mutually exclusive; long used in northern parts of Mesopotamia, Aramaic became the major language of diplomacy in the Persian Period (538-333 BCE), and is used in Tanak in Daniel 2:4b—7:28; Ezra 4:18—6:18; and 7:12-26 (with a sprinkling of words and phrases elsewhere).

families, no doubt, had grown careless of their heritage during decades in foreign lands, and younger generations who had never known any homeland but Babylonia would have little or no sense of identity with Israel or her sacred traditions, unless their parents had. So what Ezra did was crucial to the continuity of the covenant people and to their religion, and perhaps later generations did not exaggerate when they looked back to his work as a kind of watershed event. Promoting the study of the Scripture and calling people back to the ancient traditions, Ezra was not unlike the warrior Joshua of eight centuries before who demanded of the tribes that they put away the gods they had served "beyond the River,"[13] and commit themselves wholly to the Lord. It is not without reason, at any rate, that Ezra has been called "the father of Judaism"—by virtue of his appeal to *torah* as the basic authority and his insistence on teaching and understanding *torah* as indispensable to the Jewish way of life.[14]

To return briefly to the question of the book that Ezra expounded, I must mention one item of external evidence that is sometimes used to argue for it as the complete Pentateuch: the Samaritan Bible. This ancient text contains the five books of the *Torah,* and only those—the full extent of the Scriptures for the Samaritan community even to this day. On the basis of Nehemiah 2:9-20, 4:1-9, and other references to the enmity with Sanballat and Tobiah, we might suppose that the Jews and Samaritans parted company, leading to the establishment of a separate cultic center on Mt. Gerizim about 432 BCE. Thus it could be argued that the Samaritan Bible testifies to a corresponding five-book canon among the Jews by that time. But—alas!—the evidence for the date of the Samaritan schism is not unanimous. Josephus, for example, puts it at least a century later.[15] Weighing the merits of such testimony here would take us beyond our immediate objective; let us leave open for the moment the question of the contents of Ezra's book, and recognize the significance of what I have already implied—that by 400 BCE the Jews had taken a large step to-

---

[13]Joshua 24:14, where "the River" refers to the Euphrates, long-standing demarcation between the peoples of Mesopotamia and those of Canaan.

[14]See John Bright, *A History of Israel,* 2nd ed. (Philadelphia: Westminster Press, 1972) 392: "The distinguishing mark of a Jew [henceforth] would not be political nationality, nor primarily ethnic background, nor even regular participation in the Temple cult . . . but adherence to the law of Moses." From this point on it is appropriate to speak of the people as "Jews"—a name derived from *jehudi,* resident of Judea.

[15]Flavius Josephus, *Antiquities* xi, 7.2; 8.2.

ward becoming "the people of the book," looking to "the law of Moses" (whatever its exact form) as *the* norm and definition of their faith and practice.

Another two centuries pass before we come to what I regard as a third milestone in the process of canonization. This is not to ignore completely scattered hints in the postexilic sources, such as Zechariah 1:4 (mention of "the former prophets"), which suggest growing recognition of a Prophetic corpus, possibly as early as 500 BCE. But we know that the collection was not yet complete by that date, and because we must allow for a considerable interval between composition and canonical authority (based on the evidence so far), we should not expect to find "the Prophets," as a whole, set alongside "the Law" much before the third century BCE.

In fact, it is from around 180 BCE that the clearest signs appear, in the prologue of the Wisdom of Jesus son of Sirach, also known as Ecclesiasticus (but *not* to be confused with Ecclesiastes). Originally composed in Hebrew, this book was translated into Greek by the author's grandson some fifty years later (ca. 130 BCE). The prologue (added by the grandson) refers three times to a three-part collection of books, comprising the "great teachings" to which Sirach was devoted. The reference each time, with only slight variation, is to (1) the Law, (2) the Prophets, and (3) the "others that followed them" or "other books of our fathers." The third category lacks definition or title, but it is clear that the writer is using terms for the first two—the Law and the Prophets—which are definitive, familiar to his readers, and thus need no explanation. It is a good indication that by the time of Sirach—or of his grandson, at the latest—both *Torah* and *Nebi'im* were well defined and widely accepted collections, already set apart by the faithful as sources of "great teachings" and authoritative guidance for the community.

An interesting sidelight here is the openness of that third category—the "others." No doubt the grandson of Jesus had no good designation for that set of books, because it was still growing, and because it already embraced a variety of things—an assortment hard to name: psalms, proverbs, a story-poem (Job), a priestly history (Chron.), and so on. Curiously, the writer of the prologue even hints that Grandfather Jesus' book might also take its place in that growing collection, to provide "instruction and wisdom" to contemporary readers. Certainly there is not yet any idea of a "closed canon," to which nothing should be added nor taken away.

For the first two milestones—that of Josiah's book of the covenant, and that of Ezra's "law of Moses"—I am able to see special relevance for "canonizing" in the historical context: in the seventh-century BCE it was a step taken in crisis, in Judah's attempt to bring about a "revival" of the Mosaic covenant and to avert the judgment of God that had befallen Israel; in the fifth century, the crisis was of a different order, and yet there, too, it was a matter of survival—not of the nation, but of the traditional faith—against new threats of absorption, syncretism and apathy. If we take our third milestone as marking the recognition of the Prophetic books, in addition to Torah, should we expect to find in the historical backdrop some similar crisis or emergency precipitating that recognition? Some scholars have so theorized, contending that throughout the process of canonization the community's recognition of certain books as Scripture follows close upon some such threat to the community's survival or identity.[16] The theory has its merits, but whether it fits as neatly in the case of the Prophets as in other cases is still debatable. Proponents point to the oppressive Seleucid government under Antiochus IV (Epiphanes) in the years 176-164 BCE as the most likely provocation of this new step in canonization. There is no doubt that those were times of crisis for the people of Judea, suffering as they did from the Syrian ruler's efforts to impose Hellenistic ways on his subjects, and facing finally overt persecution for practicing their Judaism—circumcision was outlawed, and sacred books were confiscated and burned! Such conditions provoked the faithful to resistance that eventuated in what is known as the Maccabean Revolt; they also produced fiercely patriotic writings like 1 Maccabees (part of the Protestant Apocrypha) and, probably, the apocalyptic book of Daniel. It is *possible,* of course, that they also called forth the final definition of "the Prophets," to help rally the faithful against the oppressor and perhaps to make clear what were sacred books and what were not. The difficulty with this lies in the fact that in the prologue of Ecclesiasticus the writer speaks of the law and the prophets (at least) as books accepted as sacred *already* in the day of his grandfather (180 BCE)—before the Syrian persecutions. While this could be explained as a simple anachronism on the translator's part, it seems much more reasonable to understand that prologue—in fact, the whole book—as testifying to a fairly long-standing recognition of the prophetic canon, and one that did not necessarily await the coming of Antiochus Epiphanes.

---

[16]For example, E. C. Colwell, *The Study of the Bible,* rev. ed. (Chicago: University of Chicago Press, 1964) 8-14.

What we take for the next milestone in the growth of the Hebrew canon seems somewhat more easily related to contemporary pressures, although it must be emphasized that any attempt to fix a precise date to this stage will be arbitrary. The usual date assigned to this step—for those who like to have such records—is 90 CE, marking a time when leading Jewish rabbis, driven out of Jerusalem, settled in the countryside and engaged each other in scholarly discussions. One such town was Yabne, or Jamnia, where the learned assembly turned its attention to questions of grave moment, and in particular to questions about which books "defiled the hands"—i.e., which were sacred and which were not. It is said that out of such deliberations came the "official" recognition that eventually determined the limits of the third division in the Hebrew Bible, "the Writings." Again, the background is all-important; what led to expulsion of the Jews from Jerusalem and created the "crisis" that precipitated such deliberations?

Two things for sure, and perhaps a third, help account for this step. First and most obvious was the conflict between the Jews of Palestine and their Roman overlords. Years of discontent and increasing corruption among Roman governors finally pushed Jewish zealots into open revolt in 66 CE; the outcome by 70 was utter defeat and the devastation of Jerusalem, including the Temple. Jews were banished from their city, which was rebuilt and renamed Aelia Capitolina. Once again, as in the Babylonian Exile, Judaism was forced to do without its Temple and the priestcraft that normally went with it. But this time there were ready-made synagogues to receive the refugees and take up the slack in cultic and spiritual leadership. It was here that the Pharisaic tradition, with its scribes and diligent students of Scripture, proved itself. Sacrifice may cease, but Judaism would continue, for it had "the books."

Second, there was the spreading "sect" of Christians and its increasing independence of the synagogues. It became obvious to Jewish leaders, perhaps before the fall of the Temple, that the followers of Jesus could not be contained or intimidated by ordinary disciplinary actions. Moreover, Christian missionaries in their preaching appealed to the old Scriptures, finding *testimonia* (we might say "prooftexts") in the Torah and Prophets and Psalms (cf. Luke 24:44) to support their claims that "the Messiah was Jesus."[17] And to make matters worse, from the synagogue's point of view,

---

[17]Acts 18:5, 28, may preserve the authentic word order of apostolic preaching to Jews, in which an expectation of Messiah (Christ) might be presupposed, but identification of Jesus as the expected One would need to be "proved."

after 70 CE many Christian writings began to circulate, representing a potential rival or challenge to their own canon. To devout Jewish rabbis, like those at Jamnia, the demand for clear definition of what was and was not sacred was never more urgent.

A third factor that might help to account for the move to define the Writings by the end of the first century is one already noted in describing the Greek version, the Septuagint. For at least two centuries Greek-speaking Jews had read their sacred books in that version, and it was only natural that it became the standard text of Christians as they moved out into the Hellenistic world. But the Septuagint contained a wider assortment of books than the Hebrew collections, books later to be designated Apocrypha by Protestant Christians. And though language was probably not the chief objection to those "additional" books, since indeed some of them were originally composed in Hebrew, not many Palestinian Jews of that period would have looked kindly on those known only in the language of the Gentiles. More important, perhaps, was consideration of the late date of certain books, whether in Greek or in Hebrew, and the notion that "prophecy had ceased" with Ezra, thus creating suspicions about books (like Jubilees or 1 Enoch in the Pseudepigrapha) known to be of recent origin. In short, it was a complex cluster of factors, not one simple crisis, that brought the Hebrew Bible to its final three-part definition.

Back of the whole process, of course, was the usage of the books in the ongoing life of the religious community. It cannot be stressed too much that what ultimately creates Canon is not that "official seal of approval" given by a body of scholars, but rather the love, devotion, and reverent obedience given the books by many generations of readers—or, better, *hearers*—since many of them would not have had the ability to read for themselves. A few learned experts might, as at Jamnia (85-90 CE), be called on to settle certain disputed cases in times of unusual urgency, but back of them and their little moment were the multitudes of ordinary believers, who through the years (and even centuries) treasured the familiar books as the source of their strength, their hopes and their dreams. For the most part, then, Jamnia represents simply a confirmation of the preexistent consensus of the Jewish community, embracing without question most of the variegated collection of "books, rolls, and others"—the traditional subheadings assigned to the Writings.[18] And even in the problem cases, books on

_____

[18]The "books" are Psalms, Proverbs, Job; the "rolls" are Song of Songs, Ruth, Lamentations, Ecclesiastes, Esther; the "others" are Daniel, Ezra-Nehemiah, Chronicles.

which opinion was divided, long-standing usage and popularity must have weighed heavily in favor of acceptance, even in the face of scholarly disapproval. Such, indeed, seems to have been the case with Esther. Certain rabbis in the second century objected to Esther, because it did not even mention God, let alone promote "religious values." In this light it may not be mere coincidence that among all the books (or parts of books) found at Qumran—the Dead Sea Scrolls—every book of the Tanak is represented *except* the book of Esther. Yet, that Esther was retained after all the debate speaks volumes for its hold on the imagination of the people, and to some extent the popularity of the Feast of Purim with which the book had become inseparably linked.

Step by step, then, ever so gradually the Hebrew Bible grew—first, Torah, then Prophets, and Sacred Writings—the historical stages at last reflected in the tripartite arrangement of the books. All we can see now are a few milestones, momentary glimpses of that long process, but enough to plot the course of the hidden dynamic that produced it. At least three elements of that dynamic have emerged: (1) the pull of traditions (and the desire to maintain them) as a means of national or religious identity; (2) external pressures, crises, or challenges to be met, demanding redefinition of "the standards"; and (3) usage by the community of books that nurture and promulgate the traditional faith and order. In and through all, of course, there was the consciousness of being led by God, of being addressed by the Spirit—a dimension we call "inspiration," which will need elaboration in another place.

(B) New Testament: the Christian Books as Canon

Our sketch of the process so far should make it clear that at the time of Jesus (4 BCE–30 CE) there was not yet a fixed or "closed" Canon for the Jews, even in Palestine. Judging from the teachings of Jesus in the gospels, we assume that he was well-versed in the Scriptures, and his quotations or allusions to the books reflect knowledge of all three parts of what was to become Tanak. Although his use of the Scriptures in his teaching was characterized by a certain freedom, Jesus obviously had a great reverence for "the Law and the Prophets," and there can be no question of their authority for him, as for any faithful Jew, as God's word. And the same applies, as far as we can tell, to his disciples and to the earliest Christians in general. *Interpretation* of the Scriptures very quickly divided the

Christians from the non-Christian Jews, but *not* the canon itself. On that they were agreed—at least, for a while.

Christians were content at first to proclaim their ''good news'' of Jesus as Messiah by word of mouth, feeling no urgency to write it down, until perhaps the late 60s. But from the very beginning, as passages in Acts and in Paul's letters indicate, Christian preachers and teachers drew on the Law and the Prophets (and sometimes the Psalms)[19] as evidence that God had promised to Israel the coming of *this* Messiah, Jesus of Nazareth. It is not unlikely that written collections of these ''prooftexts''—sometimes called *testimonia* —existed years before there were any full-scale gospels; that of Matthew, in fact, makes use of such texts very obviously—whether in written form or not. But in all the Gospels we find in varying degrees the same desire to show that all Jesus did and said was in some sense a fulfillment of the promises in Scripture.

The earliest parts of the New Testament were the letters of the Apostle Paul, and it seems appropriate to start with them in attempting to trace the development of the Christian canon. Recall the list of those assumed to be authentic[20]—Romans; 1, 2 Corinthians; Galatians; Philippians; Colossians; 1, 2 Thessalonians; Philemon—and those thought to be the pseudonymous work of a Paulinist—Ephesians; 1, 2 Timothy; Titus. Since our modern distinction scarcely figures in the ancient testimony about Paul's letters, we can afford to ignore it for the moment and treat all thirteen together. As a matter of fact, it was as a group, and not as individual ''books,'' that the Pauline Corpus finally came into the discussions of early Christian leaders and others whom we now call to witness to the canon. Not that all of the letters of Paul were equally well known from the outset, or always equally admired. Chances are that after they served their original and immediate purpose(s), the letters found various resting places—some in local church records (assuming such were kept), others in somebody's personal papers, still others possibly in the ancient counterpart of our ''file thirteen.'' Earlier I discussed the patchwork assembly of the Corinthian cor-

---

[19]See Luke 24:44 (a reference to law, prophets, and the psalms), which some interpret as evidence of a three-part canon by Luke's day (ca. 90 CE), since ''the psalms'' could be used here as a caption for the whole of the Writings—Psalms being first in the list. In any case, the Psalter by itself was frequently quoted as ''prophetic''—as in Acts 4:25-26 or Hebrews 1:5-9.

[20]For a more complete account of the scholarly arguments, see ch. 5.

respondence; how many other letters of Paul may have perished without trace, we cannot know. Years, maybe decades, passed before somebody, now unknown to us, gathered the surviving letters (or copies of them) and made the first collection.[21] Strange as it seems now, in view of Paul's tremendous impact on the Christian movement, the Acts of the Apostles (ca. 95) traced the travels of Paul in much detail but made no mention at all of his letter writing or of his letters.

It is from the same decade, however, that we get our first clearly documented notice of *one* letter of Paul that can be identified—1 Corinthians. The notice appears in another letter, known as 1 Clement (counted as one of "the Apostolic Fathers") and addressed to "the Corinthians"—presumably heirs of Paul's correspondence to that church.[22] In that letter (47:1-3) Clement, a leader of the Roman church, rebukes the Corinthian Christians for their factiousness, saying, "Pick up the letter of the blessed apostle Paul . . . under the Spirit's guidance he wrote to you . . . because even then you had formed cliques." He also alludes to "Cephas and Apollos" (names mentioned by Paul in 1 Cor. 1:12) and to other matters in Paul's letter, making it virtually certain that he had a copy of 1 Corinthians; and he assumes his readers also have a copy, and moreover uses it to support his brotherly admonitions. Even so, Paul's letter is not yet on the level with *Scripture* for Clement, because he seems to reserve that term for the Tanak, to which he refers in 45:2—"you have studied Holy Scripture, which contains the truth and is inspired by the Holy Spirit." So while Clement could ascribe to "the blessed apostle" an authority born of divine inspiration—in fact, not unlike that claimed for his own letter (see 63:2)—he gave a higher status still to the old and acknowledged canon.

Somewhat the same inference can be drawn from the letters of Ignatius of Antioch (ca. 115), who repeatedly cites Paul's letters and personal example.[23] Ignatius seems to have six or seven of the Pauline letters now included in the New Testament, but his quotations are usually loose and never

---

[21]E. J. Goodspeed (*The Meaning of Ephesians* [Chicago, University of Chicago Press, 1933]) suggested that it was the publication of Acts that rekindled attention to Paul and perhaps prompted the search for, and collection of, his letters.

[22]See *Early Christian Fathers*, ed. C. C. Richardson, Library of Christian Classics 1 (Philadelphia: Westminster Press, 1953) 43-73. My quotations from 1 Clement and Ignatius came from Richardson's translation, unless otherwise noted.

[23]For the clearest instances see Ignatius, *Ephesians* 18:1; *Philadelphians* 3:3; *Romans* 5:1; *Trallians*, in Richardson, *Early Christian Fathers*, 87-120.

introduced by the phrase "it is written," which he reserves for citations from the Tanak. For Ignatius, Paul is obviously "a real saint and martyr" (Eph. 12:2), much to be admired and emulated, but not yet are his letters in the same class with Holy Scripture.

It is the reference to "all his letters" in 2 Peter that marks the critical point: there (in 3:15-16) we read

> So also our beloved brother Paul wrote to you according to the wisdom given to him, speaking of this [the forbearance of our Lord] as he does in *all his letters.* There are some things in them hard to understand, which the ignorant and unstable twist to their own destruction, as they do *the other scriptures.* [Italics added]

Second Peter was among the latest of the New Testament epistles, composed probably in the second quarter of the second century. By the writer's day, we may assume, Paul's letters have been collected and widely circulated; whether "all his letters" can be taken to mean all that we now have is still an open question, and it could be nothing more than the offhand equivalent of "many" or "all that I have read." It is interesting to notice, incidentally, the writer's frank admission that he has found Paul sometimes "hard to understand"—surely an opinion shared by readers through the ages.

But more significant for our purposes is that last phrase (italicized above) in the quotation. Much hinges, of course, on the precise meaning of the Greek *tas loipas graphas* —literally, "the rest of (remaining) writings." The meaning that the noun *graphai* has in most Christian documents of this period is Scripture, sacred writings. So the presumption is in favor of that meaning in 2 Peter, suggesting therefore that the writer counts the letters of Paul among "sacred writings." If so, this marks a definite elevation of status from that of the time of Clement and Ignatius, and a sign that (in some circles, at least) difficulty of contents was no hindrance to canonization.

Sayings and stories of Jesus gradually assumed a uniquely Christian literary form, the gospel. Three, the so-called Synoptic Gospels (Matthew, Mark, and Luke), had come into their final form around 90 CE, and the Fourth Gospel (John) may be dated ca. 100-110. Ignatius of Antioch, in the letters already cited (ca. 115), seems to allude to the Gospel of Matthew seven or eight times, and quite possibly to John in four places, but never by name. All his allusions are very brief phrases—seldom as much as a whole line—and more likely from memory, not from a written copy. In no case does Ignatius use them as proof texts or treat them as specially sacred sources.

One of the earliest references to a gospel by name is the statement ascribed to Papias, bishop of Hierapolis (ca. 140 CE), that "Mark became Peter's interpreter and wrote accurately all that he remembered . . . of the things said or done by Christ."[24] Incidentally, it is the same Papias whom Eusebius elsewhere quotes as saying that he much preferred "the living and abiding voice"—that is, *oral* proclamation of the gospel—over reports circulating in writing.[25] How typical of Christian contemporaries Papias was in this respect we cannot say, but his attitude runs parallel to one expressed in Jewish circles of the second century, serving to delay the written compilation of the early rabbinic traditions (Mishnah, and so on).[26] It is possible that Papias reflects a similar current among Christians, resisting for a time the full recognition of the written gospels.

But any such resistance must have been overcome by the latter half of the second century, when the testimony unanimously points to a fourfold set, widely cited as "apostolic" and normative for doctrine and practice. In the First Apology of Justin Martyr, who died about 165, we have a clear instance of this; he obviously cites the gospels in prescribing proper procedure for the Eucharist.

> For the apostles in the memoirs composed by them, which are called Gospels, thus handed down what was commanded them: that Jesus, taking bread and having given thanks, said, "Do this for my memorial, this is my body"; and likewise taking the cup and giving thanks he said, "This is my blood."[27]

Justin goes on to refer to the reading of these "memoirs" in meetings on "the day called Sunday," as though interchangeable with readings from

---

[24]Eusebius, *Historia Ecclesiastica* III. 39. 14-15.

[25]Ibid., 39:4. It is not certain that Papias was referring to whole gospels, but it is likely.

[26]*Gittin* 60b. This particular section of the Mishnah seems to explain the reticence to write down the "oral Torah" (rabbinic teachings and interpretations of Scripture) as due to a desire to maintain the uniqueness of the written Torah and to keep rabbinic teachings flexible and adaptable to new situations.

[27]Justin Martyr, *Apology* 66, ed. and trans. E. R. Hardy, in Richardson, *Early Christian Fathers*, 286. The language is influenced by 1 Corinthians 11:23-25 as well as Mark 14:22-24.

End of 2nd Cent — 3rd — What is apostolic? — must have some connection. Unbroken with events of Christ

HOW THE BIBLE CAME TO BE SCRIPTURE   83

"the prophets.''[28] It would appear that Christians have by this time made Sunday the regular day of corporate worship, and have begun to treat the gospels in much the same manner as the Jews did the Law and the Prophets in the synagogues. Though no "official" pronouncement has yet been made, such *usage* of the gospels in the developing liturgy of the Church was definitely a step toward eventual canonization.

Some years after the death of Justin, a disciple of his—Tatian by name—moved from Rome to Syria and set about combining the four gospels in one continuous book, which became known as the *Diatessaron* (literally "through four").[29] Though popular for a time in some Syrian churches, Tatian's work ran into opposition from many quarters, showing how firmly entrenched the four separate gospels were in the affections of Christians far and wide. On the other hand, the very fact that Tatian felt free to make his harmony and publish it as an alternative form testifies to the still fluid situation, before there were any formal or generally accepted limits laid down.

As it turns out, that time soon came, and the situation at the close of the second century had changed; as witness, Irenaeus of Lyons.

> It is not possible that the Gospels can be either more or fewer in number than they are. For, since there are four zones of the world in which we live, and four principal winds, while the church is scattered throughout all the world, and "the pillar and ground" of the church is the gospel and the spirit of life, it is fitting that she should have four pillars.[30]

While the logic of Irenaeus may not sound convincing today, there was perhaps an unconscious wisdom at work to keep the fourfold witness, on two counts. First, as over against the synthesizing efforts of Tatian, it meant that Christians recognized the legitimacy of variety in the Gospel, or at least were not threatened by the obvious differences among the four books. They were willing to run the risk of having disagreement in their treasured sources rather than to reduce them to common uniformity by a kind of arbitrary

---

[28]Justin Martyr, *Apology*, 67, in Richardson, *Early Christian Fathers*, 287.

[29]This work is extant only in a few Arabic manuscripts and an Armenian translation; the third-century Dura fragment preserves about fourteen lines in Greek. Some think the original was written in Syriac (a variant of Northern Aramaic).

[30]Irenaeus, *Against Heresies* III.11.8, ed. Alexander Roberts and James Donaldson, in *The Ante-Nicene Fathers* (New York: Charles Scribner's Sons; 1925-1926), 1:428.

[handwritten margin notes: Revel. not accepted by Eastern & Syrian Christians — not widely read. 3rd, 4th & 84 cent. Councils affirmed what grassroots had already decided as scripture.]

conflation. Second, as over against the circulation of heretical teachings, some taking the form of sayings collections and—later—of Gospel-like books, most Christians seemed to recognize the priority and/or superior claims of Matthew, Mark, Luke and John. It was in confrontation with Gnostic or Docetic versions of Jesus' career, no doubt, that Christians of the more ''orthodox'' brand began to insist upon the marks of ''apostolic'' origin in their Gospels and Epistles.

The case of Marcion (ca. 150) well exemplifies the effect that heretical movements had upon canonization. Wealthy and well-schooled in Hellenistic philosophy, this son of a bishop from Pontus (Asia Minor) went to Rome and led a movement to disclaim the Jewish Bible. He rejected the God of the Tanak as a deity inferior to the Father of Jesus, and proposed that the Christian Scripture consist of one Gospel—his expurgated version of Luke—and ten Epistles of Paul, also carefully edited. It was largely in reaction against Marcion, and others like him, that the lines of ''orthodoxy'' began to be drawn and the first serious attention was given to defining ''true'' Christian books. Although the final and official delineation was still a long way off, especially in regard to the non-Pauline epistles and certain other documents, the challenge of Marcionites prompted the church to take a definite stand on the question of the Tanak, and the decision to embrace it was one of far-reaching implications. It remains here to note that by about 180 CE Christians could refer to the Jewish Scriptures as the ''Old Covenant''[31]—later to be Latinized as ''Old Testament''— making it a very natural next step to coin the phrase ''New Testament'' for the peculiarly Christian additions.

By the end of the second century Christian writers refer to various sources other than the Gospels and the letters of Paul; we need to remember, however, that mere reference or citation does not constitute evidence of canonical status. By the same token, it is risky to assume that *absence* of a title in such references means that the book was unknown or rejected. Judging from the variety of ''lists'' that scholars have made from the works of Greek and Latin Fathers of this period, we can safely say there was hardly any widespread unanimity on the outer limits of the canon, although the four Gospels, Acts (regarded as Luke's ''volume two''), and nine or ten letters of Paul seem firmly established at the center.

---

[31]The term is ascribed to Melito, bishop of Sardis, according to Eusebius, *H.E.* IV. 26.14.

Irenaeus apparently cites with approval 1 Peter, 1 John, and the Revelation to John, as well as the four Gospels. But Irenaeus also uses the Shepherd of Hermas, a curious visionary work of the early second century, which is found in one of the oldest Greek manuscripts of the Bible.[32] The Epistle to the Hebrews was known to Irenaeus, although he may have had doubts about the commonly accepted notion that Paul wrote it.[33]

Tertullian of Carthage, writing early in the third century, uses 1 Peter, 1 John, and Jude as Scripture—at least on a par with the letters of Paul. He also seems to respect the Revelation to John and, in his earlier writings, the Shepherd of Hermas as well; later, however, he repudiates the Shepherd, although the book was to remain popular in some circles for another century or so.

Clement of Alexandria (not to be confused with the author of 1 Clement) shows in his works (ca. 200 CE) that the four gospels have surpassed all rivals; among the epistles he regards as Scripture are the Pastorals (1, 2 Tim., Titus) and the Epistle to the Hebrews. Also, he cites as "apostolic" 1 Peter, 1 and 2 John, Jude, 1 Clement, and Barnabas.[34] Moreover, Clement is acquainted with books later to be branded "apocryphal"—for example, the Gospel of the Hebrews and the Gospel of the Egyptians.[35] There are quotations in his voluminous works from the Shepherd of Hermas and the so-called Revelation of Peter, and apparently with the same degree of approval as citations from the Revelation to John. In short, Clement himself makes no clear distinction between such books and those he deems "apostolic"; his is a very liberal attitude, as yet unhampered by any ecclesiastical restrictions.

His successor, Origen, representing the middle of the third century, has somewhat the same attitude but is more conscious than Clement of canonicity as a growing issue in the Church. Origen makes use of the terms

---

[32]Codex Sinaiticus, so named because of its discovery of St. Catherine's Monastery in the Sinai, is dated in the late fourth century.

[33]Cf. A. C. Sundberg, Jr., "The Making of the New Testament Canon," *The Interpreter's One Volume Commentary on the Bible,* ed. C. M. Laymon (Nashville: Abingdon 1971) 1220.

[34]"1 Clement" is the letter to the Corinthians, mentioned earlier as a witness to the circulation of Paul's letters. "Barnabas" is a tract from ca. 120-130, usually included among the "Apostolic Fathers."

[35]Extant fragments of these may be found in the *New Testament Apocrypha,* ed. Edgar Hennecke and Wilhelm Schneemelcher, 2 vols. (Philadelphia: Westminster Press, 1963).

"accepted" and "disputed" in discussing certain books. By *whom* accepted or disputed he does not always make clear; presumably he means to acknowledge a general, informal consensus among the churches of his own acquaintance. What is most interesting is that Origen knows that some of his sources are disputed in some circles, but goes on to quote them as authoritative, nonetheless—for example, James, 2 and 3 John, Jude, 2 Peter and Barnabas. Of Hebrews—long assumed to be an epistle of Paul—Origen provides perhaps the best answer to the current questions about its authorship: he says, "God knows [who wrote it]!" On the whole, the great Alexandrian scholar leaves us the impression that as yet there is no universal agreement among Christians on the matter of canon, but it is fast becoming an issue, and that his own preferences roughly approximate the contents of the Codex Sinaiticus a century later.[36]

During the next half-century we find evidence that the issue comes to focus on one book especially—the Revelation to John. It became popular among most Western churches but enjoyed little or no attention in the East. Some scholars suggest that Eastern resistance to the book was due to an antiapocalyptic current in the church, dating back possibly to earlier schismatic controversies, in which the dangers of "prophetism" (as in Montanism) with its appeal to visions had caused great concern.[37] Moreover, debate over the authorship (and, therefore, apostolic status) of the book may have given many readers the excuse they needed for discounting a book they found difficult or distasteful anyway. It should be noted, however, that Dionysius of Alexandria (ca. 260), even though he questioned its apostolic origin, held Revelation in high esteem; for him the *worth* of the book did not depend on the question of authorship.

Only as we move into the fourth century do we find the lines of a definite consensus clearly emerging. Not that all disputes over particular books suddenly ceased; Revelation continued to meet resistance among the leaders of the Eastern church,[38] a fact reflected also in the paucity of manu-

---

[36]Much of Origen's own writings have been lost; the basic source for his discussion of the books mentioned is Eusebius, *H.E.* VI.25.

[37]For references to Montanism (named for its founder, Montanus of Mysia) see Eusebius, *H.E.* V.16.7-10; Hippolytus, *Refutatio omnium haeresium* viii.19; cf. Sundberg, "The Making of the New Testament Canon," 1224.

[38]For example, Cyril of Jerusalem (d. 386) rejected Revelation, even forbidding private, as well as public, reading of it. The Christian school at Antioch apparently disapproved of it, and it was omitted from the Syriac Peshitta ("common" version) of the New Testament (fifth century).

scripts containing Revelation, as compared with other books.[39] But the tide of events leading to the toleration and Roman recognition of Christianity, then to the great ecumenical councils of the fourth century, wrought within the Church a hardening of lines both in creed and in canon. Once again, as for the centuries past, Eusebius provides invaluable testimony for this period (his own), as to which books were ''accepted'' and which ''disputed''—using the same categories as Origen. Eusebius further divides the ''disputed'' books, telling which of them he personally regards as Scripture and which ones he rejects. His own list includes the four Gospels, the Acts, fourteen letters of Paul (counting the Epistle to the Hebrews), and seven Catholic letters (noting, however, that the authenticity of James and Jude was disputed), and—in Eusebius's words, ''if it really seems proper''—the Revelation to John.[40] Overlooking his uncertainty about the last book, then, we count twenty-seven in all, precisely those that eventually compose the present New Testament.

By 325 CE, the list of ''rejected'' books has titles already mentioned, such as Barnabas and the Didache, and many that we know only by name. Many of them have disappeared; some may yet be recovered someday— as were the documents of Nag Hammadi in Egypt.[41] At any rate, we now know that a wide assortment of books was available to Christians during those formative years, and yet apparently no effort was made to repress the unacceptable or to censor them. Only the subtle pressure of moral persuasion and the appeal to growing consensus seem determinative so far.

Although the ancient witnesses cited thus far were not very explicit about the *criteria* for deciding which books were acceptable, Eusebius suggests three, according to one modern authority: ''universal acceptance, evaluation of the content on doctrinal grounds, and the claim to apostolicity.''[42] These three concerns, in varying proportion or degree of importance, seem to operate at

---

[39]Only about one-third of the Greek manuscripts of the New Testatment contain the book or any part of it. See ch. 3 for further comment on the significance of this.

[40]Eusebius, *H.E.* III.25.1-7.

[41]This collection of scrolls, discovered in 1945, was apparently the library of a Gnostic community; most of the books, containing fifty-two tractates, are written in Coptic (an Egyptian language using the Greek alphabet) but thought to be translations from texts in Greek. Cf. *The Nag Hammadi Library*, ed. J. M. Robinson (New York: Harper and Row, 1977).

[42]Sundberg, ''The Making of the New Testament Canon,'' 1224.

the level of conscious reflection and in the learned discourses of the scholars and fathers of the early Church. But we should also be sensitive to the level of the unconscious or, better perhaps, the un*self*-conscious factor—that is, the grassroots, widespread *usage* of these books over many years, which underlay "universal acceptance" among Christians, just as it did among the Jews. We emphasize this, not to deny the importance of the learned discussions of ancient church leaders, but simply to maintain a proper perspective. This survey, quoting as it does a long list of "fathers and doctors," could create the impression that canonical status was imposed upon a passive and unsuspecting rank and file by hierarchial *fiat*, or that Scripture was defined only by the deliberations of a few prominent teachers. Such is definitely *not* the case. Scholarly debate—as in argument over authorship or apostolic origin—comes relatively late in the process, and if a book has already won for itself a place in the hearts of several generations or entrenched itself in the liturgy of countless congregations, that book can scarcely be dislodged by anything that the scholars may say against it. Conversely, certain books were generally thought to be written by one or another of the apostles, but unless they endured the test of time and satisfied the needs of believers, they did not survive as Scripture.

One last witness to this process of defining the New Testament must be cited: Athanasius, the bishop of Alexandria, famous for his opposition to Arianism during and after the Council of Nicea.[43] In his *Epistola Festalis* of 367 CE he provides for his diocese a list of books held to be authoritative (no doubt implying a negative judgment against those he omitted); the list coincides exactly with the contents of the New Testament as it is known today. Even so, we should not conclude that Athanasius thought of the canon as entirely closed, for in that same letter he adds a list of books to be read by those taking instruction (presumably for admission into the church), and this list includes the Didache, the Shepherd of Hermas, and five books of the Old Testament Apocrypha.[44]

Finally, we come to what might be called the stage of *ratification* by church councils or synods (formal assemblies of bishops, and so on). The

---

[43]Arianism (from Arius, a presbyter of Alexandria) asserted that Christ was neither wholly divine (of one substance with God) nor truly human. The doctrine provoked widespread opposition among bishops who assembled in 325 and produced the famous Nicene Creed.

[44]Actually only four belong to the Protestant Apocrypha: Wisdom of Solomon, Sirach (Ecclesiasticus), Judith, and Tobit; the fifth was Esther (in its expanded form).

word "ratification" seems appropriate here, because what the various assemblies of clergy did in the latter half of the fourth century was not so much to *create* the canon as to give it an official blessing, a formal stamp of approval. They were, in effect, merely ratifying something already created through centuries of public and private usage by ordinary Christians. In most instances where the books of Scripture became matter for discussion in such meetings, that discussion was incidental to some other subject of concern, not itself the focal point of debate. Dominating the fourth-century synods, of course, were questions of Christology—how best to affirm what Christians believed about Christ, his relationship with God and with the world. But it became clear in the course of their theological deliberations that creedal affirmations needed to be grounded in the church's most authoritative witnesses, and this meant a clear and definite determination of what they were.

By the end of the fourth century, then, that emerging consensus was reflected in the records of the Synod of Carthage (397 CE). Western opinion, it seems, had for the moment prevailed regarding the Revelation to John. Noteworthy, too, was the discussion in that meeting of the use of martyrologies in public worship; it was decided that reading of such books (for example, the Martyrdom of Polycarp)[45] was permissible on days devoted to the martyrs (for example, anniversaries of their death). Implied in this was a concern that appropriate distinction be made between the regular lection from Scripture and those occasional readings from other popular (but noncanonical) books.[46]

Even the official resolutions of ecclesiastical councils did not terminate all argument or impose complete uniformity of canon for all. Fifth-century records show, for example, that many Christians continued to express doubts about the value of the Revelation to John; others still disputed one or more of the Catholic Epistles. In fact, only three of the Catholic Epistles appear in the Syriac Peshitta (ca. 411), the standard version of the New Testament among Syrian churches well into the modern period. In the sixth century, however, other Syriac Bibles appeared with the full twenty-seven-book New Testament, probably reflecting the influence of

---

[45]In Richardson, *Early Christian Fathers*, 149-58.

[46]A lection (from the Latin *lectio*, "reading") is a passage from the gospels or epistles designated for use in the liturgy for a particular Sunday (or special occasions); collections of these, arranged according to the church calendar, were known as lectionaries.

the Latin Vulgate, which had become the predominant Bible of Western Christendom.

While most Syrians were content with a twenty-two-book New Testament, Ethiopian Christians embraced thirty-five books, including a so-called "Clement" (not the same as our 1 Clement, mentioned earlier) and an expanded Revelation of Peter. All things considered, it is safe to say that variation in the definition of Scripture continued to find expression long after Athanasius and the decrees of the councils; the Western consensus did not bring about a "closed" canon, in the usual sense of the word. Perhaps the term itself should be abandoned, and an image more appropriate to the dynamics of the process be used instead—something like "grew up" or "reached maturity."

For now the best conclusion is to say that somewhere along the way (probably within the fifth century) the general consensus of Western Christendom concerning the New Testament settled on those twenty-seven books and gave that definition to the canon, which many of the readers of this book will know and recognize. Once determined, the boundaries of the New Testament became a part of the fixed heritage of the Christian Faith and have become for most of us so familiar that, when we discover now what really went into the formation of "the books," what a complexity of action and reaction gave shape to our New Testament, we are moved to a sense of wonder and, perhaps, to a deeper appreciation.

Development of Canon

621 B.C. — Book of the Law - (similar to Deuteron.) - Used by Josiah as canon to determine nat'l policy

400 EZRA — time of restoration. Nationwide reading & study of Bible - "Book of the Law or the Covenant." - Is this Pentateuch

180-150 Ecclesiasticus or "Sirach"-refers to Law & Prophets & others

A.D. ~100 After 1st Jewish Revolt & destr. of temple & scattering of people. Locations such as Jamnia discussed what books defiled the hand.

For Further Reading

Samples of the "Apostolic Fathers" (cf. C. C. Richardson, *Early Christian Fathers,* The Library of Christian Classics 1 [Philadelphia: Westminster Press, 1953]):
1 Clement (of Rome) 44–end
Letters of Ignatius: Magnesians, Philadelphians
The Didache (Teaching of the Twelve Apostles)
On the Canon of the Old Testament:
Jeffery, Arthur. "The Canon of the Old Testament." In *The Interpreter's Bible.* Nashville: Abingdon Press, 1952. 1:32-45.

Koch, Klaus. *The Book of Books: The Growth of the Bible.* Philadelphia: Westminster Press, 1968.

Silberman, Lou H. "The Making of the Old Testament Canon." In *The Interpreter's One-Volume Commentary of the Bible.* Nashville/New York: Abingdon Press, 1971. Pages 1209-15.

On the Apocrypha (Deuterocanonical books) of the Old Testament, Pseudepigrapha, and so on:

Metzger, Bruce M. "Introduction to the Apocrypha." In *Oxford Annotated Apocrypha.* Revised Standard Version. Either separately bound or in the Students Edition of the whole Bible. New York: Oxford University Press, 1965. Pages ix-xx.

Rost, Leonhard. *Judaism Outside the Hebrew Canon.* D. E. Green, trans. Nashville: Abingdon Press, 1976.

On the Canon of the New Testament:
Goodspeed, Edgar J. "The Canon of the New Testament." In *The Interpreter's Bible.* Nashville: Abingdon Press, 1952. 1:63-71.

Sundberg, Albert C., Jr. "The Making of the New Testament Canon." In *The Interpreter's One-Volume Commentary of the Bible.* Nashville/New York: Abingdon Press, 1971. Pages 1216-24.

On the "New Testament Apocrypha":
Hennecke, Edgar, and Wilhelm Schneemelcher. *New Testament Apocrypha.* R. McL. Wilson, trans. Two volumes. Philadelphia: Westminster Press, 1963, 1965.

James, M. R., ed. *The Apocryphal New Testament.* Oxford: The Clarendon Press, 1950.

Relevant Passages in the Bible

(The following are chosen as samples for illustrating in English translation some of the "variant readings" of the text and the kind of decisions the textual critics have to make in such cases.)

Genesis 4:8 (see footnote)*

1 Samuel 13:1 (and footnote)

Isaiah 49:24 (where the Qumran scroll of Isaiah has figured)

RSV introduction to Jeremiah, explaining variations between Hebrew text and the Septuagint

Habakkuk 1:12 (where "*we* shall . . . " probably is a scribal emendation— *tiqqune sopherim—for* "*you* shall not die")

Psalm 100:3

Matthew 6:13 (and footnotes)

Mark 1:41 (unnoticed in the RSV footnotes is the variant "Moved with *anger* . . . "—example, perhaps, of "the more difficult reading.")

Mark 16:9-20 (and footnotes)—cf. *Gospel Parallels,* 191

John 7:53—8:11 (and footnote)

Romans 5:1

1 Thessalonians 2:7

Revelation 13:18

---

*The footnotes referred to here are those of the *Oxford Annotated Bible,* Revised Standard Version (RSV); the Oxford Study Edition of the *New English Bible* has virtually the same notations, but lacks reference to the Greek in its introduction to Jeremiah.

parchment - fine, thin leather
  vellum parchment - from unborn animal - finest
papyrus - from plant
scrolls
codex - folded sheets - first book
sopher - scribe - reproduce books
masoretes - standardized texts, invented vowel system
  of dots & dashes

Textual Criticism
- Reconstruct actual wrote.

Chapter 3

The Texts of the Bible
and Their Transmission

Now that I have traced the process of canonization and noted the stages by which both the Tanak (Old Testament) and the Christian New Testament became authoritative Scripture, it seems appropriate to give special attention to the ways in which Jews and Christians have preserved, copied, and translated their sacred texts through the centuries—in a word, the matter of textual transmission. This is a matter both fascinating and complex, and because it involves some rather specialized technical data, most handbooks or introductions to the Bible devote very little space to it. Consequently, many lay people have been left in the dark, or else have only the few scraps of information that their pastors and teachers let fall from sermon or Bible study, and therefore miss this fascinating aspect in the development of the Bible itself *and* of modern research in texts and translations. So, because of its importance for understanding what the Bible is and for appreciating the labors of recent scholars, I will run the risk of oversimplifying the subject and offer the following summary.

First, a few words about terminology. When scholars refer to the biblical *text* in the technical sense, as I now intend to use it, what they mean is the book or books *in the original language*. Sometimes, as in cases where it is uncertain which was the original language of a book, one may find reference to a Greek text and a Latin text (for example) of the same book, but ordinarily the term *version* is used to distinguish the known translations of books in other languages. For instance, the Septuagint was an ancient version of the Jewish Bible, and the Syriac Peshitta was an early version of the Christian Bible.

The label generally applied to people who have become experts in the study of texts, versions, and their history—involving, obviously, intimate knowledge of the ancient languages—is textual criticism.[1] "Criticism," by the way, is here a technical term, meaning simply investigation or scholarly inquiry, and carries no connotation of hostility or of any negative attitude toward the Bible.

Textual criticism is necessary because there are numerous witnesses to the text of the Bible, and no two are exactly alike in every detail. We refer, of course, to the handwritten (Latin, *manu scripta*)[2] text of the centuries prior to the invention of mechanical printing presses: the Hebrew MSS of the Tanak and the Greek MSS of the New Testament plus some Greek MSS that contain (or once contained) the whole Christian Bible. While the variations among all these documents are sometimes very minor—for example, a simple spelling variation or an accidentally omitted line— sometimes they are significant, and in any case the cumulative effect is to raise the question at certain points: what *is* the original wording?

The earliest manuscripts of the Bible are *copies* dating no earlier than the fourth century of our era (for the whole Bible), although there are a few individual books of the Old Testament for which the Dead Sea Scrolls provide an earlier witness.[3] Some papyrus MSS, many of them fragmentary, have recently come to light to give us some third-century copies of Paul's letters. But all are copies, more or less distantly removed from the actual documents (what the scholars refer to as "autographs") of the original au-

---

[1]This field of scholarship is also called by some writers "lower criticism," as distinct from "higher criticism"—those areas of inquiry into oral and literary sources, redaction, authorship and dates of books, or even the historical background and occasion for the writings—matters said to be "higher" only in the sense of prior to the production of the text itself.

[2]Hence the convention of abbreviating the word "manuscript" as MS, and the plural as MSS. Until about 1450, books were published only by this slow and laborious method: either a scribe at his desk would transcribe by sight from his exemplar, or a number of scribes would take "dictation" and write down the text as read to them aloud by a reader or lector.

[3]Such, for example, is the book of Isaiah, preserved on leather scrolls and protected for centuries in pottery jars, dating from about the second century BCE. Two copies—one of which is remarkably intact and complete—provide a witness to the text of Isaiah that is nearly one thousand years older than any known before 1949, when the scrolls came to light.

thors. Those original documents, written no doubt on parchment or papyrus[4] apparently did not survive the ravages of time and climate. The wonder is not that those first MSS disappeared but that so many old copies of them *have* survived. In fact, by comparison to the state of the text of many Greek writers of the classical period, the New Testament text has the advantage of not only more numerous witnesses but also MSS of a date much nearer to the time of original composition. For example, while the plays of Aeschylus (fifth century BCE) are preserved in not more than fifty Greek MSS, and these from times at least 1,300 years after Aeschylus, there are about 5,000 Greek MSS of the New Testament, whole or in part, and perhaps more than 200 of them derive from times within four centuries of the original writings.[5] In the case of Hebrew MSS of the Tanak, we are not quite so fortunate, since the earliest parts stem probably from the tenth-century BCE, and of the approximately 2,500 MSS known to us hardly any come from a time before 800 CE with the notable exception of some fragments from about the sixth century and the scrolls of Qumran and Murabba'at.[6]

But the existence of so many manuscripts is not entirely comforting. In fact, that is part of the problem: the greater the number of different manuscripts, the more variations there are among them. And thus the task of the textual critic is to search through the multiplicity of witnesses to ascertain the best possible text—that is, what most *probably* was the original wording. For it is largely a matter of probabilities, very rarely certainties, and yet I hasten to point out that the total amount of doubtful or problematic readings in proportion to the amount of text that is unquestioned is perhaps less than five percent. Moreover, the vast majority of these variant readings are of such a character as to leave doctrine virtually unaffected; seldom if ever, is any major theological affirmation of Jew or Christian jeopardized by the kind of judgments the textual critics have to make.

---

[4]These were the two primary materials used for writing in the period of the Bible's composition; parchment was made from the skins of animals scraped or rubbed smooth, and usually sewn together to form a scroll, while papyrus was made from the stem of an aquatic plant, cut into strips and pressed flat. Sheets of this material could also be joined to form scrolls and, later on, to form the codex—the ancestor of our present books.

[5] F.G. Kenyon, *Handbook to the Textual Criticism of the New Testament,* 2nd ed. (Grand Rapids: William B. Eerdmans, 1951) 3, 5.

[6]John Reumann, "The Transmission of the Biblical Text," *Interpreter's One-Volume Commentary on the Bible* (Nashville: Abingdon Press, 1971) 1228.

But before pursuing further the modern scholar's investigations, let me now turn back to the work of those ancient scribes or copyists who were responsible for producing and transmitting what we now have. A survey of their contributions will help greatly to explain the problems of latter-day readers, translators, and interpreters of the Bible, and—indeed—explain the tremendous debt that readers today owe to their care and industry.

Preservers of the Ancient Hebrew Text

To find a specific date for the final assembling of the Tanak, and thus for the publication of the whole collection as a unit, is probably impossible, since Jewish practice for centuries into our era was to treat the Scriptures as a collection of "the books" and *not* as a single book. Most of the books in an early Jewish synagogue—and private ownership was virtually unknown—would be on separate scrolls, except for the shorter books (for example, the twelve "minor" prophets) gathered into one scroll. When the wear and tear of many years began to show and a new copy was needed, it was generally one book at a time that was replaced. It is not likely that any one scribe would copy the whole Bible, unless under unusual circumstances he were especially commissioned to do so. The worn book was often ceremoniously "retired" to a special resting place, called a *geniza,* indicating something of the sanctity that surrounded the very material on which God's Word was written.[7]

It was this conviction that "the books" were holy that provided the dominant impetus not only for their preservation, in the sense of replacing worn-out copies, but also for the meticulous care with which the new copies were made. The evidence suggests very strongly that the tendency to "fix" or standardize the Hebrew text grew apace with the notion of that text's special holiness and canonicity. Not just anybody was qualified to handle these sacred books, either in the synagogue services or in the work of copying; the job could be entrusted only to those properly authorized and approved by the Jewish community or its leaders. Tradition traces this attitude back to Ezra and "the men of the Great Synagogue"[8] but whether

---

[7]One remarkable example of a synagogue *geniza* was discovered in the 1890s in Cairo; "buried" there were numerous fragmentary MSS, some dating back to the sixth century. Some scholars have been inclined to think of the caves of Qumran as primitive instances of the same practice, but the objections to such an interpretation are fairly strong.

[8]*Pirke Aboth* (Sayings of the Fathers) 1:1. For an English translation of this ancient Jewish tract, often published as part of the Mishnah, see the edition of R. Travers Herford (New York: Jewish Institute of Religion, 1945).

or not it started so early in actual fact, by the opening of the Christian era
the office of the professional scribe had become one of great dignity and
responsibility. Not without cause do the gospels refer to them often as
"lawyers," for their work involved far more than the labor of transcribing
manuscripts; scribes had become the experts in expounding the *meaning*
of the books as well as in copying their text.

The job of transcribing, in itself, was no mean task. It required years
of training, sitting at the feet of a learned teacher who no doubt instilled in
his disciples both technical precision and a real love for the work. It had
to be a labor of love, as we now reflect on it, for otherwise what the scribes
did is simply incredible.

In the period from the first century BCE through the fifth century of our
era, records refer to these Jewish scholars as *sopherim* (literally "bookmen").[9] Because the word *sopher* (scribe) comes from a Hebrew root
meaning "to count," some scholars think that the basis for that title was
the practice of counting the number of letters on a page or in a book.
Whether or not that is the best etymology, those ancient bookmen did indeed count and tabulate the Hebrew characters on the pages of their completed copies, in order to make sure that they had not missed a single letter—
not even a *yodh* or a tittle.[10] They kept tables to indicate how many lines
or even letters there were to the midpoint of each book, the better to locate
the fault, in case counting turned up either too many or too few letters on
the page.

To these early scribes belongs the credit for taking the first major steps
toward "standardizing" the Hebrew text—reducing differences among
existing MSS by correcting orthography (spelling), for example, and generally lending authority to their preferred readings where choices had to be
made. Even though they gave meticulous care to detail, most scribes were
fully aware of the sense of the words they copied, and were quick to recognize mistakes in their exemplar. Sometimes they must have taken the
liberty to make corrections by replacing the offending word in their new

---

[9]A. Cohen, *Everyman's Talmud* (New York: E. P. Dutton, 1975) xvi.

[10]Behind the familiar "jot and tittle" of Matthew 5:18 (Greek: ἰῶτα ἓν ἢ μία κεραία,
lit. "one iota or one hook") lie the Hebrew character *yodh* and the word for a decorative
flourish sometimes added to a letter. If by *yodh* is meant the smallest letter of the alphabet,
the saying could apply only to the Aramaic (square) script and not to the older form, where
the *yodh* was larger.

copy, leaving their exemplar untouched; other times they might try to re-
touch the exemplar as well, perhaps by scratching off the old ink and writing in the new wording, but more often (judging from the practice of later
times) it seems the correction would be penned in above the error or written in the margin. The tendency that prevailed was apparently one of conservatism: more and more the scribe would let the error stand, even copy
it into his new text, but add the marginal correction to show that he knew
how the text *should* read. Thus an early attempt at textual criticism was
made by the ancient scribes themselves.[11]

It was also during the period of the *sopherim* that the style of writing
found in nearly all Hebrew MSS of the Bible was fully developed and
adopted. An older, more rounded form of character, often called "cursive," gave way to the "square" script, often called Aramaic or Assyrian,
no doubt as a result of the predominance of the Aramaic language as the
vernacular of Palestine and much of the Middle East. It is likely that many
of the difficult textual problems represented by medieval MSS of Tanak
are ultimately due to the difficulty some scribes had in copying from texts
in the old script. In this chart I can illustrate the differences in a mere sample of the alphabet.

SOUND	HEBREW NAME	CURSIVE SCRIPT	SQUARE FORM
b	beth	𐤁	ב
z	zayin	𐤆	ז
k	kaph	𐤊	כ or ך
l	lamedh	𐤋	ל
n	nun	𐤍	נ or ן

It takes no special training in Hebrew to see among these five characters many possibilities for miscopying. How easy, for example, for a scribe
accustomed to forming his *lamedh* in the new style to mistake the old *kaph*
for that letter, or to confuse *kaph* and *nun* in the old script. Of course, the
new script also afforded its own opportunities for confusion, quite apart

---

[11]By the Middle Ages this habit of distinguishing between the word "to be read" (*Qerê*)
and what was "written" (*Kethîv*) became a formally recognized practice, clearly marked
by appropriate abbreviations in the margins.

from the difficulty of using two scripts. Similarities between certain square characters required an alert mind and a keen eye to distinguish them; for example, compare ד (*daleth* or "d") and ר (*resh* or "r"), or ה (*he* or "h") and ח (*cheth* or "ch" as in the Scottish *loch*). When one considers that Hebrew was written with *consonants only*—no vowels[12]—then one has some idea of the task of the *sopherim,* and no little amazement at the patience and skill with which they pursued it.

Another contribution of scribes in that early period was the marking of sense divisions in the text, either by leaving spaces between words (where formerly none was used, nor any marks of punctuation) or by marks in the margins, or perhaps by both. Certain references from rabbinical literature suggest that such marks were meant to show the reader where to pause or to end the lesson for the day. Although a fully punctuated text with verse divisions, as we know them today, developed only later, we may suppose that the *sopherim* set that development in motion. It is noteworthy that in the larger scroll of Isaiah, found at Qumran, there are spaces between words and wider spaces to mark some sectional divisions—anticipating later "chapters" in some cases—but very few marginal symbols or other scribal signs.[13]

During the period between 500 and 900 CE the work begun by the *sopherim* was continued, refined, and formalized by their scholarly successors, who came to be known as "masters of the *Masora* (Tradition)" or "Masoretes." Their care and concern for accurate preservation of the sacred text virtually eliminated all would-be rivals to their "standard" copies, so that the basis for nearly all medieval MSS, and all modern editions of Tanak, is the Masoretic Text (often abbreviated in scholarly works as "MT").

Among the refinements of the scribal art in the period of the Masoretes was the notation system whereby the reader would be warned not only of the proper beginning and end of a lesson but also of alternative readings. Thus instead of removing a defectively spelled word or correcting it in the

---

[12]Two Hebrew consonants—the ו (*vav*) and the י (*yodh*)—could double as vowels (one for "o" or "u," the other for "i" and certain diphthongs), and as time passed the use of these consonants as vowels to insure proper pronunciation seemed to increase.

[13]Some ten different marks can be distinguished, but without discernible pattern or regularity; some scholars question whether these marks were made by the hand of the scribe who penned the scroll. *The Dead Sea Scrolls of St. Mark's Monastery,* ed. Millar Burrows (New Haven CT: American Schools of Oriental Research, 1950) 1:xv-xvi.

text itself, scribes marked the spot in the margin by signs indicating *Kethîv* (the written word) and *Qerê* (to be read). Sometimes, by other signs, they noted variant readings and called attention to the use of words for "god" or "gods" that did not demand special reverence in reading, as did the sacred name (written יהוה—*YHWH*—but pronounced as if it were '*Adonai*— "my Lord"), and even the more common '*elohim* when referring to Israel's God.

The Masoretes also developed a full set of cantillation signs—marks to aid the reader or cantor in inflection and phrasing, something of a mixture of punctuation marks (mostly interlinear) and accent marks for pause or stress. In this way, the actual sound of the synagogue reading tended to become standardized, along with the written text, and one listening today to the cantor in an Orthodox Jewish service of worship hears very much the same intonations as did the people of Medieval Europe.

Most remarkable of all the Masoretic achievements, next to copying the sacred text with such marvelous care, was the perfection of the system of vowel pointing. The Masoretes inherited a text composed almost exclusively of consonants. For centuries, no vowels had been necessary,[14] but as the knowledge of spoken Hebrew began to decline and, in some cases, to be forgotten, ways of insuring the proper sense and sound of the Scriptures were devised. Two or three different systems seemed to compete for a time, but finally one of these, known as the Tiberian system, prevailed. It made use of dots and dashes in various configurations under the consonants, plus the *vav* and *yodh* already serving as vowels, in order to provide the full range of vocalization. Once this system became predominant, it made possible further standardization of the text, removing many lingering ambiguities that were inherent in the unpointed MSS of earlier times. Not that all scholarly debate ceased nor all questions of proper reading were answered. Indeed, it is to the credit of the Masoretes that they recognized and clearly marked the spots that to them were dubious or defective—technically known now as "corruptions"—for the most part due to errors of copying that had occurred centuries before their own time. Piety and respect for the sacred books demanded fidelity to the Tradition that they inherited and in turn passed on, even faithful transmission of the admittedly

---

[14]See n. 12 above. There is a record of a movement among Babylonian Jews of the sixth century CE to supply vowel signs, perhaps influenced by earlier efforts of Syriac-speaking Christians to do so.

The beginning of the Ten Commandments (Exodus 19:24-20:17a) on MS 4445, a "Masoretic" manuscript written on sheets of vellum and bound in a codex during the tenth century of the Common Era. The Hebrew text reads from right to left. Note the scribal notations and corrections in the margins and between the columns and the "pointing" of the vowels. Before the library of Qumran was discovered, MS 4445 was among the earliest exemplars of the Hebrew Bible. (Photo reproduced with the permission of The British Library.)

faulty parts. Often they passed along to modern scholars very perceptive corrections or emendations, but some of their suggested readings have not proved so valuable. Yet, on the whole, the Masoretes were responsible not only for the very preservation and transmission of the Hebrew Bible but also for invaluable pioneering efforts in what was later to become the science of textual criticism.

Preservers of the Ancient Greek Text of the New Testament

Turning now to trace the beginning of the Greek New Testament, I leave aside for the moment consideration of the Greek translations of the Jewish Bible, to which of course I must return, since they were most likely the first Bibles that Christians had. Indeed, some of the oldest and most valuable of the Greek MSS contain (or once contained) both Old and New Testaments. But here, to avoid possible confusion and needless complication, let me concentrate attention on the text of the New Testament alone.

This collection of writings, like the Tanak, was formed gradually over many years, and scholars do not know precisely when the several books first became joined and began circulating together. In the strictest sense, the textual history of the New Testament begins with the history of each individual book, but of course our extant MSS—except for a few rare fragments—all represent somewhat later stages of development. Most of the Greek MSS came from the period of 500 to 1400 CE, well after the question of canon had been settled and the twenty-seven books were known collectively as New Testament. We have good reason to suppose that smaller collections and groupings of books (for example, the four gospels) had been made much earlier, possibly by the middle of the second century. A collection of Paul's letters was known to Ignatius of Antioch and to the writer of 2 Peter (cf. 3:15-16). Somewhat later, possibly by the end of the second century, it became customary to group together the Catholic Epistles and the Acts of the Apostles, the eight-book collection called ''Praxapostolos'' (from the Greek *praxeis*—''Acts''—and *apostolos*—''apostle,'' referring to Peter, John, James, and Jude).

Who first copied and transmitted the Greek texts, we can only surmise. Unfortunately for us, those early Christian scribes never gained the prestige or notoriety of their Jewish counterparts, the *sopherim* or Masoretes, and never formed themselves into anything like a professional school. This does not mean that they were any less dedicated or less skilled than those who transmitted the Hebrew text; it simply means that they were less self-conscious (in the earliest stages) of their work and left behind no "masora" by which we might assess their technical proficency. Indeed, it is likely that early Christian copyists took their technique and their standards of excellence from none other than Jewish scribes, just as Christians borrowed from the Jews much of their forms of liturgy and system of organization.[15]

Although we lack firm documentary evidence from the earliest stage of New Testament textual history, what we get from later times points back to two important impulses, both of which bear on the development of the Greek text. First, there was the impulse toward canonization, which prompted both the process of reproduction of copies and the desire to minimize variations among the MSS—two somewhat competing tendencies, as it turned out. Second, the rapid spread of Christianity over the vast Roman Empire (and adjoining areas) must have prompted the tendency toward variation of texts rather than that toward uniformity. As Christians scattered and settled in widely separate centers like Antioch, Alexandria, Rome and Ephesus, scribes in each locality would reproduce their own "local" texts. Before the rise of Roman Catholicism, with its hierarchical structure, there was no effective means of exercising ecclesiastical control over such matters and thus preventing textual diversification.

Such diversification did in fact take place, modern textual criticism now shows, in that the extant Greek MSS of the New Testament tend to fall into fairly well defined "types" and "families." Sorted on the basis of kinship—common variations—the various types of text seem to stem from certain "ancestors" representative of distinct localities or areas. Thus one may find reference to a Byzantine text, an Alexandrian type, a Western type and so on.

It was apparently in the fourth century that the church began to grow sensitive to the problems of textual diversity and to make some effort to control it. It was natural that attention to the details of the text should increase apace with attention to questions of canon and creed. Underlying all these concerns was the church's need to determine the nature and source of ecclesiastical authority, especially in its new status under Constantine.[16]

---

[15]See Birger Gerhardson, *Memory and Manuscript* (Copenhagen: Gleerup, Lund, and Munksquaard, 1961).

[16]After a century or more of persecution of Christians, the Roman Emperors Constantine and Licinius issued the Edict of Milan in 313 CE, allowing Christians "free and unrestricted practice" of their religion.

Compelled not only to affirm its faith in creedal formulae for the world to see, but also to establish its own polity and ''chain of command,'' the church looked to its Scripture as a source of doctrine and polity. And this in turn made it essential to have a text that was as ''catholic'' as the church itself—a standard by which to adjudicate the varying views and doctrines then competing for a place in Christian teaching.

Meanwhile, however, the opposite tendency had gained momentum; favored and protected by the state, the church's scribes reproduced more copies of the Bible than ever before. By this time, also, many could afford the more expensive writing material—parchment or even vellum—for their MSS; the use of papyrus began to decline, eventually to disappear completely. The *form* of the book had changed, too—as early as the second century—from the scroll to the *codex* (from the Latin for ''block''). This kind of book proved to be far more useful for study and handy for reference than the scroll. It was formed by folding sheets of parchment (or papyrus) in the middle and sewing them together in quires, at the fold, then stacking and fastening several quires together, making a book much like those we use today. The codex form is represented by some ancient papyrus sheets of New Testament books, now housed in the Chester Beatty Library (Dublin), the University of Michigan (Ann Arbor), and elsewhere, but preeminently by surviving parts of the whole Greek Bible, such as the great fourth-century MSS Vaticanus and Sinaiticus.[17]

As a result of this situation—more profilic copying coupled with growing demand for standardizing the text—there was a net gain insofar as the more obvious errors and new corruptions in the text were reduced. But the character of the Greek New Testament had already been established by now, and not much could be done about the many little corruptions from the earlier period that went unnoticed and, indeed, became a part of the standard (or, as modern scholars say, ''received'') text for centuries to come. Also, as one of America's leading textual critics argued, those scribes who consciously endeavored to standardize the biblical texts sometimes made a choice between two or more readings on the basis of personal whim or, at

---

[17]Prominent among reasons for the adoption of the codex by Christians was the need for easier reference to, or finding of, a given passage for reading; the difficulty of turning from one passage to another in the roll is too obvious to need description. No scrap of early Christian literature survives on a roll; see E. G. Turner, *Greek Papyri: An Introduction* (Princeton NJ: Princeton University Press, 1968) 11.

best, theological bias, hardly ever on the basis of solid documentary evidence. Moreover, well meaning as they no doubt were, the most earnest revisers may have discarded and destroyed MSS that contained texts superior, on the whole, to those they produced.[18] At any rate, the diversity of Greek texts was there to stay, or to await the emergence of better scholarly methods for solving its problems.

In the period from 400 CE to about 800, the MSS of the New Testament were characterized by the distinctive style of lettering known as *uncial*[19]— block-like "capitals" without ligatures (linking lines). If we are to judge from our earliest (and in some respects best) specimens, scribes gave great care and painstaking effort to their work, taking pride in the appearance of the finished page as well as in the accuracy of the text itself. In some of these uncial MSS we find the beginnings of the practice of illumination, at first by enlarging and adding color to the initial letter of a book or its title,[20] then with the use of decorative designs and figures in the margins, by way of illustrating the subject of the book. Thus the Christian Bible became in many instances a work of art, meant to be protected as a treasure and kept for only the most solemn ceremonial occasions.

About 800 CE or soon after, the elegant but slow style of uncial lettering began to give way to a freer, more flowing style called cursive or minuscule. Much like normal handscript of today, the letters were smaller and joined together. Practical convenience and speed in copying seem to have won out over more aesthetic considerations. The monks, who were the usual custodians and copyists of the books, devised numerous shorthand signs and abbreviations for much repeated words like "God" and "Lord." And the rate of reproduction, though still far from rapid, must have increased noticeably over the next three centuries. By far the greatest number of our Greek MSS (over 2,500) come from the ninth through fifteenth centuries. Unfortunately, as we have already suggested, where

---

[18]Ernest C. Colwell, *The Study of the Bible,* rev. ed. (Chicago: University of Chicago Press, 1964); see also his article "Text and Ancient Versions of the New Testament," in *The Interpreter's Bible,* vol. 1 (Nashville: Abingdon Press, 1952) 72-83.

[19]Derived from the Latin *uncialis*—literally, having to do with an inch—the term may have applied to letters said to be (by exaggeration) "inch-high." If, however, the term was first applied to letters incised in stone and literally inch-high, it is merely a matter of transferred meaning, from the size of the lettering to the style.

[20]Such letters or words were often reddened with vermilion ink—hence our word "rubric" (from the Latin *ruber* meaning "red").

manuscript transmission is concerned "more" is not necessarily "better." The quality of product during the medieval period varied greatly from place to place and from scribe to scribe, but on the whole the Greek text suffered from the mistakes of careless copyists as much in this period as in the earliest, if not more.

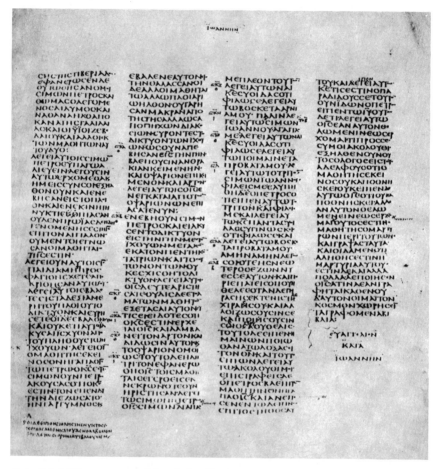

John 21:1-25 on a page of the Codex Sinaiticus (אׁ), a magnificent example of the great uncial codices prepared under the patronage of the Emperor Constantine early in the fourth century of the Common Era. Still considered to be one of the earliest and best of the manuscripts of the Christian Bible in Greek, Codex Sinaiticus was probably written at Alexandria and was corrected at Caesarea in the seventh century. Several hands are visible in the corrections between the columns of text. (Photo reproduced with the permission of The British Library.)

To summarize, the Greek text of the New Testament (often together with the Greek Old Testament) passed through three main stages, corresponding to the chief material used and the style of writing most prevalent—(1) the earliest stage when MSS were mostly of papyrus, mainly scrolls, with uncial characters in tightly packed lines (no spaces between words, little punctuation); (2) when uncials continued in use, but predominantly on parchment codices (the plural of codex), often with spacing of words and sometimes initial letters in red; and (3) the stage of cursive lettering, with more use of punctuation and abbreviations, paragraphing and illuminations. Some 70 specimens of the papyrus MSS survive; about 250 examples of the uncial period, and more than 2,500 of the minuscule, have been catalogued and classified by experts. In addition, Christian scribes (mostly from ninth century on) produced the *lectionary,* a collection of readings from the New Testament, arranged for use in church worship according to the needs of the ecclesiastical calendar; about 2,000 of these are known, giving modern scholars yet another valuable group of witnesses to the ancient text.[21]

The Ancient Versions of the Bible

In the modern critic's attempt to recover the best text of either testament, his first and fundamental material, of course, is the mass of MSS now available in the original languages. But there is a second body of material, almost as valuable as the first in some respects—namely, the ancient translations from the Hebrew or Greek into other languages. Here, again, the biblical scholar has a distinct advantage over those who work at restoring any other ancient text. Not only has the Bible been translated into more languages than any other book, but the process started very early and we now possess copies of versions made just as early as some of our oldest MSS in the original, if not earlier. Most notable of examples are copies of the Greek Septuagint, the translation of the Hebrew Bible, made some five centuries earlier than the Masoretic Hebrew MSS. And, taking these copies as witnesses to the state of the Hebrew text when first translated into Greek (third to second centuries BC), we gain highly valuable, if indirect, evidence of readings that help to correct the errors of intervening centuries.

---

[21]These books usually contained only excerpts from parts of the New Testament, and quote from the Gospels more often than the Epistles.

The reader has already been introduced to the Septuagint, in the chapter on the Hebrew canon, but here a few more remarks about that version are in order. It arose out of the need in Alexandria for copies of the Jewish Scriptures that Greek-speaking Jews could read and understand; the highly legendary story in The Letter of Aristeas probably contains a core of truth when it claims that the Greek translation was made for the royal library of Ptolemy Philadelphus (285-247 BCE), but this would be more likely in reference to the end of the process than to the beginning. The name was used first of the books of Torah only, which were doubtless first to be translated, and it may have been many years before the Prophets, then the writings (with expanded contents), came into circulation. Close analysis of the various parts proves that the Septuagint, like the Tanak itself, had many different writers, from a wide span of time, and the quality of the translation ranges from very good (as in Lev. and Deut.) to very poor (as in Dan.).[22]

As we have noted, it was this Alexandrian Bible that became the version preferred among the earliest Christians—at least, among those who wrote the New Testament. Quotations from the Old Testament by the author of Hebrews or by the writer of Luke-Acts are almost certainly from the Septuagint, and not from the Masoretic Hebrew. Even the "very Jewish" Gospel of Matthew, in its many citations of the Old Testament, used the Septuagint or another Greek version very close to it.[23]

There were other translations in Greek, known from the second century on, suggesting that Jewish acceptance of the LXX was less than unanimous. As already noted, the Alexandrians had come to embrace a larger collection of books than was acceptable to Palestinian Jews at Jamnia. But there may have been other grounds for dissatisfaction with the LXX. When closely compared with the Masoretic Hebrew it shows numerous differences, many going beyond the ordinary, expected results of translation, so that some scholars insist that the LXX was based on a Hebrew text substantially different from the ancestor of the Masoretic text. If by the second

---

[22]Also the Psalms seem to be carefully done, while most of the Prophets appear in a very loose, paraphrase-like translation; cf. Arthur Jeffery, "Text and Ancient Versions of the Old Testament," *Interpreter's Bible* 1:58-59.

[23]For example, Matthew's quotation of Isaiah 7:14 (Matt. 1:23) as "a virgin shall conceive . . . " conforms only to the LXX reading, whereas the Greek translations of Aquila, Symmachus, and Theodotion more accurately render the Hebrew word as "young woman."

century Jewish scholars began to campaign for conformity to the preferred (proto-Masoretic) text, it stands to reason that the Septuagint (representing a rival tradition) should lose favor. Moreover, as it became identified more and more with the Christians, the LXX could not long continue unchallenged or unchanged.

One challenge came from the school of Rabbi Akiba, which early in the second century made a new edition of the Tanak. This became the basis for the translation of Aquila of Pontus (ca. 130 CE), whose work was noted for being extremely literal, simply matching Hebrew and Greek word for word, and virtually unreadable. Another translation (ca. 175-80) was made by Symmachus, whose style and method were far superior to Aquila's; this version was said to be highly regarded by Jerome.[24] A third appeared a few years later from the hand of Theodotion, whose style was somewhat paraphrastic, but whose work on the book of Daniel proved so successful that it eventually replaced the LXX version of that book. Only fragments of any of these translations are still extant.

One further edition of the LXX should be mentioned, if only to illustrate how even the most prodigious work of scholarship can have unexpected, even disastrous, consequences. This was the edition called the Hexapla, composed by the Alexandrian scholar Origen ca. 230-40. He undertook to gather the existing versions of the Greek Old Testament, no doubt intending to make what would amount to a critical text for his day. But Origen chose to publish his work in a six-column book—hence the term *hexapla* (six-fold)—putting side by side the Hebrew text, a transliteration in Greek letters, and the four Greek translations: Aquila, Symmachus, the LXX, and Theodotion. In his fifth column (the LXX) Origen had freely made alterations of his own , often conflating two variant readings from some of the other versions, but these he clearly marked with an asterisk. It was indeed a remarkable feat, although his work on the text of the LXX was left in an unfinished state. He probably never intended it to be taken for the finished edition of the LXX, but here precisely is where the unfortunate consequences come. Because the huge work was so unwieldy, copyists copied only the fifth column and left out the rest; moreover, most of them did not bother to copy Origen's critical signs and notes, and thus they presented their MSS as true copies of the LXX! The widespread dissemination of these curious, misbegotten MSS through subsequent cen-

---

[24]Jeffery, "The Text and Ancient Versions of the Old Testament," 59.

turies has proved to be a major hindrance to the recovery of that great translation.

While Greek remained the dominant language of culture in the first three centuries of our era, the Bible went with Jews and Christian into lands where the native tongue was not Greek, and where the inhabitants soon demanded a version in the vernacular. In antiquity, as now, evangelism provided a major incentive for translations of the sacred texts. Thus, by the second century, Christians in Syria and Mesopotamia began to translate parts of the Bible into Syriac, a Semitic language closely related to Aramaic. Some scholars believe that Tatian's *Diatessaron* was originally written in Syriac. A manuscript of the Gospels in Syriac from the fourth century was discovered at Mt. Sinai (St. Catherine's Monastery) in 1892, and another, representing a different type of text, ca. fifth century in date, turned up in the British Museum. Known long before these MSS, however, were copies of what came to be called the Syriac Peshitta,[25] representing fifth-century efforts to standardize the earlier texts. It translated the whole Old Testament (lacking the Apocrypha) and all the New Testament except the Revelation and four Catholic Epistles (which, the reader will recall, were never accepted as canonical by Syrian churches).

Also in the second century came the beginnings of translation into Latin. First in North Africa, then in Italy, parts of the Old Testament were translated for Christians whose first language was Latin; of these efforts—representing what scholars call the Old Latin (to distinguish from the Vulgate or later MSS)—very few scraps remain today. From these we may presume that a Greek version, not the Hebrew, was the usual base text. In the Western parts of the Empire knowledge of Hebrew was extremely rare.

The situation that confronted Jerome in the fourth century, when he was commissioned by Bishop Damasus to make a revised Latin edition of the Bible, was not promising. As Jerome himself remarked, "There are almost as many versions (of the Latin Bible) as there are manuscripts."[26] Jerome was an able scholar, competent in Greek, but he knew no Hebrew,

---

[25]*Peshitta* is the Syriac word for "simple" or "common." It is not clear whether the term was meant to indicate "simple" in contrast to a Syrian edition of the Hexapla or "common" in the sense of "standard" (as with *Vulgate*).

[26]From Jerome's letter to Damasus, prefaced to the completed revision, which can be found in the full Latin text in Wordsworth and White's *Latin New Testament* (Oxford, 1911 and later); for a partial translation into English, see F. C. Grant, *Translating the Bible* (Greenwich CT: Seabury Press, 1961) 36-38.

and so his first efforts were based on the LXX, issuing first in a translation of the Psalms, which he later revised on the basis of Origen's text. This appeared ca. 386. By this time Jerome, with a sensitivity rare for his day, felt the need to refer to the original Hebrew, and finding no reputable teacher at hand he made the journey to Palestine and engaged in the study of Hebrew there. By the year 392, he had mastered enough of the language to revise his Psalter on the basis of the Hebrew text and to complete other portions of his translation, using both Hebrew and Greek MSS. Jerome's work on the New Testament had been done quickly, and the result was a rather conservative revision of the Old Latin, but his work on the Old Testament was very deliberate and thorough, completed only in 405. In many ways Jerome's translation departed from the familiar Old Latin versions, and thus offended the conservative tastes of many in the church. Opposition to his Bible persisted for many years, indicating not only how much the Old Latin had replaced the Hebrew and Greek originals in the Western church but also how quickly that church became defensive about the very wording of its familiar and accepted translation. And yet—one of history's most notable ironies—Jerome's work eventually proved its worth and ousted all rivals, becoming the standard version—the *Biblia Vulgata*[27]— for Western Christianity for more than a millennium. Indeed, one can hardly exaggerate the importance of the Vulgate in terms of its influence on Roman Catholic doctrine, liturgy, and hymnody, an influence that no doubt lives on today.

From the third and fourth centuries came translations of the Bible into Coptic, the language of Christians in Egypt. Manuscripts of the Coptic Bible are mainly of two types—those in the Sahidic dialect (Upper Egyptian) and those in the Bohairic (Lower Egyptian) dialect. These translations were apparently made directly from the LXX. Likewise, an Ethiopic and an Armenian version seem to be derived from the Greek, although a few MSS may show signs of revisions based on comparison with the Hebrew or, perhaps, the Syriac; these came from the fifth through tenth centuries. Also, from the latter part of that period we have a number of Arabic copies of the Bible, but they represent, for the most part, a great mixture of texts— some from the Greek, some from Syriac, others from Coptic. Obviously

---

[27]This label became the customary designation only in the thirteenth century, though Jerome's Latin Bible had won acceptance among Catholic authorities long before this.

these versions, important as they are in their own right, have very unequal value in the overall task of recovering the best text.

Quotations from Extrabiblical Sources

I have now referred to the two main sources of material for textual criticism: MSS in the original languages and ancient versions. In addition to these there is a third source of evidence, which I will sketch briefly: quotations from books of the Bible made by other ancient writers.

As I have already noted in reference to the formation of the canon, we can learn much about the history of the Jewish and Christian Scriptures from the way the ancients themselves treat those books—for example, how second or third-century writers quoted, alluded to, or commented on them. So with questions of text, scholars have a valuable checkpoint in the vast array of Fathers, Apologists, and later churchmen who directly cite the Scriptures in their own writings. Occasionally even opponents of the church, sometimes those later branded as heretics, would quote from the Bible, and these also prove useful to the textual critic. In a recent critical edition of *The Greek New Testament*[28] the editors listed more than two hundred sources of such quotations that were used at one point or another in that edition.

Obviously, such evidence has its limitations and must be treated with care. For one thing, we know that the early church leaders often quoted very loosely, and sometimes with little regard for exact wording. Moreover, their own writings have been subject to the same textual corruptions through the ages as the biblical texts; this becomes especially noticeable in MSS that derive from a time after about 500 CE, when conscious efforts were made to conform Greek Bibles to a ''Byzantine'' type of text. There are signs that even quotations in certain patristic writings were retouched to bring them into conformity.

But when due allowance has been made for these limitations, the quotations can serve the critic well as supplemental testimony to the reading of some troublesome passage, perhaps supplying evidence of a date earlier than the extant MSS themselves. Rarely, if ever, will the quotations by themselves settle the issue in any given instance of variant readings; their

---

[28]*The Greek New Testament,* ed. Kurt Aland, Matthew Black, Carlo M. Martini, Bruce M. Metzger, and Allen Wikgren, 3rd ed. corrected (New York/London/Edinburgh/Amsterdam/Stuttgart: United Bible Societies, 1983, ³1975).

value lies rather in supporting or confirming the strictly textual or ver-sional evidence, and often in providing "missing links" or filling gaps in the lines of textual relationship, which the critics try to reconstruct. Of spe-cial importance are the works of prolific writers like Origen (early third century) or John Chrysostom (fourth century), whose sermons and com-mentaries were full of quoted biblical material. To cite only one example of this kind of evidence, there is the interesting variant reading of Matthew 27:16-17 (two references to the prisoner, Barabbas). English readers, if they consult *Gospel Parallels*[29] at that passage, will see that the critical appa-ratus lists a dozen witnesses to the reading (simply) "Barabbas," but notes that two MSS, a Syriac version, and Origen support the variant, "*Jesus* Barabbas." While the *Gospel Parallels* (based on the Revised Standard Version) sides, in this case, with the majority of witnesses, textual critics will agree that in their business the majority does not always rule.[30] Many recent critical editions of the New Testament, in fact, prefer the reading "Jesus Barabbas" in both occurrences, and the support of Origen in this weighs heavily in that preference. Also entering into consideration in this case is the question of motivation: why would one add, or omit, the name "Jesus"? By this line of reasoning, many scholars argue that it is much more likely that pious copyists *removed* the name, out of reverence for their Lord, from their texts, than that they added it (for no perceptible reason). On this reading, then, Pilate gave the people a choice between *two* Je-suses—between the one called Barabbas (which was patronymic) and the other called "Christ."

In drawing to a close this brief sketch of the ancient texts and their transmission (including some of the earliest versions), we need to reiterate that our concern here has been to trace the formation of the Bible (or, better Bible*s*) through the period of handwritten reproduction; I have in the next chapter to deal with the beginnings of printing and an entirely new era of Bible transmission that follows. There I shall also turn attention to the be-ginnings of the English Bible and to the whole matter of *translation*. What I must emphasize at this point is the difference between the modern schol-

---

[29]*Gospel Parallels,* ed. B. H. Throckmorton, Jr., 4th ed. rev. (Nashville/New York: Thomas Nelson, 1979); this is a synopsis of the first three gospels, arranged in parallel col-umns, and supplying a brief and easily readable critical apparatus at the foot of each page.

[30]For a discussion of methods and principles involved in textual criticism, see John H. Hayes and Carl R. Holladay, *Biblical Exegesis* (Atlanta: John Knox Press, 1982) ch. 2.

ar's work of textual criticism and the work of the translator, whether ancient or modern. Textual criticism is concerned primarily with the establishment of the best, most reliable *text*—what the original writers wrote in the authors' own languages (Hebrew or Greek).[31] This work is made necessary because the original works survive only in numerous copies, among which many differences now appear. Textual critics try to examine the wealth of materials available—MSS, versions, quotations—in order to explain, if possible, not only the several particular variants in a given MS, but also to trace its history or its "family connection" with other MSS. This work is like a giant, interlocking puzzle, in which each small piece we add makes us revise the emerging picture, and in turn helps us better to find the missing pieces.

In the strictest sense, and perhaps ideally, the textual critic's work is done when he has produced his critical edition of the Hebrew Bible or the Greek New Testament.[32] Here (again ideally) the work of the translator begins. No translation can be any better than the text on which it is based. The job of the translator is different from that of the textual critic, but he cannot be indifferent toward the results of the latter's labors.

---

[31]To be more precise, the original languages include Aramaic as well as the other two, because a major part of Daniel, two small bits of Ezra, and a verse of Jeremiah stand in Aramaic within the Hebrew context.

[32]Examples of recent editions include *Biblia Hebraica Stuttgartensia,* ed. Karl Elliger and Wilhelm Rudolph (Stuttgart: Deutsche Bibelstiftung, 1977), another in a long line of editions of Rudolf Kittel's *Biblica Hebraica* (Stuttgart: Württemburgische Bibelanstalt, [13]1962, [7]1951, [3]1937, [1]1906); and the third corrected edition of the Greek New Testament mentioned in n. 28 above. Work on both texts, however, continues without ceasing among scholars of many countries and of various religious affiliations.

For Further Reading

Gospel Parallels: A Synopsis of the First Three Gospels. B. H. Throckmorton, Jr., ed. Fourth edition revised. Nashville/New York: Thomas Nelson, 1979: identifies many of the MSS used by the RSV for the Synoptic Gospels, explains the critical apparatus, and so on—see especially iv-xvi.

Hayes, John H., and Carl R. Holladay. "Textual Criticism." In *Biblical Exegesis: A Beginner's Handbook.* Atlanta: John Knox Press, 1982.

Kenyon, Frederic G. *Handbook to the Textual Criticism of the New Testament.* Second edition. Grand Rapids: William B. Eerdmans, 1951. Especially 1-44.

_____ . *Our Bible and the Ancient Manuscripts.* Fifth edition revised by A. W. Adams. London: Eyre and Spottiswoode, 1958.

Metzger, Bruce M. *The Early Versions of the New Testament: Their Origin, Transmission, and Limitations.* London/New York: Oxford University Press, 1977.

_____ . *The Text of the New Testament: Its Transmission, Corruption, and Restoration.* Second edition. New York/London: Oxford University Press, 1968.

Reumann, John H. P. "The Transmission of the Biblical Text." In *The Interpreter's One-Volume Commentary of the Bible.* Nashville: Abingdon Press, 1971. Pages 1225-36.

Roberts, B. J. "The Textual Transmission of the Old Testament." In *Tradition and Interpretation.* G. W. Anderson, ed. London/New York: Oxford University Press, 1979. Pages 1-30.

For a relatively nontechnical account of the scrolls of Qumran and their value for textual criticism:

Vermes, Geza. *The Dead Sea Scrolls: Qumran in Perspective.* Cleveland OH: William Collins and World Publishing Co., 1978. Especially 198-209.

Relevant Passages in the Bible

(It is recommended that these samples be examined in two, three, or even four different versions or translations; among those that offer the most fruitful comparison are the King James Version, Revised Standard Version, New English Bible, The Jerusalem Bible, The New American Bible, and Today's English Version.)

Psalm 23	**Mark 6:1-3**
Psalm 51	**John 7:53-8:11**
Job 19:17-27	**Acts 15:1-35**
Genesis 1:1-8; 3:1-7	**1 Corinthians 13**
Ecclesiastes 12:1-8	**Philippians 2:1-13**
1 Kings 18:17-46.	**Hebrews 11:1-3**

Chapter 4

The Bible
in English Translations

A casual reader, browsing among the stacks in a public library or among the well-stocked shelves of the modern bookstore, must be aware of the vast array of English Bibles now available. Scarcely can today's reader imagine, faced with the abundant and varied supply at his fingertips, how far different was the situation of his ancestors, and how complex and convoluted the course of events that led to our present state. We have to remind ourselves, for one thing, of the world-shaking effect that the printing press had, making possible mass production of books and consequently changing the patterns of education in ways undreamed before 1450. Reading, once the hobby of the privileged and the priesthood, became the right and responsibility of common folk, fanning the fires of revolution in both church and state. Thus the great rebirth of humanistic learning we call the Renaissance, and the revolt of Protestants known as the Reformation, are very much a part of the story behind the translation of the Bible into English.

But beyond that we must also remind ourselves of the less sensational, pre-printing-press times and the labors of those—mostly unknown by name—who made the first efforts to put the Bible into English. For this we have to recall the period when that language itself was just emerging as a distinctive national tongue and beginning to produce its own literature—works like the famous *Beowulf*. In the evolution of the language historians refer to this as the period of Old English (ca. 450-1150).[1] Most people in the land of the Angles (hence the name England) were illiterate, depending on word-of-mouth communication, and little caring for books of their own. It sufficed the common people to listen to tales of traveling minstrels or to occasionally eavesdrop on the reading (aloud) of their feudal lords. In the Middle Ages, as indeed in more ancient times, traditional lore and bits of "the news of the day" circulated in poetic, lyrical form, and it is not at all surprising that much of surviving Old English literature is in the form of songs.

Legend has it that the first English translation (or poetic paraphrase) of the Bible took that form: the lowly cowherd, Caedmon, working at the monastery at Whitby in Yorkshire, was said to have received a vision of Christ calling on him to sing, and as a result Caedmon was enabled to put into simple English verse the stories and lessons he had heard from the monks as they read from the Bible. Caedmon himself could not read or write, but his simple and singable paraphrases apparently inspired those who could, and soon thereafter (ca. 670) poems based on Genesis, Exodus, and Daniel, and certain psalms in Anglo-Saxon made the rounds of the English countryside.

While Caedmon's efforts, strictly speaking, were to paraphrase—that is, to capture the gist or rudiments of the story without following the wording of the original—later efforts were to stick more closely to the Latin Bible (the predominant version in Britain) and count as proper translation.[2] Credit for one of the earliest translations of the Psalms goes to Aldhelm, the Abbot of Malmesbury, and a gifted musician, whose work appeared ca. 700. About the same time the English Bishop Egbert produced an interlinear translation (Old English between the lines of Latin) of the Gospels, and it is supposed that the famous Lindisfarne Gospels, a beautifully illuminated MS now in the British Museum, comes from the same period.

The Venerable Bede, perhaps the most notable scholar of the eighth century and author of an *Ecclesiastical History of the English People*, also put his hand to the task of translation, but unfortunately nothing remains

---

[1]From 1150 to ca. 1500 is the period of Middle English, and from 1500 on, Modern English; cf. A. C. Baugh, *History of the English Language* (New York: Appleton-Century 1935).

[2]The line between "translation" and "paraphrase" is not always clearly drawn; the distinction will be further explored later.

of his work. The oft-told story of Bede's translation of the Gospel of John comes to us through the writings of Cuthbert, said to be present during the last stages of that translation, as Bede lay on his death bed. As Bede's strength faded he struggled to dictate the last remaining chapter, interrupted by many well-meaning visitors, but managed to complete the final sentence just before he died. This was on the Eve of Ascension Day, 735.

Remarkable to note, it was not only the monks and cloistered scholars who fostered the translation of the Bible. We have already mentioned the illiterate laborer, Caedmon. Here we have to note that royalty, as well, joined the movement—if we can dignify it with that term. In any case, the exceptional King Alfred (aptly called "the Great") has to be counted among those early translators. In the late ninth century Alfred actively promoted a revival of learning in England, seeking and providing books that he judged most valuable for his people, and even setting them an example by studying Latin himself. Apparently he learned enough Latin to write a translation of Exodus 20-23 (the Ten Commandments and other laws) and incorporate this into his *Book of Laws* (ca. 890); he was said to have started on a translation of the Psalms in English when he died in 901. Though King Alfred's writings have long since perished, his influence lived on to inspire numerous tenth-century efforts, some of which are represented by extant MSS and fragments. An impressive example, the Rushmore Gospels, may be seen today in the Bodleian Library at Oxford.

Some of the extant examples of Old English translation may be copies of the work of Abbot Aelfric (later Archbishop of Canterbury), who was known to have produced an Anglo-Saxon version of the Pentateuch, Joshua, Judges, Job, and other parts of the Old Testament (ca. 1000). It is said that he took editorial liberties, omitting parts that he considered unimportant or lacking in interest, and the few remains of his work (two MSS containing the Pentateuch and Joshua) may fall into the category of paraphrase rather than translation.[3]

Then came the Norman Conquest which, as one scholar has put it, "changed the whole course of the English language."[4] In the wake of William's victory at Hastings in 1066, there was a time of great social upheaval and an even longer time of adjustment to the incursions of French

---

[3]See F. C. Grant, *Translating the Bible* (Greenwich CT: Seabury Press, 1961) 52.

[4]Baugh, *History of the English Language,* 131.

customs and—especially—language. Over the next century or so, Old English gave way to Middle English, a language less Teutonic and more Romanic than the Old. It was only toward the close of the twelfth century that English literature began to revive, and from about 1300 comes a psalter in metrical English, and from a little later a Latin Psalter with an English gloss, attributed to the "hermit of Hampole," Richard Rolle. It is noteworthy how prominently the Psalms figure in the story—from the days of Caedmon on, the English people expressed their faith in song and naturally those parts of the Bible meant to be sung became favored texts for translation or paraphrase.

As far as scholars now know, no complete Bible in English was produced until the late fourteenth century. It appeared against a backdrop of religious and political discontent that was sweeping England and parts of continental Europe. It was the day of growing nationalism, new social and economic aspiration, and many were beginning to taste the heady wine of that humanistic movement, already flourishing in Italy, called by later ages the Renaissance. In part, of course, it was a look backward, a revival of classical learning, a new appreciation of Greek and Latin models. But what people discovered in that backward glance was essentially a new spirit of inquiry, of questioning, that was bound to upset or challenge the *status quo.* Just as it fed the smoldering fires of political unrest among those who were oppressed, it also contributed to an undercurrent of certain Christians who complained of abuse or corruption in the church. Moreover, in the new wave of interest in sources (including the Bible in its original languages) new questions had to be raised about the adequacy or accuracy of the Latin Vulgate. People, whose doubts or suspicions about the morality of clergy would have remained silent in centuries past, now found their voice. And in the Scriptures, freshly understood, they claimed they found their support and mandate for reforms.

One of those who became most vocal in calling for reforms was the Oxford scholar John Wyclif (1328-1384). From both lectern and pulpit Wyclif decried what he took to be errors in the church's theology and abuses of ecclesiastical authority. To back up his protests he appealed to "the Law of God"—as found in the Scriptures—as opposed to the laws of church and pope. To suggest that these could be so opposed to each other was, to say the least, an audacious position for any man of the cloth and Wyclif was by this time Rector of Lutterworth. But, thanks in part to friends in high places, Wyclif managed to dodge direct recrimination long enough to begin work on a fresh English translation of the Bible and to set his followers moving into the streets and byways of England. Called ''poor preachers'' and ''Lollards'' (probably a derogatory term) these followers did much to prepare the way in England for the later Protestant Revolt.

Wyclif's personal contributions to the work of translation are not easy to determine now, since much of his original work was lost or destroyed, and because he was assisted in his labors by two followers, Nicholas of Hereford and John Purvey. It was their revision, published after Wyclif's death, that circulated widely and focused public attention on the controversial translation. The New Testament, primarily the work of Wyclif himself, had appeared about 1380, and the Old Testament was done, with the collaboration of Hereford (and, perhaps, of others), by 1384, the year Wyclif died. Those first editions were said to be of ''uneven'' style,[5] but on the whole a very straightforward and often literal rendering of the Latin text. It was John Wyclif's desire to make known to the common people what he regarded as the simple teachings of ''holi writ,'' and he never understood why there was such a storm of protest against his English translation.

From our perspective, of course, the question is not so hard to answer; Wyclif lived and died before the crucial days of Luther, Calvin, Zwingli and others of the Reformation, and before the Roman Catholic Church had solidified its own position regarding translation of the Bible into the vernacular. It was actually twenty-four years after Wyclif's death (1408) that Archbishop Arundel finally voiced official disapproval of such translations and decreed that offenders, when caught, should suffer ''the pain of excommunication.'' In 1414 the Catholic Council of Constance made a similar resolution, forbidding all unauthorized translations. The reason was now clear: to put the Bible in the hands of the laity opened the church to new and widespread criticism, and in effect encouraged what the hierarchy saw as a misguided attack on the authority of the church and its institutions. It was a risk too great to run, and the church moved decisively to squelch it wherever possible. In 1415, the Council of Constance, not satisfied with a public denunciation of Wyclif's writings (along with other

---

[5]Two obvious reasons for the inconsistencies are (1) the still-fluid state of the English language (with hardly any recognized standard for spelling), and (2) the fact that some of Wyclif's work was edited by others before publication and some was not.

"heretics"), ordered that Wyclif's bones be disinterred and burned, as a gesture of warning to others so inclined.

Another century was to pass before the next dramatic step towards the complete Bible in English. But this was the century that embraced the introduction of the printing press into England and the maturing of the Protestant Revolt. Movable type on wooden blocks had been used in the Orient by the thirteenth century, and it is said that Koreans were able to cast type in metal in the fourteenth century, but practical use of such techniques spread to Europe only in the mid-fifteenth century. Credit is usually given to Johannes Gutenburg, whose press produced a two-volume Latin Bible at Mainz in 1456. It was truly the opening of a new era in Western civilization: one man and one machine could now turn out in two days what would have required in Wyclif's day forty-five copyists working steadily for two years. And the labor-saving aspect of this was only a beginning, far overshadowed by the long-range effects on the lives of people who could for the first time afford to buy a book or who now had incentive to read and write. Education began to flourish, and nothing short of a cultural revolution was underway.

Then, in the sixteenth century, the movement already outcropping in the works of Wyclif and Hus two centuries earlier gathered steam and swept all Europe into ecclesiastical conflict. Both humanist scholars and reformers of the church advocated the distribution of Scripture in the language of the people, and—by implication—the right of the common layman to read it for himself, unassisted by clerical interpretation. This was the position of the Oxford-educated William Tyndale, who made the famous vow that one day he would cause even a ploughman to know the Scriptures better than the scholar. Tyndale seemed ideally suited for the task of translation, for he was not only a gifted linguist and expert in Hebrew and Greek but also a master of style in English prose. But the opposition of the Catholic clergy, supported by most officials of state, made it almost impossible for Tyndale to carry out his plans in England. So he went to Germany, encouraged by the efforts of Martin Luther, whose German translation of the New Testament appeared in 1522. There, with the financial aid of a few wealthy British merchants, Tyndale managed to complete his English New Testament in 1525, although enemies discovered his printer's location and caused a delay in the publication of his work. In one of the oddest episodes of international intrigue known to us, Tyndale's British friends smuggled his translations into England, and one London merchant even sold copies to the Bishop of London—who promptly had them burned—and passed the profits along to Tyndale, in order to have more printed and smuggled into England!

Tyndale had intended to translate the Old Testament, too, and made a beginning, publishing a translation of the Pentateuch and the book of Jonah, when his persecutors caught up with him. He spent about eighteen months in a prison near Brussels, working all the while on his translation, until the authorities finally decided that he must die for his crimes. In October 1536 he was strangled and his body was burned at the stake; tradition recorded his last words as a prayer, "Lord, open the King of England's eyes."[6] These words remind us that in England in 1536 so much depended on the king (at that time Henry VIII), who had made a break with the Pope and was now declared by Parliament "the only supreme head in earth of the Church of England." Strangely enough—and tragically for Tyndale—some moderation in the royal and ecclesiastical opposition to the Bible in English was already indicated by the acceptance of Miles Coverdale's edition of 1535, and the ultimate irony of it is that Coverdale incorporated much of Tyndale's work in his translation.

While Coverdale was not the equal of Tyndale in his talents as linguist and translator, he apparently excelled in diplomacy and was able to win the support of no less a person than Thomas Cromwell, the king's chief agent in ecclesiastical affairs, as well as the favor of leading churchmen. Coverdale's Bible removed some of the controversial features of Tyndale's New Testament,[7] and, on the whole, stayed closer to the wording of the Latin Vulgate, which was the basic text behind his Old Testament. He made use also of the Zurich Bible (1529) and the German Bible of Martin Luther (1534). Thus the first complete Bible to be printed in English was not at all a fresh translation from the original languages (as was Tyndale's) but a mixture of previously published works, translated and revised.

Even so, the Coverdale Bible proved surprisingly popular, and by 1537 a second edition appeared, printed this time in England rather than on the

---

[6]John Foxe, *The Acts and Monuments of the Church* (London, 1641) rev. by J. Malham and T. Pratt (Philadelphia: J. J. Woodward, 1836) 544.

[7]Tyndale's "Protestant bias," showing up in his choice of words like "repentance" for "penance," or "congregation" for "church," had annoyed readers of his work; Coverdale reverted to more conventional wording.

Continent, where the first had been published. Other editions followed in rapid succession, once that hurdle was past and officials of both church and state, responding no doubt to a growing popular demand for Bibles in English, began actively to promote their publication. The stage was set for an edition that could claim the royal "seal of approval," and official license that had so far been withheld from any translation. Oddly enough, in 1537, there were two such editions, each claiming to have "the Kinges most gracyous lycence," in the wording of one title page.[8] One of these was the Coverdale Bible, reprinted by James Nicolson, and the other was a Bible ascribed to a "Thomas Matthew," a name now believed to be a pseudonym for John Rogers, Cambridge scholar and close friend of William Tyndale, who later died in the persecutions of "Bloody" Mary Tudor. The "Matthew Bible" caught the fancy of the Archbishop of Canterbury, who in turn enlisted the support of Cromwell in gaining the king's approval. Whether it was recognized at the time or not, the translation was essentially that of Tyndale himself; now, only ten months after that scholar's execution the shifting tides of fortune paid posthumous (though perhaps unconscious) honor to his work by licensing it to be sold and read without fear of reproach.

Revisions of the Matthew Bible soon followed: one by Richard Taverner, a lawyer and ardent admirer of Tyndale's New Testament, made some modest changes, mostly in favor of a more idiomatic style; the other was a more thorough revision undertaken by Miles Coverdale with the aid of "dyverse excellent learned men" whose identity is now unknown. Both appeared in 1539, but the latter publication quickly overshadowed the former, mainly because of the sponsorship of Cromwell and many ecclesiastical leaders who had for some time desired a Bible officially authorized for public use in the churches.[9] Printed on large sheets of high quality paper, this new edition earned its label "The Great Bible," and by royal appointment it was established as the first "authorized" English Bible. Marginal notes (which had been used in earlier translations) were omitted, probably by clerical orders, in an effort to reduce the objections of those

---

[8]This appears on the title page of the Matthew Bible; cf. Geddes MacGregor, *A Literary History of the Bible* (Nashville: Abingdon Press, 1968) 131.

[9]The Matthew Bible was only "licensed"—that is, individual readers were permitted to use it with impunity. "Authorization" meant approval for *public* use by the churches and presumably implied that no other Bible should be so used in the pulpit.

who were still suspicious of Bibles in the vernacular. Best suited to pulpit use, because of its size, the Great Bible apparently exerted little influence beyond a small circle of scholars and others of the privileged class, although it passed through seven editions between 1539 and 1541.

About this time it seems that the fickle tides of church politics changed again, and King Henry himself was powerless to stop extremists in both Catholic and Protestant camps from harrassing and killing each other. In this time of turmoil the movement to put the English Bible in the hands of the people suffered considerable setbacks; in 1543 the government placed restrictions on the reading of the Bible, and soon thereafter efforts to ban any but the authorized version led to the burning of Bibles in great numbers. Only after the death of Henry in 1547, in the reign of Edward VI, a ruler of Protestant sympathies, was there a respite from this kind of intemperance.

The respite, however, was short-lived. The reign of Mary Tudor, who came to the throne in 1553, became a reign of terror for all conspicuous Protestants. Many fled for their lives to the Continent and to Geneva in particular, where the great French Reformer John Calvin ministered to his staunch colony of Protestants. There the English-speaking exiles set about to make their own translation of the Bible. They found a willing and able leader for this work in the person of Calvin's brother-in-law, William Whittingham. He produced his New Testament in 1557, which was much indebted to Tyndale, and finally the Old Testament in 1560. For the latter the Great Bible served as the basic text, though some attention was given to the Hebrew and to a few Latin MSS. Thus appeared the first edition of what soon came to be known as the Geneva Bible.

Because of its influence on readers at the time and on translations yet to come the Geneva Bible proved to be a watershed publication. Its appearance was timely, coinciding with the abolition of papal jurisdiction in Scotland, and answering the needs of Protestants far beyond the colony of exiles in Geneva. In fact, it won a following among English Puritans and eventually made its way with the Pilgrims to the coast of the New World. Quotations and allusions to Scripture found in the works of Shakespeare and of John Bunyan are derived mostly from the Geneva Bible.

This revision represented a marked improvement over earlier versions in a number of respects. First, the translation was carefully done, without the tremendous pressure that had often attended the preparation of texts printed under threat of penalty and cover of secrecy. Also, it was the first

English Bible to use the Roman type instead of the Gothic, making for much easier reading. The Geneva Bible adopted the practice, already well-known, of making chapter divisions, but further divided chapters into verses. Another innovation for English Bibles was its use of italicized words to indicate words not in the original language, but necessary for the English idiom or grammar. Moreover, the Geneva Bible set at the top of the page captions to show at a glance the main content of the text on that page. Memorable phrases from such captions have become a part of common English speech—for example, "a mess of pottage" is the caption above the story in Genesis 25 about Esau's selling his birthright to Jacob. One of the more curious examples—and a classic bit of understatement—is the caption given for the story of the beheading of John the Baptist as a result of Herod's promise to Salome (Mark 6:14-29): it reads "the inconvenience of dancing"! Captions like this no doubt tell the reader more about the ethical outlook of the editors than about the content of the biblical text.

Of all the special features of the Geneva Bible perhaps the most valuable to readers of that late sixteenth century was its array of annotations. These explanatory comments on the text reflected the best scholarship of the day, no doubt owing much to the biblical studies of John Calvin. In the earlier Bibles of Coverdale and the Matthew Bible such annotations had frequently served to advocate Reformation principles and to attack "papist" doctrine or practice. To curb this polemical commentary the annotations were altogether eliminated from the Great Bible. But with the Geneva Bible marginal notes became a vehicle of Protestant propaganda,[10] and though somewhat more restrained than in previous versions, the notes were bound to give offense to Roman Catholics and stand in the way of any official recognition of the Geneva Bible. Still its popularity was such that it went into more than one hundred editions in fifty years and left its undeniable mark on translations for many generations.

Meanwhile, in the reign of Queen Elizabeth I, efforts were underway to provide for an English Bible acceptable to the Church of England but without the controversial features of the Geneva Bible. Matthew Parker, then Archbishop of Canterbury, formed a panel of scholars, mostly bishops of the church, and assigned "parcels" of the Bible to each, undertaking a considerable portion himself. The resulting edition, largely a revision

---

[10]This word is to be understood here in its original (neutral) sense—what is to be propagated or taught.

of the Great Bible of 1541, appeared in 1568 and was called "the Bishops' Bible," appropriately enough. Three years later it was formally endorsed by the English Church Convocation, becoming the second "authorized" version of the English Bible.

The Bishops' Bible, however, fell short of the mark it was intended to reach. The work of revision had been done hastily, and it proved to be of uneven quality, reflecting both the variety of individual talent among the dozen or so translators and the lack of a strong editorial hand on the whole. As if to compensate for this weakness, the editors included a vast number of "helps"—chronological and genealogical charts, maps, pictures, and abundant marginal annotation. Even though explicit rules had been set forth, discouraging "controversie" or "bitter notis" on the text, some polemical remarks—a few drawn from the Geneva Bible—found their way into these notes.[11] As one example, to indicate the short distance between Geneva and London on certain issues of the day, whereas the Geneva Bible had commented on Revelation 9:11 by identifying "the angel of the bottomless pit" as "Antichrist the Pope," the Bishops' Bible was only slightly more moderate, finding the "beast out of the earth" (Rev. 13:11) to mean "the pompe of the romish bishops."[12]

Such inflammatory comments did not go unchallenged. But to counter the Protestant attack Roman authorities came to realize that they would need an English translation of their own. One of the first to advocate this was William Allen, himself an exiled priest and founder of a college at the Flemish town of Douai. With the help of some former Oxford colleagues he set to work on the New Testament, but because of political pressures the work had to be completed at Reims, where it was published in 1582. It was not until 1609 that the Old Testament was published, and by that time the college had returned to its quarters at Douai, so that the complete Bible came to be known as the Douai-Reims Version.[13]

Through its copious notes, both in the margins and at the close of chapters, the Roman Catholic Bible retaliated against "the corruptions of divers late translations," and railed at Protestant "heretics" with the same fervor as the Geneva Bible had expressed against "papists." While some

---

[11]A. W. Pollard, *Records of the English Bible* (Oxford: Henry Frowde, 1911) 298.

[12]MacGregor, *Literary History,* 156.

[13]Sometimes called "Rheims-Douay."

Greek MSS were consulted, the basic text was of course the Latin Vulgate, which the preface elaborately defended as accurate and supported by the Fathers of the Church. In some respects, as it turns out, the claim that the Vulgate was superior to many texts used by earlier translations was true. The time of scientific textual criticism had not yet come, and as indicated in the previous chapter, versions like the Vulgate sometimes do preserve readings closer to the original than certain of the Hebrew or Greek MSS available in the sixteenth and seventeenth centuries.

The translation as a whole, however, was marred by its almost slavish adherence to the Latin, often simply transliterating a term instead of using truly current English. In the Lord's Prayer, for example, the Rhemish New Testament has: "Give us today our supersubstantial bread" (Matt. 6:11), virtually lifting from the Vulgate the Latin *supersubstantialis,* rather than attempting to find an English word for the admittedly obscure Greek.[14] Similarly, where Paul wrote of Jesus (Phil. 2:7) that "he emptied himself" (as most English Bibles have it), the Douai-Reims has: "he exinanited himself." Fortunately, this latter term gave way in later editions to the more customary, and more understandable, language. But, even though numerous improvements were made in the course of subsequent centuries, the Douai-Reims Bible gave little competition to the other translations in the affections of the English people, and except for the vigorous criticism it provoked among certain Protestant leaders, it left minimal impression on the mainstream of biblical interpretation.

As we have seen, each new English translation from Tyndale's on was in reality a revised edition of its predecessor; even in the New Testament of Reims one can discover some influence of previous English Bibles, including the Geneva. In the first century of printed Bibles, while each one may show a few distinctive features in style, choice of words, annotations and the like, there was an inevitable "family resemblance" due to the shared scholarship of the revisers as well as to the limited textual resources then available. Thus when we turn to the best-known, most-influential English Bible (at least until this century), we find that it, too, belongs to that same family. Though indisputably superior in the elegance of its style and turn of phrase, the great King James Version was itself a revision of earlier editions, based mainly on the Bishops' Bible.

---

[14]The Greek word ἐπιούσιον is best rendered "of the morrow," as in daily rations, for so it is used in certain papyri of Hellenistic times.

Various handbooks and histories of the English Bible now detail the steps leading to the commissioning and, seven years later, the printing of this great version,[15] and we must not attempt here to repeat the full story. Much less can we deal with the interesting but complex question of King James I and his role in the story, except to make it clear that James himself figured in the actual labor of translation not at all. In fact, aside from his interest in literature and a taste for theological discourse, the king had no special competence for judging either the need for a new translation or its adequacy, once completed. But largely because he saw an opportunity to placate certain Puritans and to gain credit for being a patron of scholarship, James consented to the project, when it was suggested by John Reynolds, the Puritan president of Corpus Christi College, Oxford, in 1604. The King promptly appointed a committee of "fifty-four learned men," which apparently began full-scale operations only in 1607.[16]

According to the plan of procedure, the translators were divided into six groups, each with assigned portions, and each with the liberty to seek help, if required, outside the ranks of the committee. Many of the participants were well qualified for their task by training and position, and it appears that, in spite of the wide range of persuasions represented, they worked together with extraordinary unity and, considering the results, amazing speed. After only three years the work of the separate groups was ready to assemble for review and final proofreading; by 1611 the first edition was printed by Robert Barker, "printer to the King's most Excellent Maiestie." Complete with a flattering dedicatory epistle to the King who had commissioned it, with numerous tables and charts, as well as marginal notes and prefatory chapter summaries, it was a Bible of imposing appearance, befitting the historic occasion.

The King James Version, or (third) "Authorized" Bible, as it first came to be known, was remarkable in many respects. Not least of these was the fact that very strict regulations had been imposed on the translators at the beginning, bringing individual preference or theological bias of the various scholars under constraint, yet without entirely stifling their creativity. Although, for instance, the Bishops' Bible was the prescribed "base" for the revisers, they were free to use other editions—Tyndale, Coverdale, the

---

[15]MacGregor, *Literary History*, gives a very thorough account; cf. Grant, *Translating the Bible.*

[16]MacGregor, *Literary History*, 183.

Geneva, and others,—"when they agree better with the text than the Bishops' Bible."[17] An important step in the required procedure was for each translator's work to be reviewed by the whole group, and when agreement could not be reached within that company, the case was to be referred to a meeting of "the chief persons of each company" for final decisions. No doubt much of the resulting consistency and smoothness of style is due to a careful following of such rules.

The regulations specifically ruled out annotations other than those intended to explain the underlying Hebrew or Greek. There seems to have been a genuine effort to minimize the kind of partisan polemic that had characterized older English Bibles and to produce one that might at last win the respect of several factions among English Christians. Even so, it is likely that the Puritans were not entirely satisfied with the version of 1611, though their cause had been ably represented in the committee. One rule laid down to guide the translators was that "old ecclesiastical words" ought to be preferred—that is, "congregation" should not replace "church"— as it apparently had in the common understanding of many Puritan interpreters. In any case, for them and for most nonconformists of the day, the Geneva Bible was already firmly established and would hold first place in their affections for generations to come. Like other versions of more recent date the King James Bible did not meet with immediate or uniformly enthusiastic approval; only after many years and much opposition would its virtues be properly recognized.

Not that the workmanship was without its flaws. The first edition had, in fact, many defects—mostly, to be sure, printing errors, archaic spellings, and inconsistent translation of proper names. For example, one finds the prophet's name as "Elijah" in the Old Testament, but spelled "Elias" in the New. This was due to a close adherence to the original languages— Hebrew in the Old and Greek in the New Testament—but is the kind of inconsistency that most later English versions managed to avoid. As for archaic spelling, it must be pointed out that in 1611 the English language had not yet reached the level of uniformity it would later achieve—due largely indeed, to the pervasive influence of the King James Version. It was still in a fluid state, both in grammar and spelling, and therefore we might expect to find—as we do—numerous changes made in subsequent

---

[17]Rule 14 (of a total of fifteen); see the full list in MacGregor, *Literary History*, 184-85.

editions: for example, shortening words like ''soule'' by dropping the silent ''e,'' or a tendency to use a final ''y'' on words like ''mercie'' and ''charitie.'' On the other hand, the translators of the first edition probably meant to be conservative in this regard, as in others, mindful as they were of the peril of adopting the ''latest fashion.'' Older spellings might knowingly be kept in the interest of maintaining a literary elegance and in keeping with the dignity of the subject matter itself.

The printing errors, of course, are no fault of the translators, and yet they seem to be the kind of defect by which versions are remembered. A notable case in point derives from the different translation given in two printings of the same verse—Ruth 3:15. One issue read the last part of that verse: ''and he went into the citie,'' and the other read ''she'' instead of ''he''—giving rise to the designations ''He Bible'' and ''She Bible.''[18] The latter edition also confused readers in the story of Jesus in Gethsemane (Matt. 26:36) with the misprint: ''Then cometh Judas [instead of Jesus] with them . . . and saith unto the disciples, Sit ye here, while I go and pray yonder.'' Was the typesetter guilty of wishful thinking, or had he simply anticipated Judas's entry on the scene by some eleven verses? The edition of 1631 contained an even more startling error by omitting ''not'' in Exodus 20:14, producing the commandment ''Thou shalt commit adultery.'' Not unexpectedly that edition was nicknamed ''The Wicked Bible.''

In spite of numerous errors like these, mostly eliminated in later editions, the King James Version gradually gained support in England and Scotland, and by 1644 it had appeared in more than 150 different printings. Though known as the authorized version, and no doubt somewhat bolstered by ecclesiastical promotion, there was never any legal mandate, no official act of Parliament or the like, requiring its exclusive use in the churches. Its growing popularity and eventual dominance over other versions in the late seventeenth century, as the historians tend to agree, were largely due to its own intrinsic excellence. Geddes MacGregor has well summed up the matter.

Not even Shakespeare has more deeply affected English literature. The King James version is unique among the literary wonders of the world . . . its influence has bequeathed to us a noble standard and tradition of literary

---

[18]While textual variants may not have figured in this case originally, there is some textual evidence for the feminine pronoun in certain Syriac and Latin versions, and the Revised Standard Version and the New English Bible both prefer that reading.

style, . . . its cadences are echoed in thousands of now everyday turns of speech, even where their origin has been forgotten by many who use and delight in them.[19]

In view of the excellence of the King James Version and its continuing popularity over the centuries, the opposition to its publication in 1611 and the persistent criticism that followed will surely puzzle the vast throng of readers who still regard it as "the Bible." Part of the explanation, already mentioned, was simply partisan opposition to any new version of the Scriptures regarded by some as needless tampering with Holy Writ. Many faithful Roman Catholics, even after the publication of the Douai-Reims Bible, steadfastly held to the Vulgate as the only authorized version and would be opposed to translations in principle. Many Protestants, especially Puritans or other nonconformits, were satisfied with older versions, like the Geneva Bible, and were convinced that no revision was needed. Some objected to inclusion of the Apocrypha in the new version, and apparently persuaded certain printers to omit these books despite the express ruling of Archbishop Abbot (1615).[20] It became an issue of such importance that in 1644 the Long Parliament passed a decree that only "the canonical books" (not including the Apocrypha) should be read in the church. In Scotland, where Presbyterianism flourished, even omission of the Apocrypha failed to quiet the opposition, and a few disconsolate Scots were calling for thorough revision of the King James Bible as early as 1655, but nothing came of this.

One further instance of opposition, though not the last, was certainly one of the loudest: it came from a learned biblical scholar, Hugh Broughton, who had years before started work on his own translation. A gifted linguist, competent in Hebrew and in Greek, Broughton was not invited to take part in the revisions of 1604-1611, and was no doubt deeply hurt by the obvious rejection. Reasons given for the exclusion of Boughton seem to cluster about two things: (1) he had long ago proven himself a contemptuous critic of the Bishops' Bible (1568-72) and supporter of the Geneva Bible; (2) he was notoriously impatient and ill-tempered with those who dared to disagree with him. Something of Broughton's disposition

---

[19]MacGregor, *Literary History*, 218.

[20]The archbishop set a penalty of one year's imprisonment for anyone producing the Bible without the Apocrypha; cf. F. F. Bruce, *The English Bible* (New York: Oxford University Press, 1961) 110.

shows in these words of critique, sent to an officer of the king after he had seen a copy of the new Bible: "tell his Majesty that I had rather be rent in pieces with wild horses, than any such translation by my consent should be urged upon poor churches. . . . The new edition crosseth me. I require it to be burnt."[21] Aside from the element of personality conflict here, the incident stands to underscore the importance for Bible translation of the team effort in contrast to that of individuals working alone. The remarkable achievement of the "fifty four learned men" in cooperation across various lines of background and training established a precedent—indeed, a model—for all those who in subsequent times would set their hands to this task.

For nearly a century the only modifications of the King James text were minor corrections of printing errors or spelling peculiarities like those already mentioned. But during the eighteenth century there were several independent translations, a few of which merit naming. One was the New Testament of John Wesley, founder of Methodism in England, who produced a conservative revision of the King James text "for plain unlettered men who know only their mother tongue."[22] In that same year (1768) a Presbyterian minister, Edward Harwood, published his own *A Liberal Translation of the New Testament*—actually a paraphrase in the "stilted, verbose style" characteristic of that period.[23] Perhaps the Harwood version of John 3:16 (the familiar "For God so loved the world that he gave his only begotten Son . . . " KJV) will be enough to illustrate.

> For the supreme God was affected with such immense compassion and love for the human race, that he deputed his son from heaven to instruct them in order that everyone who embraces and obeys his religion might not finally perish, but secure everlasting happiness.[24]

Surely that edition served later translators only as an example of how not to go about the task.

In the Catholic camp, during this period, the efforts of Bishop Richard Challoner are noteworthy. The Vicar Apostolic of London, who had once

---

[21]As quoted in ibid., 107.

[22]See MacGregor, *Literary History*, 197.

[23]Bruce M. Metzger, "The Revised Standard Version," in *The Word of God*, ed. Lloyd R. Bailey (Atlanta: John Knox Press, 1982) 29.

[24]See ibid., 29.

been a Protestant, recognized the defects in the Douai-Reims Bible and set about to produce a more readable and understandable revision of it, eliminating (for example) the offensive Latinism of Philippians 2:7 ("he exinanited himself") and generally improving the style throughout. His first revision appeared in 1749, and further editions appeared until 1772, each successive effort indicating a gradual assimilation of the vocabulary and style of the King James Version. In 1810 the Douai-Reims-Challoner Bible was finally authorized for use by Roman Catholics in the U.S.A.[25]

In the New World English-speaking colonists had brought with them whatever books the rigors of travel might permit, and most were content to use the familiar Geneva Bible (if Protestant) or Douai-Reims (if Catholic). It is remarkable, however, that the first Bible to be printed in America was not in English but in the dialect of American Indians of Eastern Massachusetts—a translation made by the missionary John Eliot. It was 1743 before the first Bible in any European language was printed on this continent, and that was the German Bible of Christoph Saur in Pennsylvania. Aside from the expense and technical difficulties involved, American printers before 1776 had to contend with royal restrictions against unauthorized publication of the King James Version—in effect, the British government still held the "copyright." Not until after the American Revolution, in 1782, was the first English Bible printed on this side of the Atlantic: it came from the press of Robert Aitken of Philadelphia, and still has the distinction of being the only edition of the Bible recommended by act of Congress for use in the American churches.[26]

Up to this point in my survey of English Bibles I have traced what amounts to a genealogy, mainly of one "family," leading from Tyndale to the Authorized Version of 1611, with a few sidelong glances at parallel developments among Roman Catholics and certain private translators. The story to this point has been largely one of revision by various scholars, at various times and places, of basically the same kind of text. The manuscripts, ancient versions and other material available to the King James committee were essentially the same (in quality, if not quantity) as the material available to Miles Coverdale. Progress in the sequence I have traced was measured primarily by (1) improving the clarity of meaning through

---

[25]Bruce, *The English Bible*, 126.

[26]Bruce M. Metzger, "How We Got the Bible," in *Introduction to the Bible*, The Layman's Bible Commentary 1 (Richmond VA: John Knox Press, 1959) 139-40.

choice of appropriate English words, and (2) improving literary style through attention to refinements such as cadence, and so on—what the seventeenth-century rhetoricians called "felicity of expression."[27]

Though by far the fairest flower of that family tree, the epitome of literary elegance, the KJV (scholars now know) was based on a very poor text. No translation can be more accurate than the text on which it stands. Of course, the translators (revisers) of 1611 were not to blame; they could use only what they had at the time—a few medieval MSS of the Old Testament, the Greek New Testament (1516) of Erasmus, the 1550 edition of Stephanus, and the Greek text (1582) of Beza.[28] One of the greatest ironies is that the Greek Bible now known as Codex Alexandrinus, a MS older and in many ways superior to any used in the KJV, had been sent as a gift to the king of England from Cyril Lucar, Patriarch of Constantinople—only a decade too late! In fact, delays in shipment made its arrival in England (1627) too late for King James even to see; that monarch died in 1625, and the gift was received by Charles I. The codex eventually passed to the British Museum, where it may still be seen.

Although it was discovered too late to make any difference to the KJV, and perhaps too soon to bring about serious reappraisal of the *Textus Receptus*—the "text received" as standard to that date—knowledge of Alexandrinus served to alert scholars to the possibility of finding other ancient MSS and called attention to a need for fresh translation, not just revision, of the Bible. Except for a few cases of independent effort,[29] really fresh translation would have to wait another century or more, but meanwhile the search for better textual sources began to bear fruit, and in the process the special linguistic skills of outstanding scholars were applied to the study and collation of the new material, marking the beginning of modern textual criticism.

Codex Vaticanus, a Greek Bible from the late fourth century, had been listed in a catalogue of the Vatican Library as early as 1481, but it was closely guarded by Roman officials and not available even for scholarly perusal until the nineteenth century. In fact, it was only after the MS was taken "as a prize of war" by Napoleon and lodged in Paris that the real

---

[27]One of the enduring charms of the King James Version is how well suited it is for reading *aloud;* its rhythms please the ear as well as the eye.

[28]See Grant, *Translating the Bible,* 88.

[29]Cf. Bruce's examples (*The English Bible,* 130-33).

age and value of Vaticanus were made known. Even after its return to Rome in 1815, the Vatican was unwilling to grant more than sample readings to outsiders, perhaps anticipating its own publication of the text.[30]

It was the dramatic discovery of another Greek Bible, or parts of it, that gave decisive impetus to the movement to reassess the *Textus Receptus* and to give translators a better base for their work. This was the unexpected result of a visit by the German scholar, Constantin Tischendorf, in St. Catherine's Monastery at Jebal Musa in the Sinai.[31] He noticed in his wastebasket several sheets of parchment, apparently intended for starting fires, but on closer inspection they proved to be pages from an ancient manuscript, written in Greek uncial letters. Tischendorf saw enough to recognize portions of a very early copy of the Septuagint, and on inquiring about the rest of the MS was told that they had already served as kindling. Torn between his indignation at such acts of negligence and his excitement over the prospect of further finds, he pursued his inquiries and found elsewhere in the monastery portions of three other books belonging to the same MS and eventually he was able to "borrow" forty-three leaves to take back to Germany for closer study. Tischendorf published his findings in 1846, and a few years later returned to St. Catherine's hoping to salvage still more. This time he came away disappointed, almost despairing of his search. But on a third visit, in 1859, a casual comment of a servant led him to find much of the missing MS—the whole New Testament, portions of the Old Testament, plus the Epistle of Barnabas and part of the Shepherd of Hermas. The steward apparently had kept it wrapped in a napkin in his own quarters for fifteen years! Tischendorf, as F. G. Kenyon tells it,

> obtained leave to take the precious manuscript to his room; and that night, thinking it sacrilege to sleep, he spent in transcribing the Epistle of Barnabas, of which no copy in Greek was previously known to exist.[32]

In a delicate exercise of diplomacy Tischendorf persuaded the monks to let him take the MS to Cairo long enough to make a transcript, and eventually to present it to the Tsar of Russia, then Protector of the Greek Or-

---

[30]F. G. Kenyon, *Handbook to the Textual Criticism of the New Testament*, 2nd ed. (Grand Rapids: William B. Eerdmans, 1951) 78.

[31]Jebal Musa is Arabic for "Mount of Moses," and one of the places traditionally identified as Mt. Sinai (Horeb).

[32]Kenyon, *Handbook*, 62.

thodox Church. By 1862 the reassembled parts of the MS were published in facsimile, and the scholarly world could examine a copy of the Greek Bible dating from the fourth century, perhaps even older than Vaticanus. The MS itself, beautifully written on vellum, four columns to the page, rested for a time in the Imperial Library of St. Petersburg (later Leningrad), but after the Bolshevik Revolution the Soviet government sold it to the British Museum, where it may be seen to this day. As a fitting reminder of its timely discovery, ''Codex Sinaiticus'' became its name, and the Hebrew character א (*aleph,* first letter of the alphabet) is used to designate it in the catalogues and critical texts.

The cumulative effect of such discoveries, along with the refining of critical methods and the advances of scholarship in general, was to set the stage for a new chapter in the history of the English Bible. At last the door was open for a thorough revision of the underlying text rather than superficial improvements in literary style. Careful study of the manuscripts like Sinaiticus and Alexandrinus demonstrated the need for a better textual base than the *Textus Receptus,* and in 1870 the Convocation of Canterbury adopted a proposal for a revision specifically to correct readings based on faulty or wrongly translated texts. Committees were appointed, and rules were laid down, in effect making the Authorized (King James) Version the model in matters of English style. American scholars were invited to participate, and from 1872 about twenty Americans were actively engaged in the project, meeting in the headquarters of the American Bible Society in New York City. Metzger notes that among these Americans were representatives of nine different denominations.[33] Because of distance and difficulty of travel, it turned out that the American contribution was little more than a list of proposed readings, some of which were accepted, and the rest of which relegated to an appendix in the finished work. But it was agreed that after fourteen years the Americans could legally publish an edition of their own, incorporating all their preferences. The British work appeared in three installments: the New Testament in 1881, the Old Testament in 1885, and the Apocrypha in 1895. Known as the English Revised Version, its publication received great notoriety both in Britain and the United States;

---

[33]Metzger, ''The Revised Standard Version,'' 31.

one source estimates that within one year sales of the new Bible reached three million copies.[34]

In some respects the results were disappointing, on both sides of the Atlantic. Much of the familiar King James phrasing and rhythm suffered at the hands of the revisers, and while there were notable improvements—more accurately representing a better text—in style and rhetorical effect the Revised Version was poor. "Strong in Greek, weak in English" was the comment of the famous English preacher, Charles H. Spurgeon, speaking of the New Testament in particular. Revisers had somewhat slavishly followed the Greek order of the sentence, often inverting the natural order in English, and creating a generally awkward result.[35]

The American revisers, meanwhile, pursued their separate way and produced in 1901 what came to be known as the American Standard Version. It went further in removing archaisms, preferring for instance "Holy Spirit" over "Holy Ghost," and rendering the Greek *agape* (as in 1 Cor. 13) as "love" rather than "charity." But the American revisers substituted "Jehovah" for "Lord" (printed with a capital "L" and smaller caps in the English Bible) to indicate the sacred tetragrammaton.[36] But again the outcome was, at best, mixed. Though greeted at first with enthusiasm the American Standard Version never replaced the King James Bible in the affections of those who were most sensitive to matters of style, and on the other hand it never really satisfied those who were most aware of matters of accuracy or clarity of meaning.

The early twentieth century saw remarkable progress in biblical studies of all kinds, but especially significant for the work of translation were further discovery and collections of manuscripts, and vast improvement in the understanding of the biblical languages as a result of newfound documents

---

[34]*A Ready-Reference History of the English Bible*, rev. ed. (New York: American Bible Society, 1979) 33.

[35]Metzger, "The Revised Standard Version," 31, cites an example from Luke 9:17: "And they did eat, and were all filled; and there was taken up that which remained over them of broken pieces, twelve baskets."

[36]This sacred name is called a "tetragrammaton" because it is written in four Hebrew characters: יהוה. But because Jewish readers of the Hebrew said *'adonai* ("Lord") instead of verbalizing the ineffable name, it became a custom to insert the vowels of *'adonai* into the four consonants, producing "Jehovah." "Yahweh" is a much more likely pronunciation.

from the Middle East.[37] Just as Tischendorf's finds led to the researches of Westcott and Hort and the publication of their critical Greek text (1881), so the subsequent discovery of Syriac, Coptic, and Greek papyri led to new refinements in the principles of textual criticism and, on the whole, to a better knowledge of the meaning of the New Testament. Thanks largely to Egyptian papyri, translators became aware of the character of *koine* (common) Greek, as used in the New Testament: far from being "literary" or classical Greek, like that used by fifth-century Athenian philosophers, or some peculiar form of "biblical" Greek, it turns out to be simply the ordinary spoken language of the marketplace and forum, inelegant but very expressive and widely used as an international and ecumenical tongue. This fact by itself seemed to call for a drastic reappraisal of English translations which appeared to be bent on making the writers of the New Testament sound like academicians.

In short, many things conspired to demand yet another effort to put the Bible into English in the late 1920s and early 1930s. The International Council of Religious Education, having acquired the copyright of the American Standard Version, authorized a committee to undertake a revision "in the light of the results of modern scholarship" and yet one that would remain in the "simple, classic English style" of the KJV. It was a large order, to be sure, and fulfillment was made all the more difficult by the outbreak of World War II. Hopes for making it an international project had to be abandoned, but the team of American scholars persevered through those war years and in 1946 published the New Testament in the Revised Standard Version (RSV), to be followed in 1952 by the Old Testament and in 1957 by the Apocrypha.

The RSV was avowedly a revision of a revision; its lineage is clearly stated in the preface: "The Revised Standard Version of the Bible is an authorized revision of the American Standard Version, published in 1901, which was a revision of the King James Version, published in 1611."[38]

---

[37]Not just biblical documents but various secular writings—on clay, parchment, papyri, and even stone—have provided materials for expanding enormously the lexicon of Semitic languages and enriching our understanding of Hebrew words and phrases as never before; likewise, from the sands of Egypt have come numerous Hellenistic papyri (business records, receipts, personal notes and letters) that have helped tremendously in interpreting New Testament Greek. Cf. Adolf Deissmann, *Light from the Ancient East*, trans. Lionel R. Strachan (London: Hodder and Stoughton, 1927).

[38]See the 1973 printing of the RSV by Oxford University Press, xi. The whole preface is a good review of events leading to the RSV and a summary of its distinctive features.

The RSV thus stands in the great tradition of Tyndale and Coverdale, although the revisers took seriously their charge to incorporate the best of modern scholarship in the work. Many corrections or "conjectural emendations" of the textual base were made on the evidence of recently discovered MSS, and even though the Old Testament went to press only four years after the sensational discovery of the Dead Sea Scrolls, it managed to make some use of the larger scroll of Isaiah, the Habakkuk Commentary, and a few other MSS, as scattered footnotes ("one ancient Ms") indicate. Far more obvious to the reader, of course, were the many ways in which the RSV simplified and modernized the English in both testaments. It reverted to LORD (small caps) in place of "Jehovah," and reduced various kinds of antiquated idioms, making all pronouns of the second person "you" and "your," not "thou, thee, thy," except in prayer to God. Punctuation, quotation marks, and paragraphing followed modern usage.

Modernizing, however, is apparently a questionable virtue to many people where the Bible is concerned. The publication of the RSV was met in some quarters with great opposition, ranging from mild indignation to massive campaigns to collect and burn copies of "the new blasphemous Bible." One of the major targets for criticism was the "irreverence" toward Jesus, said to be indicated by the RSV's failure to *capitalize* pronouns referring to Jesus or Christ in the New Testament, as well as by the use of "you" and "your" instead of "Thee" and "Thy" in addressing him. Some critics were further outraged by the translation of Isaiah 7:14— "Behold, a *young woman* shall conceive and bear a son . . . " (accurately rendering the Hebrew noun)—because it seemed but one more sign of the revisers' sinister plot to demote Jesus or to deny his divinity and the Virgin Birth. It was no consolation that the RSV retained the traditional reading of Matthew 1:23, quoting the *Greek* of Isaiah 7:14 ("a virgin shall conceive"), because it seems that consistency of doctrinal interpretation counted for more than accuracy of translation in some circles. But underlying most of the attacks, it now appears, was a widespread suspicion about the motives of the National Council of Churches (and its Division of Christian Education), under whose auspices the RSV was published—suspicions aroused in part by developments in the nation far removed from the revision of the Bible. It was a time of stress, of charge and countercharge, over the threat of Communism and questions of loyalty in America, the era of Joseph McCarthy and his investigating committee, who tried to implicate certain members of the revision team in allegations that were eventually dismissed as groundless.

It is perhaps testimony to the intrinsic merit of the RSV that it managed to survive the storm of protest and to gain in popularity both here and abroad. While it lacks the rhetorical elegance and charm of the King James Bible, the RSV has been widely acclaimed for its straightforward, colloquial and readable style. In the mid 1960s, following the historic Vatican Council II and in the new ecumenical atmosphere of that day, Roman Catholic leaders agreed to publish an adaptation (amounting to only "67 slight changes in the wording")[39] of the RSV New Testament, which appeared in 1965, and the whole Bible, called the Revised Standard Version, Catholic Edition (CE), followed in 1966. In the Old Testament, of course, the deuterocanonical books (which Protestants call Apocrypha) were placed in their traditional positions, not set apart as in earlier editions. But even with that difference and the Roman Catholic annotations included, the existence of an English Bible approved for reading by Catholic and Protestant alike marked a considerable stride away from the polarization that characterized its early history. And since that date Catholic-Protestant collaboration has produced an edition of the RSV known as the "Common Bible," not only omitting the Catholic annotations but also segregating the deuterocanonical books (between the testaments),[40] and further negotiations, which included the Eastern Orthodox Churches, resulted in 1977 in the publication of an expanded edition (including III and IV Maccabees, Psalm 151) of the RSV: *The New Oxford Annotated Bible, with the Apocrypha.*[41]

So far, then, we have traced a long succession of revisions, all belonging to one "family" of English Bibles, and mostly initiated by Protestants. Here we must take note of a few remarkable efforts lying outside that line of successsion, some of which were sponsored by Protestants, others by Roman Catholics. The first such effort by Protestants to produce a *fresh* English translation of the Bible since Tyndale's New Testament began about the same year that the New Testament of the RSV appeared

---

[39]See Metzger, "The Revised Standard Version," 35.

[40]Significant preparation for the "Common Bible" came with the imprimatur of Cardinal Cushing, Archbishop of Boston, on the *Oxford Annotated Bible, with Apocrypha* (1966). The "Common Bible" was published by Collins Press in 1973.

[41]Published by Oxford University Press in 1977.

(1946). The war that had prevented British-American collaboration on the RSV was over, and there was growing sentiment in the United Kingdom that a completely *new* translation could and should be undertaken. Delegates from the Church of Scotland (Presbyterian), the Church of England, and the Methodist, Baptist and Congregational Churches met and formed a Joint Committee, which divided the work among four panels and drew on the expertise of outstanding British biblical scholars and of "recognized masters of current English."[42] In fact, one of the four panels was charged with responsibility for matters of literary style, aiming to insure a consistently dignified yet contemporary level of language, steering between anachronistic or "churchy" language on the one hand and overly familiar and voguish expressions on the other. The special care thus given to the fluency of the English, as most reviewers seem to agree, paid handsome dividends in the resulting publication of the *New English Bible*. The New Testament, as usual, came off the presses first (1961), followed in 1970 by the Old Testament and the Apocrypha.[43]

Protestant readers of many denominations welcomed the *New English Bible* (NEB), and in spite of a liberal sprinkling of anglicisms and the expected British spelling of words like "colour" and "honour" it has captured the fancy of many Americans, expecially as an alternative Bible for study alongside the Authorized Version or the RSV. The freshness and vigor of the NEB stem not only from the careful attention to English style but also from the bold use of the textual base, often departing from the *Textus Receptus* or Masoretic Text in preferring the versional reading or choosing freely to conjecture in cases of divided evidence. One notable weakness in this regard, as critics have pointed out, is the inadequacy of notes to explain all these preferences and conjectures, although later editions have served to correct this to some extent.[44]

---

[42]So described by Roger A. Bullard, "The New English Bible," in *The Word of God,* 47.

[43]The University Presses of Oxford and Cambridge, acting jointly, published the NEB. The chairman of the Joint Committee in 1970 was Donald Coggan, the Archbishop of York, later of Canterbury, whose name appears under the "Preface" as Donald *Ebor(acensis)*— Latin for "of York." By 1970 the Roman Catholics of England, Wales, Scotland, and Ireland had joined as sponsors of the project.

[44]Cf. Bullard, "The New English Bible," 57. See also the Oxford Study Edition of the NEB, ed. Samuel Sandmel, M. Jack Suggs, and A. J. Tkacik, complete with annotations and "special articles" by scholars of Canada and the U.S.A. (New York: Oxford University Press, 1976). This edition bears the imprimatur of Bishop Flanagan of the Catholic Diocese of Worcester.

Meanwhile in France there was a new surge of interest among Roman Catholic scholars to make a fresh translation from the original texts, not just another patchwork revision of the *Biblia Vulgata*. In the early 1950s a number of internationally recognized scholars contributed to a series of French translations, a book or two in each fascicle, and in 1956 a one-volume edition was prepared under the direction of *l'Ecole Biblique* in Jerusalem, later to be called *La Bible de Jérusalem*. This work was remarkable, not only for its daringly fresh approach to translation but perhaps primarily for its introductory articles and annotations, which made use of modern critical principles to an unprecedented extent.

It was this Bible which became the basis for the publication in English of *The Jerusalem Bible,* released simultaneously in Britain and the USA in 1966.[45] The British editors acknowledged their debt to the French translators but insisted that their work was an independent translation from the original Hebrew, Aramaic, and Greek texts. Introductions to the books and most of the footnotes were simply borrowed directly from the French, and in some instances the English translation itself owed much to that of the earlier French. But, on the whole, *The Jerusalem Bible* marked a new day for English-speaking Catholics, offering many for the first time the fruits of recent centuries in biblical scholarship and a Bible at last divested of peculiarities endemic to the Douai-Reims-Challoner tradition. Among the more obvious departures from that tradition was the spelling of proper names such as Isaiah and Jeremiah—giving up the accustomed "Isaias" and "Jeremias" of older editions—and the adoption of "Yahweh" for the sacred name of God. Gone are the excessive Latinisms (vestiges of the Vulgate's dominance) that plagued the Douai and its readers, and the English style—especially in the narrative and reported dialogue[46]—is idiomatic and fluent.

Somewhat parallel to the movement that produced *The Jerusalem Bible* was a basically American project, initiated by the Bishop's Committee of the Confraternity of Christian Doctrine. They had sponsored and published an English New Testament, freshly translated from the Latin Vulgate, as early as 1941, and intended to work in the same way on the Old

---

[45]*The Jerusalem Bible,* Alexander Jones, gen. ed. (Garden City NY: Doubleday, 1966).

[46]As with the NEB, the translators of JB invited and received the help of writers like J. R. R. Tolkien, whose competence was in English expression; cf. Bruce Vawter, C.M., "The Jerusalem Bible," in *The Word of God,* 109-11.

Testament. With the encyclical of Pope Pius XII (*Divino Afflante Spiritu*, 1943),[47] in effect lifting restrictions on translation from the Hebrew and Greek, plans were changed and the Catholic Biblical Association of America was charged with responsibility for making an entirely new translation from the best available texts. In the tide of ecumenism surrounding and following the Second Vatican Council, four non-Catholics (three Protestants and one Jew) were invited to participate alongside about forty Catholic scholars, and after years of careful preparation the first edition of *The New American Bible* appeared in 1970.[48]

Professor Walter Harrelson has described the NAB (to adopt the convenient abbreviation) as "a fresh translation marked by restraint in the use of conjecture or in departures from the Masoretic Hebrew text."[49] It is in that respect more like the RSV than the NEB, as he says, although the translation may lack the smoothness and consistency of either of those. Like *The Jerusalem Bible* the NAB breaks with the "Catholic" spelling of proper names, uses modern paragraphing, and relegates verse numbers to the far left margin of the page. Explanatory notes, most reviewers agree, are helpful and, for the most part, nondogmatic in tone. Most of the more technical and textual matters have been reserved for an appendix, and it is in many ways a very useful Bible for liturgy, study, or devotional purposes.

The story of the English Bible is not yet finished, but we must bring this survey to its conclusion with only the briefest notice of three other publications of recent date, leaving the reader to examine each of them firsthand, if possible, or at least to consult the reviews. Already, of course, we have omitted from consideration here a number of older, yet very valuable, translations without intending any disrespect; the limitation of space simply demands selectivity, and we must take account here of those Bibles

---

[47]An encyclical is a papal "open letter" to the church, a traditional means of setting forth important doctrinal or pastoral teaching. This particular document marked a drastic modification of Catholic attitude toward modern study of the Bible, commending archaeological, historical and literary studies to Catholic scholars as never before; cf. R. E. Brown, "Our New Approach to the Bible," *New Testament Essays* (Garden City NY: Doubleday 1968) 30.

[48]Its full title is: *The New American Bible, Translated from the Original Languages with Critical Use of All the Ancient Sources by Members of the Catholic Biblical Association of America: With Textual Notes on Old Testament Readings* (Paterson NJ: St. Anthony Guild, 1970).

[49]Walter Harrelson, "The New American Bible," in *The Word of God*, 140.

that in the last decade or so have proved most popular or useful, in addition to those just mentioned.[50]

First, in the 1960s Tyndale House published a series of paraphrases, which in 1971 were compiled and printed in one volume as *The Living Bible*. As the editors carefully state in the preface, the work is *not* strictly a translation but is a paraphrase, and, we must add, a very *free* paraphrase, guided in large measure by a very "conservative" theology.[51] Many of its readings are admirable examples of colloquial, even "folksy," American English, but the editors have often sacrificed the original sense or ignored the accepted norms of exegesis for the sake of style or doctrine. There is a real danger that unwary readers will mistake *The Living Bible* for one of the translations or revisions described above and thus be misled.

Second, there is the popular and widely used *Today's English Version*, also known as the *Good News Bible*, prepared by the American Bible Society. The New Testament was published in 1966, the same year *The Jerusalem Bible* appeared, and was printed with the title *Good News for Modern Man*. This was in its fourth edition in 1976, when the whole Bible came out. In many respects the TEV is highly paraphrastic, using what Eugene Nida calls the principle of "dynamic equivalence" (as opposed to "formal correspondence")[52] and striving to reproduce the *meaning* of the original in the language of today, which necessitates the substitution of a modern idiom for the ancient. The result is, on the whole, a lively and readable rendition, and yet one that runs much the same risk as *The Living Bible*, and tends to lean more heavily on the interpretational bias of the translator than a more literal translation does. On the other hand, as far as exegetical responsibility is concerned, there is no question of the competence and integrity of the editors of the *Good News Bible*, and if used with caution (and preferably along with the RSV or NEB) it may provide the reader refreshing insight into the ancient texts.

---

[50]With regret I have had to omit such notable items as *The Bible: An American Translation*, ed. J. M. Powis Smith and E. J. Goodspeed (Chicago: University of Chicago Press, 1935); the Bible of James Moffatt (1913-1924), and the work of J. B. Phillips (1952-1964), to name but a few.

[51]See James D. Smart, "The Living Bible," in *The Word of God*, 134-38.

[52]As a translation consultant for the American and United Bible Societies, Nida discusses his principle in "Why So Many Bible Translations?" in *The Word of God*, see esp. 20-25.

Finally, mention must be made of *The New International Version,* which was published in 1978 by Zondervan. Early promoters of this new translation included conservative Christians who had vigorously opposed the RSV, and it is likely that some vestige of that animus can be detected in the NIV's statement of objectives, if not in the work itself. From those objectives—for example, "to do for our time what the King James Version did for its day"—it is clear that only "evangelical" scholars, committed to a "high view of Scripture," were asked to join in the project.[53] Though the English style and phrasing are sometimes reminiscent of the KJV, more often than not the NIV resembles—ironically—the Revised Standard Version, which it originally set out to repudiate and replace.[54]

In conclusion it should be noted that the demand for Bibles, not only in English but in the language of virtually every nation that has a written language, continues to grow. As long as human speech is living, it changes, and with those changes comes the need to retranslate the sacred texts, or to revise even the best of versions. For that reason sponsoring bodies and translation teams in this century usually continue to function long after they have published their Bibles, planning new editions, incorporating the latest scholarly data or newfound MSS. One contemporary movement now urging modifications in the English Bible would reduce instances of "exclusivist" or "male-oriented" language. A committee of RSV translators and editors has already planned to produce an edition that makes less use of "man" or "men"—for example, "Blessed is the man who . . . " would become "Blessed are those who . . . "—and makes clearer the generic sense of Hebrew and Greek nouns for "mankind." Another committee, under the auspices of the National Council of Churches, in October 1983 published an *Inclusivist Language Lectionary,* which goes much farther in that direction, rewording many references to God as masculine and otherwise attempting to remove allegedly offensive "sexist" imagery. Already, as one might guess, the reaction of the public is mixed, and opposition has been strong. The lectionary, of course, is intended specifically for liturgical use, and it would be up to each denomination whether

---

[53]"High view of Scripture," the phrase used in promotional literature (point 6 in the objectives), is further explained: "as set forth in the Westminster Confession of Faith, the Belgic Confession, and the Statement of Faith of the National Association of Evangelicals."

[54]Cf. the review of the NIV by Robert G. Bratcher in *The Word of God,* 152-65.

or not to experiment with it in worship. Whether the liberties taken there can be taken with translations of the whole Bible (or *should* be) is another matter. But, in any case, the difficulties that this movement tries to address are very real, and no doubt they will tax the ingenuity of translators for years to come.

For Further Reading

Bailey, Lloyd R., ed. *The Word of God: A Guide to English Versions of the Bible.* Atlanta: John Knox Press, 1982. Examines nine modern English Bibles and evaluates them.

Bruce, F. F. *The English Bible.* New York: Oxford University Press, 1961.

The Cambridge History of the Bible, volume 3: *The West from the Reformation the Present Day.* S. L. Greenslade, ed. Cambridge: Cambridge University Press, 1963.

Grant, F. C. *Translating the Bible.* Greenwich CT: Seabury Press, 1961.

MacGregor, Geddes. *The Bible in the Making.* Philadelphia: Lippincott, 1959.

_____ . *A Literary History of the Bible.* Nashville: Abingdon Press, 1968.

May, Herbert G. *Our English Bible in the Making.* Philadelphia: Westminster Press, 1952.

Metzger, Bruce M. ''How We Got the Bible.'' In *Introduction to the Bible.* The Layman's Bible Commentary 1. Richmond: John Knox Press, 1959.

Price, Ira M. *The Ancestry of Our English Bible.* Third edition revised by W. A. Irwin and A. P. Wikgren. New York: Harper, 1956.

Another reference work, outstanding for its graphic display of historic Bibles, title pages, and other illustrations, is *The Bible Through the Ages.* Harry T. Frank, Charles William Swain, and Courtland Canby, eds. Cleveland OH: World Publishing Co., 1967.

A GENEALOGY OF ENGLISH BIBLES

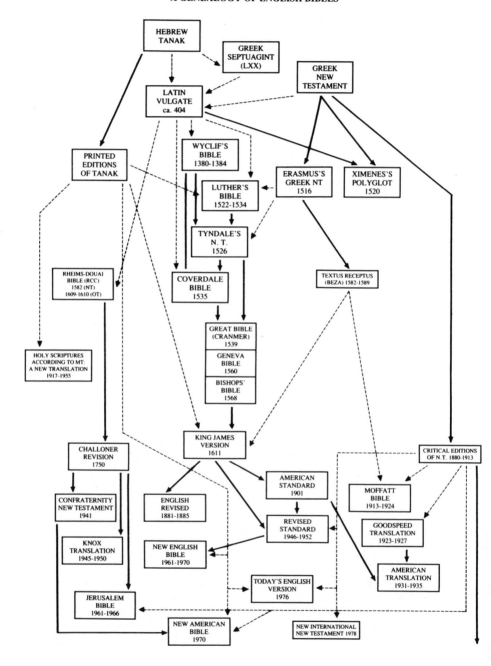

Chapter 5

How the Bible Has Been,
and Is, Interpreted

The Question of its Meaning

To say a comforting word at the outset, the intention of this chapter will be somewhat less ambitious than the title might suggest. Obviously, it would require considerably more than a few pages to give a full survey of all the ways people throughout history have tried to understand and interpret the Bible—what a vast and variegated panoroma that would be! Nor is it possible in one chapter even to summarize all the efforts of recent biblical interpreters, deserving though they may be. So we shall have to be selective both in the historical periods we choose to treat and in the instances of modern disciplines that will engage us, leaving the reader to seek more light from the reading suggestions found at the close of this chapter.

The elementary, but indispensable, fact with which we begin is that the Bible *requires* interpretation. Its meaning (or meanings) will not leap forth from the printed page with crystalline clarity without some aids or without some efforts on the reader's part. As we have already noted in the previous chapter, every translation of the Bible is in some respects itself an effort to interpret, to explain what the original text says. The most helpful translations will do more than set a Hebrew or Greek text into words of another language; in the very process of choosing the proper words the translator gives expression to what he has already discerned as *the meaning* of the original text. A good choice of words is one that captures that meaning and carries it across the gap between the ancient text and the modern reader.[1] To that extent the translator is an interpreter; he is engaged in what is known as the *hermeneutical process,* the business of eliciting meaning from what has been written.[2]

What has been said to this point could, of course, apply to other books we must read in translation, as well as to the Bible. But for readers of the Bible, translation is only the beginning. Because it is a book (or collection of books) from ancient times, the product of a people and a culture in many ways remote from our own, it requires a bit more in the way of interpretation. Even with the best possible English translation in hand the perceptive reader will be conscious of a certain strangeness in the thought forms and point of view of its writers. This is why editors of many versions over the years have included notes, introductory comments, maps and other "helps" of various kinds. These are attempts to deal with the Bible's special peculiarities, devices meant to aid the reader in the quest for meaning.

The very *age* of the Bible creates problems of interpretation. Already today's readers are nineteen centuries removed from the time of Jesus and separated from the patriarchal age by as much as thirty-five centuries! But by any calculation it is an ancient book, and what registers with most new readers today is the Bible's *remoteness* from the present. This in itself can be a real obstacle to serious study, because the temper of *our* times is to value literature for its novelty, not its antiquity. Thus we are conditioned to suspect anything as old as the Bible of being utterly out of date and out of touch with "reality." While such suspicions can be put to rest after better acquaintance with the Bible, they do serve as an important indication that our hermeneutical problem has *two* sides, not just one: there is the Bible's antiquity on one side, and our own modernity on the other. In other words, in interpreting the Bible we shall need to make allowances for the historical conditioning of *both* the writers *and* the readers.

One commonly cited instance of the distance between us and people of ancient times is the difference in worldviews or cosmology. The Bible obviously comes from what we call "prescientific" times; it reflects presup-

---

[1]Our word "translate" is derived from the past participle of the Latin verb *transferre,* "to take or carry across."

[2]Hermeneutic(al), adjective, and hermeneutics, the noun, are often used today in reference to the process of interpretation or to the principles and presupposition of it; the Greek verb from which these terms come is ἑρμηνεύειν, "to translate, interpret."

positions about the world that are radically different from our own. The prevailing notion, in both testaments, is of a flat disc (earth) underneath a vaulted canopy (heavens, sky) and afloat, as it were, on "the great deep" or surrounding ocean. In the Old Testament there are references to *sheol*, a kind of pit deep in the earth, the place of the dead (cf. Pss. 30:3; 55:15; Amos 9:2). By New Testament times certain details were modified—for example, the underworld became the abode of demons or evil spirits—but the structure of the universe remained essentially the same "three-storey" arrangement for Jews and early Christians alike.

Furthermore, the world was full of mystery for the people of those times, innocent as they were of "laws of nature," and it was reasonable for them to explain what was marvelous or otherwise inexplicable as miracles—or, as they often put it, "signs and wonders," mighty acts of God. Not bound by our concept of secondary causes, and with a logic all their own, biblical people could as easily account for a fortuitous rainfall, ending a long drought, by saying "the Lord has blessed us," as they could blame various kinds of disease on the demons. Lacking the interest in such speculations as characterized the Greeks (for example, mathematics and philosophy), biblical writers sometimes seem careless of figures—counting things in round numbers, measuring things by the "cubit," etc.[3] This was their way of thinking, strange as it may seem to us today, and those who wish to make sense of their books will have to reckon with it.

The distance between the biblical writer and the modern reader is not merely a matter of time; it is also a matter of cultural distance as well. Even as early as the third century of the Common Era some of the Greek Fathers (though much closer in time to biblical events) had trouble with the cultural strangeness of the Old Testament. Indeed, even before that, Marcion and others had faced the gap between Tanak and their own thought-world and decided that it was too wide to be bridged—the God of the Old Testament was an inferior deity, and Tanak was to be discarded in favor of an abridged Gospel of Luke and a few (expurgated) letters of Paul. Though his proposal was extreme and—fortunately for us—rejected by most Christians,

---

[3]A *cubit* was the length of the forearm, which varied of course with the individual but became sufficiently standardized by Solomon's day to be utilized by his builders (cf. 1 Kings 6:1-6, 7:2-12). Modern estimates put the equivalent at about 444 millimeters or between 17 and 18 inches. Ezekiel, however, refers to a "long cubit" (Ezek. 40:5, 43:13) in his visions of the restored temple, each being about 20.5 inches.

AN ILLUSTRATION OF ANCIENT HEBREW COSMOLOGY

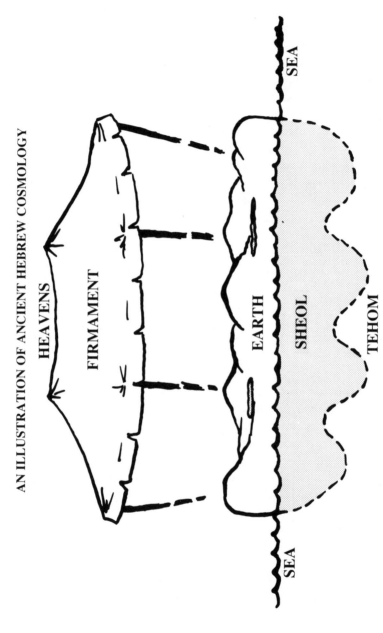

HEAVENS

FIRMAMENT

EARTH

SHEOL

TEHOM

SEA

SEA

In ancient Hebrew cosmology a "Firmament" (or, sometimes, "firmament of the heavens," Genesis 1:14) stretched like a canopy or tent across the sky or "heavens" (cf. Psalm 19:4, 104:2; Isaiah 40:22). Earth, like a disc afloat on Tehom, "the great deep" (Genesis 1:2, 7:11; Proverbs 8:27), seemed to be surrounded by the mysterious Sea. Sheol, the underworld, was imagined as the abode of the dead or their spirits.

Marcion at least recognized the very real difficulty posed by the adoption of Scriptures from another culture.

The scene of the biblical story, after all, is set within lands of a definitely *Eastern* orientation, among peoples whose roots and social character are quite different from those of today's English-speaking interpreter. Whatever may be said of the Bible's transcendent values and timeless truth, we must acknowledge that these are mediated to us through the peculiar story of a people in many ways strange. To ignore these cultural differences, to assume an all-too-easy transference of meaning across the gap, can be as foolish a solution to the hermeneutical problem as was that of Marcion.

The history of biblical interpretation is dotted with instances of this kind of failure, and one reason for giving some attention to the efforts of interpreters of ages past is to warn against their mistakes. This should not be taken as arrogance or contempt for all ancient efforts, as though the latest scholarship is *ipso facto* best, but the undeniable truth is that the gains made in recent decades of Bible study are such as to constitute a kind of revolution of human knowledge, especially our knowledge of the ancient Semitic languages, customs, laws—in short, the very culture that for so long proved mysterious and baffling to interpreters of ages past. It is only in the past century or so that archaeological discoveries in the Middle East have enabled students of the Bible—the Old Testament in particular—to discern the real sociopolitical milieu of ancient Israel and to see its history in the proper context of relations with its neighbors. Links with other, kindred peoples have now been established, serving to reduce considerably that cloud of mystery or aura of unreality that often attended our reading of, say, the patriarchal stories in Genesis. Gains in the understanding of kindred languages, based on the recovery of long-buried texts, have greatly improved our ability to translate the biblical Hebrew and Aramaic and to make sense of formerly puzzling passages. Thanks to the manuscripts of Nag Hammadi and the scrolls from the Judean desert,[4] we have enormously enlarged our picture of intertestamental Judaism and early Christianity in the past forty years, making possible many new insights into the meaning of the New Testament. There is available to the modern interpreter a vast store of knowledge and potentially useful aids in the hermeneutical task that, unfortunately, were not available to our immediate predecessors.

---

[4] Here I have in mind the Dead Sea Scrolls from Qumran and scrolls and fragments from Wadi Murabbaat, eleven miles to the south.

Interpreters in Ancient Times

It is good to look backward, then, as sympathetically as one can, to those who have wrestled with questions of meaning in the ages past. Somewhat arbitrarily we begin with the opening of the Common Era; it may be a reasonable starting point, however, since it was a time when Jewish scribes and scholars were formulating rules of interpretation that would eventually harden into written form as the *Mishnah,* and when the Christian movement was in process of reinterpreting Tanak and Jewish tradition in the light of its understanding of Jesus of Nazareth. This was a parting of the ways for most Jews and those who followed Jesus, and the beginning of two distinctive ways of interpreting the Scriptures they still had in common. In terms of literary expression, one way led to the *Talmud* of Judaism and the other to the New Testament of Christianity.

At this point it may be useful to define some terms—including those just mentioned—that are too important to be relegated to the footnotes. I begin with the generic term Rabbinic literature, the vast corpus of teaching and interpretation ascribed to generations of Jewish rabbis, or teachers. "Rabbi" was a title of honor (literally, "my great one") applied to men who proved themselves diligent students of Torah and qualified to transmit their learning to others. Jewish tradition understood these teachers as spiritual heirs of Ezra the scribe, who was credited with the return to Torah (ca. 400 BCE) already discussed in another context, forming in effect a continuous chain of faithful transmission of oral torah.[5] It was the accumulation of this teaching which was finally organized and codified about 200 CE in the *Mishnah,* comprising sixty-three tractates, arranged by topic under six headings (Hebrew: "orders").[6]

Rabbinic literature continued to grow, and a number of supplements to the *Mishnah* appeared after 200 CE, and gradually a body of commentary on the *Mishnah* itself—called *Gemara* ("completion")—came to be added, forming by around 500 CE the voluminous *Talmud* ("study"), which took

---

[5]See *Pirke Aboth* (Sayings of the Fathers) I.1: "Moses received the Law from Sinai and committed it to Joshua, and Joshua to the elders, and the elders to the Prophets; and the Prophets committed it to the men of the Great Synagogue." "Great Synagogue" is usually understood as the succession of teachers from Ezra on.

[6]Three Jewish scholars have been singled out as primarily responsible for the *Mishnah:* Rabbi Akiba (d. 132, a casuality of the Roman Wars), Rabbi Meir, who produced a written edition of oral torah, later used and expanded by Rabbi Judah "the Prince" (d. 219).

two forms: (1) a Palestinian Talmud (using Western Aramaic), and (2) a Babylonian Talmud, larger and using Eastern Aramaic. Embodying the accumulated wisdom of many generations, and touching on every conceivable aspect of Jewish thought, law, philosophy, and history, it represents an effort to capture the *meaning* of Scripture (Tanak) for Jews of that age, and as such counts as a monumental hermeneutical work. "In a real sense," admits one modern-day rabbi, "it is not the Bible, but rather the *Talmudic interpretation* of the Bible, which sets the framework for all Jewish activity."[7]

During this ancient period there were many, less ambitious writings, which have survived until our day or, once lost, have been found in recent years. Some of these were similar to our modern commentaries, efforts to expound the meaning of specific books of the Tanak, and are called *Midrashim.*[8] Among the recently recovered "Dead Sea Scrolls" were documents—for example, the so-called "Habakkuk Commentary"—purporting to state the *meaning* of biblical texts for the covenanters of Qumran. Strictly speaking, such sectarian writings, often blatantly at odds with Jerusalem-based Judaism, cannot be counted as "rabbinical" but still serve to illustrate the very dynamic and varied character of interpretation among Jews of that period.

From this wealth of material what can we tell about rabbinical interpretation, its methods or motives? One thing, perhaps basic to all the rest, was a widespread notion of the Tanak as the all-sufficient revelation of the will of God for humankind, and its corollary, that there could be no human problem (however novel or strange) that the Bible, properly interpreted, did not address. It was, therefore, the task of the skilled teacher or rabbi to show people how to live by an ancient, unchanging Torah in new situations and changing conditions. This was what motivated the continual study of Torah and the multiplication of precepts or laws based on it. The idea was to bring all personal and corporate life under obedience to Torah and thus under the Reign of God.

---

[7]Rabbi Meir Belsky, Headmaster of Yeshiva of the South (Memphis TN), in his 1974 letter, responding to this author's queries about the curriculum of Jewish Studies at the Yeshiva (Academy). Italics added.

[8]*Midrash* (the singular noun) comes from the Hebrew דָּרָשׁ (to search out, to inquire); the best examples are the commentaries on Exodus, Leviticus, and Numbers (severally), and the *Midrash Rabbah* ("large") on the Pentateuch and the five *megilloth.*

The growth of the oral torah was also the result of efforts to make the written laws as specific as possible in order to leave no room for misunderstanding and unwitting disobedience. *Pirke Aboth* (I.1) refers to this rabbinical principle, saying, "Make a fence around the Torah." Just as a hedge was often planted along property lines, especially where a public path or thoroughfare passed, to keep pedestrians from straying and trespassing on others' lands, so there was need for clarity in the interpretation of the Law to prevent even accidental trespasses. Thus, by rabbinic teaching the meaning of the commandment—"Remember the sabbath day, to keep it holy"—was spelled out quite specifically: it was forbidden to engage on that day in any of thirty-nine different kinds of work.[9] If one were not sure what time it was—the Sabbath began on Friday at sundown—preparations should be made well in advance to leave a margin for error, and many of the specific rules (Hebrew: *halachoth*) of rabbinical teaching have that character. They are, in effect, the "ounce of prevention" against transgressions of divine Law.

In this light it becomes understandable that this development of oral tradition was viewed (at least, by Pharisaic Judaism) as simply an extension of written Torah, and not as something superfluous or "merely human invention" and lacking divine authority.[10] The prevailing attitude can be seen exemplified in a story from the Talmud, concerning the famous Rabbi Akiba ben Joseph (d. 132), who was noted for his exposition of the Law of Moses that contributed eventually to the formation of the Mishnah. The story has it that Moses (in heaven) got the Lord's permission to visit earth and sit in a class with the disciples of Akiba—invisibly of course. Moses was said to be unable to follow all the rabbinical arguments. But when disciples questioned Akiba as to the source of his teaching, he replied, "It is a law given unto Moses at Sinai," and Moses, we are told, "was comforted" and returned to heaven, singing the praises of Akiba's ability to find such undreamed-of meaning in his words.[11] It was as if Moses himself was unaware of the fuller implications

---

[9]*Shabbat* 7.2.

[10]The Pharisees, noted for their dedication to the study and keeping of the Torah, were mainly lay persons (as opposed to priests) and were leaders in the synagogue and the Jewish community at large from ca. 150 BCE. Their reputation as heartless legalists or hypocrites (as often pictured in the gospels) is an unfair and, for the most part, undeserved generalization.

[11]Talmud, *Menachoth* 29b.

of the laws he had received from the Lord, implications that were "there" at Sinai but were made explicit only in the expositions of teachers like Akiba. Thus the Jew of Akiba's day—more than a millennium removed from Moses—justified the novelties of oral torah as teaching not really *new* but rather the necessary, and completely logical, continuation of the *old*. And as such these innovations carried the same authority as if Moses himself had spoken the words.

Not all Jews, we must admit, were comfortable with the position just described. In fact, if the judgment of Josephus be accepted, a basic disagreement between the popular movement of the Pharisees and the more aristocratic Sadducees involved the question of authority;[12] the Sadducees apparently did *not* extend to the rabbinical teachings the authority of written Torah, and their insistence that Torah alone should determine the way Jews were to live probably accounts for most of their other doctrinal pecularities.[13]

It must be noted, too, that the Gospels of the New Testament provide evidence of divisions among Jesus' contemporaries over the weight to be given certain oral traditions as opposed to the written Torah. For example, the question put to Jesus concerning the grounds for divorce (Matt. 19:3) reflects the well-known dispute between followers of Rabbi Hillel and those of Rabbi Shammai. Deuteronomy 24:1 provided for the husband to divorce his wife, if he should find "some unseemly thing in her," but what did "unseemly" mean? Shammai interpreted this to mean evidence of marital infidelity, actual adultery; Hillel, on the other hand, held that even burning dinner was "unseemly" in a wife and therefore grounds for divorce. The answer of Jesus as reported in Matthew 19:4-6 (cf. Mark 10:2-9) seems to indicate his refusal to be drawn into the dispute over *grounds*, insisting that divorce for *any* cause was "to put asunder" what God had joined. But when further pressed (in Matthew but not in Mark) Jesus makes a pointed contrast between the divine ideal of unbroken union and the concession allowed in Deuteronomy (that the husband grant his wife a certificate of divorce), and ends by making "unchastity" (RSV) the sole grounds for divorce (Matt. 19:7-9; 5:31-32). It was a thorny question for

---

[12]Josephus, *Antiquities* XVIII, 1.2, 4; *Jewish Wars* II, 8.14; cf. Morton Scott Enslin, *Christian Beginnings* (New York: Harper and Brothers, 1956) 112-18.

[13]Josephus, *Jewish Wars* II, for example, mentions the Sadducees' rejection of the idea of personal "immortality." In the New Testament, Luke in both the Gospel (19:27) and the Acts (4:1-2) refers to the denial of the resurrection of the dead by the Sadducees.

both Jews and Christians, as variations in the writings of both traditions clearly testify.[14] To the subject of Jesus' use and interpretation of Scripture on other matters we shall return.

Meanwhile there are a few more principles of rabbinical hermeneutics that ought to be mentioned. We have already said that one underlying idea was that Scripture, rightly interpreted, was the all-sufficient revelation of God's will, adequate for the whole of human life. Another, akin to this idea, is that *all* Scripture, properly understood, was of value in *some* way— that is, Tanak contained nothing superfluous, nothing meaningless. The point is made in an ancient midrash on Proverbs 27:18, which says, "Whoso keepth the fig-tree shall eat the fruit thereof." And the commentary: "Why is the Torah compared to a fig? In all fruits there is a part which is refuse. In dates there are stones, in grapes there are pips, in pomegranates that are husks; but the whole of the fig is eatable. Similarly in the words of the Torah there is no refuse."[15] Although, in a sense, this seems an anticipation of the later Christian notion of "plenary inspiration," the emphasis in Jewish thought was on practice rather than theory, the *utility* of biblical texts rather than their inspiration.

The notion had rather far-reaching implications for the way that specific texts came to be interpreted. In effect, it encouraged a kind of exegesis that finds "hidden meaning" in the most unexpected texts, and often in ways that the modern reader would call "hair-splitting." For if there is nothing superfluous in Scripture, then every book—indeed, every line and every word—holds a significant meaning, even though not immediately plain to see. The more obscure the passage, the more the skill or ingenuity of the interpreter is challenged to extract from that passage its treasures. To those of us not schooled in that technique the results are, to say the least, amazing. To take an often cited example, there is the story in Genesis 14 of Abraham leading a host of "three hundred eighteen men" in pursuit of his enemies. Jewish scholars, hard pressed to account for the precise figure of 318 (when round numbers usually suffice), noted that these men were said to be "born in his house," and yet the only heir of Abraham's house

---

[14]For the difference between Shammai and Hillel see *Gittin* 9.10; Josephus, *Antiquities* IV, 8.23. Within Christian circles compare Mark 10:2-9 and Matthew 19:4-9; Paul (1 Cor. 7:10) may reflect the Markan reading of Jesus' teaching, where divorce (for whatever cause) was discouraged.

[15]Cited in Abraham Cohen, *Everyman's Talmud* (New York: Schocken Books, 1975) 133.

mentioned in Gen. 15:2 was Eliezer, a slave. Cleverly, interpreters took the letters of Eliezer's name and added up their numerical values; they came to exactly 318, proving (they said) that Abraham's "army" consisted of the one servant, Eliezer![16]

Sometimes nothing more than one syllable or one Hebrew character was made to bear a terrible load of "meaning" under this kind of exegesis. In the Hebrew text of Genesis 2:7 ("the Lord God formed man . . .") the presence of a double-*yodh* in the verb, grammatically superfluous, gave interpreters a handy proof text for the doctrine of two *yetzers,* or two impulses (one good, the other bad) at work in humankind and vying for dominance. Or, in Genesis 4:10 ("your brother's blood is crying to me . . ."), because the form of the word for "blood" is plural, not singular, the meaning was said to be Abel's blood *and* that of his posterity, and was used to justify severe laws against false testimony in cases of capital offense.[17] Usually such atomistic exegesis involves many different passages of Tanak, and it is on the strength of whole *catenae,* or chains, of such interpretive links that the rabbis put forth and defended their theses.

Another consequence of the view that Scripture contained nothing useless or meaningless can be seen in a growing tendency to *allegorize.* Where the plain sense of a biblical text was either manifestly irrelevant to the times of the interpreter or posed some kind of dilemma (perhaps because of a contradictory text elsewhere), the favorite way to deal with that text and still derive "meaning" from it was to look for its symbolic or allegorical message. The same was true of certain passages deemed to be irreverent or unworthy of divine utterance, if taken at face value. No doubt some such interpretation of the Song of Songs, taking the erotic love-poems to be an expression of God's love for Israel, saved the book for the Canon. Some of the more blatantly anthropomorphic references to God troubled scholars like Philo of Alexandria, and they sometimes went to great lengths to explain the symbolic or "spiritual" significance of God's face, hands, and other parts.[18]

---

[16]Involved here is the ancient use of *gematria,* whereby each letter of the alphabet has a numerical value (א = 1, ל = 30, י = 10, ע = 70, ז = 7, ר = 200); the use of such calculation in numerology was widespread, and it no doubt figured in the Revelation's famous "number of the beast" (Rev. 13:18). Our story is cited in E. C. Colwell, *The Study of the Bible,* rev. ed. (Chicago: University of Chicago Press, 1964) 104-105.

[17]*Sanhedrin* 4.5.

[18]Philo, a Jewish scholar roughly contemporary with the Apostle Paul, devoted many

The dangers inherent in allegorizing were probably not so obvious then as they are today from the standpoint of modern scholarship. But in that ancient period it was not only possible but widely acceptable to approach Scripture with a predetermined doctrine or ethical stance and "find proof" for it in the Bible by the clever use of allegorical interpretation. This, often as not, was an instance of *eisegesis,* reading *into* the text the meaning one desired to find, rather than *exegesis* (reading *out* the intended meaning). Not that allegory in itself is mischievous; the Old Testament provides some good examples of allegory—for instance, Isaiah 5:1-7, containing the Song of the Vineyard. But a distinction must be made between what was *intended* as allegory by the author (in this case, the prophet) and other passages, where such was not the intent. The danger lies in the obliteration of that distinction so that even straightforward historical narrative, meant to be taken literally, can be forced to "mean" something far different from its plain and simple sense.

Early Jewish and Christian writers were aware of that distinction, if not always careful to observe it in their practice. Rabbinical works refer, in fact, to four distinct levels, or methods, of interpretation; a popular mnemonic device made them easy to remember, for the initial letters of the four Hebrew words spell out the consonants of "paradise"—in transliteration, thus: *Peshat* ("simple"), giving the most obvious or literal sense of the text; *Remez* ("allusion"), finding a symbolic or allegorical meaning; *Derash* ("exposition"), homiletical commentary, using *catenae* of various texts to support a proposition; and *Sod* ("mystery"), deriving a secret, esoteric meaning (as if specially revealed to a privileged few).[19] The typical interpreter of ancient times rarely used just one of these methods, or set one against another, but managed rather to combine two or more of them, depending on the situation and purpose of the moment. So, while there were basic principles and fairly well-established methods of interpretation, the system nevertheless allowed great latitude to the teacher and encouraged the use of wit and imagination in the way one tried to relate the sacred books

---

treatises to interpreting the Tanak in terms that educated (Hellenistic) readers would understand; in effect, it seems, Philo tried to make Moses sound like Plato! Cf. C. K. Barrett, *New Testament Background: Selected Documents* (New York: Harper and Row, 1961) 173-189, for excerpts from Philo, with notes and introduction.

[19]Cohen, *Everyman's Talmud,* xxxvi. Actual examples of the fourth level (*Sod*) are scarce in Mishnah itself, but appear more frequently in sectarian documents and especially in apocalyptic writings.

to the common life. As noted in the long-standing debate over divorce, so also in the arguments of other rabbis and within the Talmud generally,[20] loyalty to the biblical tradition did not impose on its scholars one narrow or restrictive set of answers to all the questions. Despite its quirks, its casuistry and convoluted arguments, the heritage of Talmudic scholarship stands even yet as eloquent testimony to the vitality of Jewish faith and its dialogue with the world.

Turning now to the Christian side of the picture, we have only to remember that Jesus himself and his earliest followers were Jews, and therefore we are not surprised to see in the New Testament numerous signs of that Jewish heritage. Just as in its organization and forms of worship the church was indebted to the synagogue, so in its attitudes towards Scripture and in its methods of interpretation. As we have already noted, Christians and Jews shared essentially the same canon, at least through most of the first century of our era. Over the crucial question of the messiahship of Jesus they differed, and their disputes grew in number and in intensity, and yet in that very controversy it is remarkable that both sides appealed to the same Bible and, very often, in a quite similar manner.

That Jesus of Nazareth was steeped in the Jewish understanding of Tanak seems very clear; in spite of the tendency in the gospels to magnify those points where Jesus challenged the scribes and Pharisees, there is ample evidence to suggest that on many points Jesus would have agreed with them.[21] Above all, however, his teachings indicate a deep reverence for Scripture as the vehicle of God's Word, as authoritative direction for human conduct. And in his ability to expound its meaning, whether for intimate disciples or for the ranks of onlookers, Jesus apparently impressed many, including some opponents, enough to be called *didaskalos* (teacher) and rabbi.[22] In fact, many of his parables and other sayings reported in the gospels are similar in form, if not in content, to those of rabbinic sources. Jesus' use of simile and argument "from lesser to greater" is standard rab-

---

[20]Hillel and Shammai were only one of a series of rabbinic "pairs" whose lively opposition (mainly first century BCE) exemplifies the capacity for variety and freedom of opinion within Judaism.

[21]Mark 12:28-34 is a case in point; on the matter of resurrection, also, Jesus was certainly closer to Pharisaic belief than to Sadducaic; cf. Mark 12:18-27.

[22]The Greek term διδάσκαλος is used of Jesus about forty times in the Synoptic Gospels. "Rabbi" (the Hebraic title) is used to address him six times in the Synoptics, six times in John, and the heightened form ῥαββουνί appears in Mark 10:51 and John 20:16.

binical procedure—for instance, in Matthew 6:26 (after the warning against anxiety about food and clothing): "Look at the birds of the air: they neither sow nor reap nor gather into barns, and yet your heavenly Father feeds them. Are you not of more value than they?" The argument here (as with the lilies and the grass of Matt. 6:38-30) is from the lesser value to the greater— if God cares for one, how much more so for the other![23]

Yet, with all Jesus' devotion to Scripture and all the affinity between his teaching methods and those of the scribes, there were undeniable differences, too. The synoptic gospels abound with examples of Jesus' opposition to the prevailing (Pharisaic) interpretation of Scripture or some practice based on it. Most numerous, perhaps, are the instances of controversy over activity on a Sabbath.[24] Even if we allow for the possibility of editorializing from the writers, the very frequency of such stories points to a real and serious quarrel. While the scribes might have agreed with Jesus in principle, that "the sabbath was made for man, not man for the sabbath" (Mark 2:27), Jesus apparently refused to stay within the prescribed limits of lawful activity on the Sabbath when human need (or divine compassion) required otherwise. To say the least, the spontaneity and free improvisation of Jesus in certain cases—as in Mark 3:1-6—stand in sharp contrast to the cautious weighing of legal minutiae so characteristic of rabbinic decisions. This contrast is dramatized preeminently in John 9, the story of Jesus' healing of "a man blind from birth." With rich irony the Pharisees (or, more frequently, "the Jews") are pictured as obsessed with the *legal* questions—whether the Sabbath was in fact desecrated, who was guilty, and so on—and hardly notice the tremendous miracle right under their noses: "whereas I was blind, now I see" (John 9:25 AV).

On other matters, too, Jesus seemed impatient with current oral tradition and even questioned its authority. Mark 7:1-23 contains a set of controversy stories and sayings, claiming in effect that oral torah may actually be a means of contravening God's commandments. By taking advantage of the current procedure of "pledging" portions of one's property to the temple fund—declaring it *corban* —a man could be excused from the ob-

---

[23]Sometimes referred to in its Latin form *a minori ad maius,* this was one of seven *middoth* (exegetical principles) set forth by Hillel the Elder (*Sanhedrin* 7.11). Another, "analogy," embraced all kinds of comparative devices—parable, simile, metaphor.

[24]Among others, Mark 2:23-28; 3:1-6; Luke 14:1-6; John 9. Note, on the other hand, the very clear disclaimer of Luke 23:56b, on behalf of the first disciples of Jesus.

ligation to provide financial support for his aged parents. Here was an act of traditional piety, no doubt encouraged by the priests, but hardly calculated to alleviate the poverty of the elderly. In fact, Jesus said, it actually worked against the spirit and intent of God's commandment to honor father and mother. It is noteworthy that later rabbinic regulations served to correct the abuses of *corban,* but Jesus' open criticism of such practices must have caused alarm among Pharisees and Sadducees alike.

The gospels all depict Jesus as a teacher with great sympathy for people on the fringes of society, the masses or "people of the land" (Hebrew *'am-ha-aretz*) who had little or no stake in affairs of synagogue or temple. Jesus identified much more closely with the poor and the outcast than with the rich and powerful, and many of his teachings are to that extent more at home in the *prophetic* tradition than they are in the *rabbinic* or legal tradition. If the common people "heard him gladly" and marveled at his "authority," it was largely because of the revival of that long-silent prophetic voice—with Jesus they seemed to hear again: "thus says the Lord. . . . "[25] And in his message of the dawning Kingdom of God, extending God's grace even to sinners and harlots, Jesus sounded a note of hope for many people who (from the strict, Pharisaic viewpoint) were reckoned as "lost." Again, it was an attitude that offended the scribes and other leaders of society, contributing to the events that culminated in Jesus' arrest and execution, but it was one that set an example for Christian interpreters for generations to come.

Of all the elements that set Jesus apart from other teachers of his day, perhaps none is so important as his proclamation: "the kingdom of God is at hand; repent and believe the good news."[26] Indeed, as modern students of the gospels have freshly demonstrated, it was Jesus' eschatological preaching which forms the ground, the basic presupposition of all the authentic teaching and, for that matter, the healing miracles as well. Because the reign of God was

---

[25]Cf. Mark 6:1-4; 12:37b, for instances of the popular response to Jesus. The phrase, "thus says the Lord," is of course a recurring formula of the Hebrew prophets, indicating that their words were a message from God. The prevailing consensus said that the age of prophecy had ceased with Ezra.

[26]Mark 1:15 (my translation); cf. Matthew 3:2. Note that Matthew prefers to say "kingdom of *heaven*" (not "of God"), but means the same thing; with Jewish sensitivity about direct reference to God, Matthew uses a fairly common surrogate. It should be pointed out, too, that the term "kingdom" is best understood as "reign" or "kingly rule," and not as a political or geographical entity.

near, and the prospect of a new Age dawning, Jesus called for "repentance"—radical reversal of life—as the only adequate response. But what
precisely this meant had to be spelled out through many a parable and saying;
the preaching was supplemented by the teaching. Thus, too, most of the miracle stories can be seen, not as just another list of "wonders" to amaze the
crowds, but evidence (for the eye of faith) that God's reign already is present
in driving out the demonic and in making people whole.

To conclude this sketch of Jesus as teacher and interpreter of Tanak, I have
to admit that many other things could be said—for example, about distinctive
features in Jesus' parables, perhaps the finer points in his understanding of the
Kingdom. Let the reader consult some of the resources mentioned at the end
of this chapter. Our purpose here was simply to trace in broad outlines both
the element of continuity—Jesus' Jewishness—and the element of discontinuity—his radical break with Pharisaic Judaism, especially in the prophetic
and eschatological character of his teachings. Jesus stood well within his heritage in affirming the authority of Tanak, as well as in the style and method
of his teaching, but over against the current proliferation of oral laws Jesus
stressed God's "original intent," and removal of legalistic bars to entrance
by "sinners" into the Kingdom. Like Deutero-Isaiah, Jesus saw God doing
"a new thing" with his people, and pouring "new wine" would call for "new
wine skins."[27]

In many respects it was this consciousness of being made *new,* of being
somehow reconstituted as "God's people of the new covenant," that best
describes the outlook and mood of early Christianity. The pivotal experience, of course, was that associated with the Resurrection of Jesus; the
Christian "gospel"—strictly speaking—began with the Easter announce-
ment: "He is risen!" By all accounts that was prior to any collection of
teachings, or even to any articulations of a Christology."[28] But from the
very outset the radical nature of the Christian movement was set by its un-
shakable conviction that God had acted in Jesus the Christ to redeem his
people, and to make with his followers a new beginning. This rudimental

---

[27]Cf. Mark 2:22, one of numerous allusions to the inability of the old institutions of
Judaism to accommodate the transforming powers at work in Christ.

[28]By "Christology" is meant a reasoned expression of the significance of Jesus as the
Christ (Messiah), Lord, Son of God, and so on. Certain statements by Paul (as in Phil. 2;
Col. 1) count among the earliest of Christologies; in some sense, the Fourth Gospel is the
fullest effort in the New Testament.

faith, far more than anything else (including Jesus' examples as teacher), determined the course of Christian interpretation, as opposed to Jewish, throughout the intervening ages.

In the light of this faith, it is fair to say, the whole of Jewish Scripture took on new meaning for Christians. They could never again read it and understand it just the way they had, before Christ, or the way the rabbis continued to do. This point emerges in Luke's story of the Walk to Emmaus (Luke 24:13-35), where the risen Jesus (unrecognized by two disciples) patiently explains "all that the prophets have spoken" to show the necessity of Christ's suffering: "And beginning with Moses and all the prophets, he interpreted to them in all the Scriptures the things concerning himself" (Luke 24:27; cf 24:32). Though the particular point here is the reinterpretation of the Messiah (Christ) as one who must suffer, it is appropriate to watch for the same kind of effect at other points and in many different parts of Tanak. Faith in Jesus as the Risen Lord "opened their minds to understand the Scriptures" as never before.[29]

One specific consequence of this was for Christian evangelists and teachers to search the Scriptures for texts to support their claims for Jesus and to *find* them even in unlikely or unpromising spots. Recall that precedent for this had been set in rabbinic use of allegory. But not content to cite prophetic passages that expressly referred to the coming of a Messiah or messianic Age, some Christians delighted in uncovering hitherto hidden allusions in virtually every book of Tanak. The writer of the Gospel of Matthew shows signs of this tendency, when (for example) he quotes from Hosea 11:1—"out of Egypt I have called my son"—as though the text were a prediction (or prefiguring) of the holy family's return from Egypt at the death of Herod.[30] The literal and historical sense—Hosea's intended meaning (God's call of *Israel* in the Exodus)—is ignored completely, and the text has found its "fulfillment" in God's son, *Jesus*. If this seems to our minds a somewhat strained exegesis (even eisegesis), by the standards of the time Matthew's use of Scripture was not so eccentric. Far more extreme cases can be cited, of which one will suffice here: recall the story of Abraham and the 318 "men of his house" (Gen. 14:14), which some Jewish interpreter explained as Abraham and *Eliezer*.[31] Not to be outdone, the

---

[29]Luke 24:45. Paul had expressed much the same thought in 2 Corinthians 3:12-15.

[30]Matthew 2:15b, cf. 1:22-23 (reinterpreting Isa. 7:14). In about a dozen places Matthew quotes texts from the LXX as being *fulfilled* by something Jesus did or said.

[31]See n. 16 above.

Christian writer of the Epistle of Barnabas (9:7-9) offered an equally ingenious explanation of the number 318. Using the Greek alphabet, he saw that the "eighteen" was *I* (*iota* = 10) and *H* (*eta* = 8), the first two letters of the name 'ΙΗΣΟΥΣ or Jesus, and the "three hundred" was *T* (*tau*), the sign of the cross. Therefore, said Barnabas, Genesis 14:14 was a forecast of the Crucifixion of Jesus!

While there were such cases of outlandish exegesis, the writers of books now in the New Testament, on the whole, took a fairly moderate line. The tendency to allegorize, of course, was evident from earliest apostolic times; certain parables of Jesus were already undergoing allegorization by the time they were committed to writing. Paul, in his letter to the Galatians (4:21-26), allegorized the Genesis account of Abraham and his two sons (Ishmael and Isaac)—"one by a slave (Hagar) and one by a free woman (Sarah)." For Paul the two women stood for "two covenants"—one leading to the "slavery" of legalism, the other to "freedom" in Christ. It is not necessary to suppose that Paul thus denied the literal or historical sense of his text; it is rather that it has been superseded by *another* level of meaning, made possible by the Advent of Christ. The two levels of meaning did not contradict each other, but were regarded as parallel and complementary. It seems that Christians, whether consciously or not, followed much the same path that led to the four levels (PRDS) of Jewish rabbinic interpretation.

One variation or refinement of allegorical exegesis was what came to be known as *typology*. Here the operative principle is the same—that the Scriptures all look forward to the coming of Christ and his church—but the particular emphasis of typology was not so much on specific promises or predictions in Tanak, but rather on *prefigurement,* a general pattern of "types" of Christ and the church of which the ancient writers themselves might be unaware. Thus, for example, even Adam was found to be a "type" of Christ in the fact that he was the "head" of the old order of mankind, whereby sin and death came in, just as Christ is the "head" of the new order and bringer of redemption.[32] In many and various texts the typologists discovered things and events said to foreshadow Jesus' Crucifixion and Resurrection, without insisting that the authors so intended them. The implication was that God himself so intended them, planting hidden clues, as it were, of a divine purpose to be made manifest "in these

---

[32]Romans 5:12-21. Paul uses the word "type" of Adam in verse 14.

last days.'' Some such notion probably explains Paul's curious statement in 1 Corinthians 10:1-5, which reads in part, "our fathers . . . all passed through the sea, and all were baptized into Moses . . . and all ate the same supernatural food and all drank . . . from the supernatural Rock which followed them, and the Rock was Christ.'' Clearly the old themes of exodus (and the Paschal lamb) and wilderness-wandering offered fruitful grounds for this kind of reinterpretation. Likewise, cultic institutions such as temple and priesthood lent themselves to Christian typology, as we see in many parts of the Epistle to the Hebrews (Heb. 2:10-18, 4:14-5:10, 7:11-8:7, 9:1-10:31; cf. Matt. 27:51). In this epistle, however, the motive is not to prove that the Old Testament prefigured the coming of Christ—this is taken for granted—but rather to argue for the superiority of the sacrifice and priesthood of Christ over that of the old covenant (merely "a shadow of the good things to come,'' Heb. 10:1).

The Fourth Gospel could be counted as a beneficiary of the same kind of reinterpretation. John presents Jesus as the provider of "living water'' (far better than the well water of Jacob) and of "living bread'' (superior to the manna of Moses), and in many other "I am'' sayings of Jesus he draws on the familiar themes of the Tanak to show how Christ fulfills and transcends them (John 4:11-15 [water], 6:35-51 [bread]; cf. 8:1, 9:5, 10:7-14, 11:25, 14:6, 15:1). Indeed, it seems that John has in effect reinterpreted the Synoptic traditions, especially Jesus' miracles, as well as the Tanak. In a series of seven "signs'' (John 2:1-11, 4:46-54, 5:1-18, 6:1-14, 6:16-24, 9:1-41, 11:1-53) Jesus is said to do mighty works which indicate not just the nearness of the Kingdom but, more especially, the *meaning* of the Word-made-flesh.

All in all, the writers of the New Testament manifest much the same ambiguity that interpreters have ascribed to Jesus himself—that is, reverence for, and dependence on, the Tanak and its promises on the one hand, and awareness of radical newness on the other. What we have called currents of continuity *and* discontinuity seems to be implicit in the very notion that Christ *fulfilled* the Scriptures; it might tend, on one side, to strengthen the ties that bound the Christian to his Jewish heritage, but on the other side, it might also tend to reduce the value of what was fulfilled and pull the Christian away from that heritage.

As a matter of historical fact, the latter tendency proved to be a significant feature in the century or two after the period of New Testament. Of course, it involved more than the question of biblical interpretation as such. It involved also the changing scene, the new cultural stance, of Christian interpreters in the second and third centuries. As Christian writings gradually became a part of the church's scriptures, alongside the Law and the Prophets, there was obviously more to be interpreted, a larger Bible in the making. But, more importantly, the church grew, too, and became increasingly *Gentile* in its constituency, its outlook, and its understanding of the Gospel itself. Obedient to the Great Commission to "go and make disciples of all nations," evangelists moved into all parts of the Roman Empire, and at the same time Graeco-Roman culture moved into the church and was bound to affect the way it read its Scriptures and declared its Faith. Needless to say, the effect of all this was to turn the current of discontinuity into a veritable torrent.

Since its consequences for later methods of interpretation prove to be important, let us take time here to describe that new incursion more fully. What we have in view is often called the "Hellenization" of the church or of Christianity. Whether or not this label does justice to the complexities of the situation, it does point to the dominant source of the new philosophy that began to prevail: Hellas (Greece). It was a Hellenistic world that surrounded Christians almost everywhere they went, since *koine* —the common, "marketplace" Greek—had long since become the international language of people throughout the Roman Empire. This fact alone does much to explain the rapidity with which the Christian message spread around the shores of the Mediterranean Sea. Beyond language, there were other elements of Greek culture that had filtered down from their heyday (fifth century BCE in Athens) and found expression in certain widely cherished notions and values among the masses. For example, their notion of deity was shaped by exposure to the ancient Greek myths and, more immediately, by contact with Stoicism or perhaps some of the popular cults like the Eleusinian Mysteries.[33] In general, this meant that God (or gods) belonged to the "spirit world," a realm quite apart from the mundane scene inhabited by human beings, and moreover God, as pure Spirit, would scarcely have created the material world or otherwise concern Himself with

---

[33]Mystery cults were characterized by a form of initiation—hence the word "mystery" (from μύστης, "initiate")—usually involving dramatic disclosure of cultic secrets. The cult devoted to Demeter and her daughter Kore (or Persephone) came to be called "Eleusinian" because of the *teleusterion* or cult center located at Eleusis, a few miles west of Athens. See Harold R. Willoughby, *Pagan Regeneration: A Study of Mystery Initiations in the Graeco-Roman World* (Chicago: University of Chicago Press, 1939).

its preservation. Matter was widely regarded as transient, decaying, a hindrance to the spiritual ''soul'' of mankind, and therefore to be renounced in this life and escaped altogether in the next. Thus the prevailing notion of ''salvation,'' as offered by certain cults of the day, was the reassurance (sometimes sacramentally granted) that initiates would finally be released from the body, and the soul would ascend to its home with God. To say the least, these notions stand in sharp contrast to the philosophical outlook often associated with Judaism and its Bible or, for that matter, with first-generation Christianity.

But these ideas (and others like them) Gentile converts brought with them into the church, producing in time an interpretational stance distinctly different from what had gone before. On this ground Christian Gnosticism flourished, promoting a concept of salvation by *gnosis* (a Greek word for ''knowledge''), and a view of Jesus that effectively denied his humanity. In the Marcionite movement, as we have seen, the current of discontinuity reached flood tide, demanding complete withdrawal from the matrix of Judaism and rejection of its Scriptures.

Though the Church survived that crisis, eventually repudiating the Gnostic and Marcionite ''heresies,'' the impact of Hellenistic culture on Christian theology and on biblical interpretation in particular was deep and lasting. We can only sketch here a few of the most prominent marks of that impact. One of the foremost was the reinforced tendency to treat the Bible, especially the Old Testament, allegorically. Jewish interpreters had no monopoly on this method; in fact, long before Philo of Alexandria there was a notable current of thought among Greek Platonists and some of the Stoic writers, applying much the same method to the myths of Homer and Hesiod. Even the motivation was similar, for just as Philo was concerned to explain Hebraic anthropomorphism and derive a philosophically respectable meaning from Tanak, so earlier Hellenistic writers had sought to remove what was offensive about the Homeric stories of the gods and still find symbolic significance in them. Thus from the Hellenistic side as well as from rabbinic custom the church inherited the practice of allegorizing in Scripture whatever seemed theologically unacceptable or embarrassing if taken literally. This practice was most prominent in Alexandria, in the Christian school headed by Clement and Origen, although not at all limited to it. Origen is said to have observed that when the devil took Jesus up to a high mountain and ''showed him all the kingdom of the earth'' (Matt. 4:8), everyone knows that there is no mountain that high; therefore the story must contain a hidden meaning behind its language. Such difficulties led Origen to propose a "threefold meaning" for Scripture—the literal (or historical), the moral, and the spiritual (or allegorical).[34]

At the hands of the Greek Fathers and Apologists the Old Testament prophets became almost exclusively foretellers of the coming of Christ, and their relevance as messengers of judgment in their own day was either ignored or explained away as typological forecast of the last judgment. Something with far-reaching implications for the later understanding of inspiration can be seen here, in the adoption of predominantly Greek notions of prophecy and the coincidental devaluation of this-worldly elements of biblical history. It meant, on the one hand, that all prophecy tended to be reduced to *prediction* of the future (and that "future" usually equated with the Advent of Christ and the Church). On the other hand, the importance of *this* world as the scene of God's redemptive activity (so characteristic of the Tanak) began to give way before the dualistic reinterpretation that would eventually make "heaven" or the world-to-come all important. As for the Bible itself, it was to become an increasingly esoteric, mysterious book, whose hidden meanings had to be expounded by the "wise" and spiritually gifted.

In all fairness we must acknowledge that such tendencies did not pass unchallenged in the third and fourth centuries. The famous exclamation of Tertullian—"What has Athens to do with Jerusalem, the Academy with the Church?"—was largely a protest against the secularism of Hellenistic philosophers, but along with that he detected in the Christian adoption of the Greek "wisdom" more subtle dangers, such as the distortion of the meaning of faith itself. Over against the rampant allegorizing of Alexandrian scholars I need also to mention the rival school at Antioch (in Syria), where the tendency of interpreters was to emphasize the historical and grammatical meaning of Scripture. Allowance was made in Antioch for the use of metaphor and parable, but of primary consideration was the meaning intended by the authors, not that imagined by the readers. Theodore of Mopsuestia, a late-fourth-century representative of the school, took Origen to task for some of his allegorical readings, accusing the Alexandrian of denying the historicity of certain Old Testament events. Theodore also held, against the prevailing opinion of

---

[34]Origen, *On First Principles* IV.2-3 (reference to the Temptation Story is in IV. 1.16). Cf. Robert M. Grant, "History of the Interpretation of the Bible: I. Ancient Period," in *The Interpreter's Bible*, vol. 1 (Nashville: Abingdon Press, 1951) 110.

his day, that the primary meaning of the prophets was to be found in the context of their own times and places, and not in long-range forecasts of the coming Messiah.[35] On many such points Antiochian scholars served to counteract the extremes of the allegorists and, in some sense, even to anticipate certain ideas of the modern period.

To conclude this sketch of ancient interpreters, it is possible to describe the course of Christian attitudes toward Scripture as a movement from Jewish beginnings, with no Bible but Tanak, to the point of separation, where New Testament writers reinterpreted Tanak in the light of their faith in Jesus as the Christ, and then to the point of rapid assimilation of Hellenistic thought, with the consequent widening of the gap between the Bible (both Old and New Testament) and its fourth-century interpreters. Inevitably, we may now say, the Church found itself compelled to deal with books both sacred and, in many respects, strange and baffling. Drawing on the intellectually vibrant legacy of Greece and Rome, preachers and teachers naturally read the Bible in ways that agreed with their own philosophical assumptions—for example, assumptions about God, leading to the Trinitarian formulations of the creeds.[36] Whereas Judaism tended to see its Scriptures as divine authority for its *practice*, Christianity looked to the Bible mainly as the source of its *doctrine*, as authority for what was believed and taught. And this use of Scripture—in the service of ecclesiastical dogmatics or apologetics[37]—was to characterize Christian hermeneutics for the next thousand years.

Interpretation in the Middle Ages

Our treatment of the medieval period will perhaps seem disporportionately brief after the somewhat detailed survey of the earlier period. Two considerations help to explain, if not to justify, this plan: (1) the ancient period was by far the more formative period in terms of setting the basic

---

[35]Grant, ''History of the Interpretation of the Bible,'' 111; cf. Edwin Hatch, *The Influence of Greek Ideas on Christianity* (New York: Harper and Brothers, 1957) 50-85.

[36]I have in mind certain affirmations, such as those of the Nicene Creed (325 CE), which uses phrases like ''essence (οὐσία) of the Father'' in defining Christ's relationship with God—phrases that reflect Greek concepts rather than strictly biblical thought.

[37]By ''dogmatics'' I mean formal, systematic attempts to declare what the Church teaches; this might take various forms—creeds agreed upon in councils or synods, papal decrees or encyclicals, essays or books of the scholars (subject to official approval), and so on. By ''apologetics'' I mean the various *defenses* of the Faith.

design and direction of biblical study for centuries to come; and (2) throughout the long period from 500 CE to about 1100 change or development in biblical hermeneutics was notoriously slow or insignificant. While the once-popular label, "the Dark Ages," should probably be discarded, it is fair to describe this period as one of little invention or innovation. To put it positively, it was an era of consolidation rather than creativity, an era which saw the church establish itself as an institution of the world ("heiress of the Roman Empire"), and provide for most of the civilized world a pattern of dogma (theology) that was to become "the Queen of the Sciences." It was certainly not a *dark* age intellectually, in view of the array of Christian and Jewish scholars whose works survive.[38] Even so, if we are looking for distinctive development, or departure from the customary, in biblical exegesis, we must look toward the end of the Middle Ages, to what is known as the Scholastic Age (roughly 1100 to 1300) and beyond, before we come to significant movement.

As mentioned in connection with the survey of ancient versions of the Bible, the work of Jerome on the Latin Bible was a watershed event. The Vulgate, completed in 405 CE, overcame the initial resistance and lodged itself firmly in the affections of Western Christians, becoming *the* Bible of Roman Catholicism. In the East, of course, the Byzantine Church still made use of the Greek Bible, including not only the deutero-canonical books embraced by Roman Catholics but also a Psalm 151, a Third Book of Maccabees, and (as an appendix) Fourth Maccabees. But very few scholars in the West followed Jerome's example of studying the original languages, so that in the Middle Ages biblical exegesis usually began and ended with the Latin text. On the positive side, the widespread use of the Vulgate did lend a unifying influence to the doctrinal discussions of Western Christianity, fostering development of the body of Tradition that grew alongside the Canon as an authoritative instrument of the Roman Church.

Once the matter of canon had been settled—and I have noted the effect of the Vulgate on that issue—the Church made increasing use of its Scriptures as a stock of "proof texts" for doctrine. The great scholar Augustine of Hippo (354-430) made an art of this in his own writings, and though he

---

[38]This was the age of the Venerable Bede, John Scotus Erigena, Alcuin, Aquinas, and Rashi, not to mention a number of bishops of Rome who were erudite scholars in their own right. See Beryl Smalley, *The Study of the Bible in the Middle Ages* (Oxford: Clarendon Press, 1941).

was inclined to allegorize and read Christian meanings *into* his text, he set a notable example for later ages in his ability to find Scriptural "ammunition" and use it effectively against heretics or other opponents of Catholic dogma. But, above all, the spiritual heirs of Augustine were far more concerned to support and defend their theological positions than to engage in any careful study of the Bible for its own sake. Bible study in this period was definitely subordinate to the task of refining and systematizing the dogma of the Church.

Not to be forgotten, however, was the more private use of the Bible as a source of inspiration and a guide for personal piety. In this, the best representatives would be the monastic orders, where reflection and meditation were basic ingredients of the daily fare, and the study of the Bible was primarily for the cultivation of the spiritual life. Here, under vows of poverty, chastity, and obedience men and women devoted themselves to the contemplative life (another echo, perhaps, of the Greek influence) and renounced secular wealth and power.[39] Needless to say, they found justification for this way of life in the Scriptures, especially in the example of Jesus and the teaching of Paul. But the main reason for the monks' use of the Bible was devotional not apologetic, practical not theoretical. Reading their texts in the context of prayer, rather than polemics, they sought in the Bible a very personal, sometimes mystical, union with God.

This leaning toward mysticism is exemplified by the work of Bernard of Clairvaux (1090-1153), who probably more than any other person epitomizes the monastic spirit of the period. He combined in himself both the ascetic ideal, renunciation of all that was "worldly," and the practical concern for honest toil and industry, which eventually brought unexpected prosperity to many monastic communities—and thus new worldly problems! But for himself Bernard longed to have the beatific vision, to lose his own will in the Will of God, and most of his surviving writings seem to be shaped by this mystical fervor.[40] Bernard wrote eighty-six sermons on—of all things—the Song of Solomon. That erotic love poetry, allegorically interpreted as God's love song to the human soul, became a model

---

[39]Typical, in most respects, was the Benedictine Order; cf. *The Rule of St. Benedict,* trans. W. K. L. Clarke (London, 1931), from the early sixth century.

[40]Bernard left many sermons, treatises, and letters, but is best known for two "classics" of Christian mysticism: *On the Steps of Humility* and *On the Love of God.*

for Bernard of the mystical union, which he elsewhere spoke of as "heavenly intercourse."

By the time of Bernard, of course, the allegorical method of exegesis was well established in all parts of the Church. Although it was widely held that there were *four* senses or levels of meaning in Scripture—(1) the literal or historical, (2) the allegorical, (3) the tropological or moral, and (4) the anagogical or "heavenly"—in actual practice we judge that allegorizing was by far the most dominant interest. And once the persons and events of a given story were interpreted as figures referring to matters of an entirely different time and place, almost *any* "moral sense" that occurred to the interpreter might be "found" in the text. Obviously, it was a custom that invited abuse, encouraging the most fanciful, even outrageous, expositions.

What held such expositions *somewhat* in check, or kept them from even greater excesses than those they did reach was the developing power of the hierarchy in the church, exercised more and more to restrict and to censor scholarship that proved blatantly eccentric or offensively independent. In the Middle Ages the bishop of Rome became "Papa" or Pope and titular head of the church on earth, the Vicar of Christ, the Successor of the Apostle Peter. This tendency to centralize authority at Rome gave impetus to the demand for conformity of doctrine, and eventually to the energetic prosecution of those who did not conform. Thus an increasingly authoritarian church, influential in the European political arena as well as in "spiritual" matters, claimed not only to have the Word of God, as revealed in the Bible, but also the exclusive power to interpret it. As guarantor of orthodoxy and Defender of the Faith, the Roman bishop had become the final arbiter in cases of disputed meanings in Scripture, and by "speaking *ex cathedra*" he could end all argument as to interpretation.[41]

Roman hierarchy had long since relied on a select few passages of the Bible as "proof texts" for their position. Basic, of course, was the "dominical charge" given by the Lord to Simon Peter (Matt. 16:18-19): "You are Peter, and on this rock I will build my church. . . . I will give you the keys of the kingdom of heaven, and whatever you bind on earth shall be bound in heaven. . . . " Romanists understood this to apply not only to the person of Peter but also to every successor to the bishopric of Peter,

---

[41]*Ex cathedra*, Latin for "from the chair"—that is, from his position as spokesman for the church in its teaching office.

thus to the whole succession of Roman Popes. For justification of the growing *secular* power of the papacy Roman exegetes appealed to such texts as Luke 22:38, where in anticipation of Jesus' impending arrest in Gethsemane the disciples say: "Look, Lord, here are two swords." Taken as a reference to two kinds of power—the "spiritual" (or ecclesiastical) and the "secular" (or political)—the two swords were lifted out of their original context and made to symbolize, at first, two separate but (more or less) equal lines of authority, both divinely sanctioned. But toward the end of this period, especially in the heated Investiture Controversy between the Emperor Henry IV and Pope Gregory VII,[42] it becomes clear that the "equality" of the two swords gave way to an exalting of the one over the other. Thus, it was argued, Jeremiah's commission (Jer. 1:10)—"I have set you this day over nations and over kingdoms"—supported the priority of the "spiritual" sword (the prophetic office identified with the papacy) over the "secular" (the kingdoms). Even the "two lights" said to be set in the firmament in Genesis 1:14-16 were interpreted as symbols of papal authority and royal authority respectively, and in the understanding of the Church there could be no question as to which was "the greater."

Even before the rise of the great universities and what we call the Scholastic Age, there were a few interpreters who drew their inspiration from Antioch rather than Alexandria, demanding more serious attention to the Bible's literal or historical sense. A number of Christian writers of the twelfth century were directly or indirectly indebted to a French school of Jewish commentators, called *Tosafists,* [43] followers of the great scholar Shlomo (Solomon) Yitzhaki, better known to us as Rashi.[44] Foremost among the contributions of Rashi was his concerted effort to clarify "the simple, natural meaning of the text" and to probe beneath the layers of popular allegory to the author's purpose. As a recent evaluation puts it,

---

[42]This struggle took place between 1075 and 1082, the culmination of a long-standing practice of certain landowners (lay persons) to invest (install) handpicked clerics in church offices; the Pope opposed this, but the Emperor ignored the decree, challenging the Pope's authority, and was deposed and excommunicated.

[43]*Tosafists* is a name derived from the Hebrew verb "to add," in token of the added comments to Rashi's works by his disciples.

[44]"Rashi" is actually an acronym formed by the initials of *R*abbi *Sh*lomo *Y*itzhaki; he was born in 1040 in Troyes, in the heart of Champagne, famous for its grapes and wine making.

In his *peshat* (simple sense), Rashi explains the text and conveys its meaning in terms of logic, grammar, common sense, and experience. This rational and logical treatment helped clarify many obscure passages and ideas, and to this day Rashi remains the most widely used commentator by students of Bible and Talmud.[45]

Among the Christian scholars influenced by Rashi was the Franciscan, Nicholas of Lyra (d. 1340), who taught at the Sorbonne in Paris. Nicholas wrote a commentary on the Old and New Testaments, in which he emphasized the primary meaning of the original Hebrew and Greek, a work that is said to have encouraged the study of biblical languages on the part of many later scholars. It is not surprising that early reform movements like the Waldensians, who had already contested the extremes of the allegorists,[46] welcomed the support they found in Nicholas's exegesis. Well known, too, is the admiration Martin Luther had for Lyra and his work, nearly two centuries later. But in the interval the universities at Paris, at Oxford, and elsewhere served to promote a more historical approach to the Bible, and with that a growing uneasiness about the traditional, dogmatic approach and "proof texts." A foundation was laid, on which both humanists and reformers would build, for a new day in hermeneutics and, in its wake, a new Age in the history of the church.

Interpretation in the Renaissance and Reformation

To understand the changes about to be described one must consider the movement that came to be known as Humanism. In some modern circles, sad to say, the term "humanist" seems to be used as a term of reproach—often linked with the adjective "secular"—and applied to those who reject or challenge certain cherished convictions of traditional piety. Thus the word has received, unfortunately, the connotation of "antireligious" or even "atheist." It is not appropriate here to quarrel with such usage, but it may be worthwhile simply to point out that, when the terms Humanism

---

[45]Samuel M. Blumenfield in *Molders of the Jewish Mind* (Washington DC: B'nai B'rith Adult Jewish Education, 1966) 65.

[46]Waldensians (or Valdenses) traced their origin to Peter Waldo, a rich French merchant who renounced his wealth in obedience to the words of Jesus—"go sell what thou hast and give to the poor"—and became an itinerant preacher. Waldo and his followers recited Scripture in French, and soon incurred the wrath of church officials, being condemned as heretics at the Council of Verona (1183). Cf. J. T. McNeill, *Makers of the Christian Tradition* (New York: Harper and Row, 1964) 145-50.

and humanist first arose, they carried no such sinister connotation. They arose out of that new intellectual ferment in European universities, fostered and promoted mainly by good Catholic teachers and scholars, which led to new emphasis on *studia humanitatis ac litterarum*.[47] Humanism was in the first instance an *educational* movement, dedicated to recovery of the literature of classical antiquity, and inspired by its values. The glimpses of classical culture, long obscured through the Middle Ages but newly discovered in works of Aristotle, for example, intrigued scholars and prompted the search for others.[48] Even the great theologian Thomas Aquinas, epitome of the Scholastic Age, was greatly indebted to the logic and the teleology of Aristotle, and his monumental *Summa Theologiae* was in many respects "humanistic" in the sense that it shows a deep appreciation for the classical virtues, for the value of human life, here and now.

Something of the same blend of Christian and classical thought found artistic expression in the *Divine Comedy* of Dante, whose admiration for the poet Virgil (his guide through Hell) was second only to his love for Beatrice (guide through Paradise, and symbol of divine grace).[49] Most of the early (fourteenth-century) representatives of Humanism, far from being antireligious, were inclined rather to claim for Christianity the worldly wisdom of Athens and Rome, or at least to redeem and revive the best of their literary remains. Even if later, in the High Renaissance of Italy, Humanism became independent, and even critical, of the church, this was less a conscious design of its proponents than it was a consequence of their studies. There was a notable shift of interest from the "*other*-worldly" to the "*this*-worldly," but it came about as a result of humanistic inquiry and its interaction with other movements, not because of any premeditated plot.

In biblical interpretation Humanism's main contributions included (1) the revival of interest in old manuscripts, and (2) the revival of Hebrew

---

[47]A phrase said to be Cicero's: "the study of humanity and letters." In the same vein we speak of "the humanities"—for example, as a division of the university curriculum.

[48]Many of the works of Aristotle, previously unknown in the West, came to light first in Arabic texts and commentaries, leading eventually to the search for and discovery of the Greek originals, in turn opening up vast "new" areas of the long-obscured classical world.

[49]For a good translation, with even better commentary, see Dorothy L. Sayers, *The Comedy of Dante Alighieri the Florentine* (New York: Penguin Books, 1980).

and Greek in the West, with the resulting interest in biblical philology.[50]
The search for ancient Greek and Latin books took scholars like Petrarch
and Boccaccio to various libraries, and some of these were found in out-
of-the-way monasteries, where once-valuable MSS often lay untouched for
centuries, sometimes to fall victim to the ravages of mice, mildew, and
human neglect. But even when rescued from ruin, copies of the Bible in
the original languages would have been illegible to Western scholars before 1400, because knowledge of those languages had virtually disappeared, and there were no qualified teachers. It was only after a concerted
effort, funded largely by Florentine bankers, that teachers from the East
were attracted and, in the fifteenth century, Greek became a part of European education. While Hebrew, of course, had survived with the Jews
of Europe, little attention was given to it by Christians, except for the French
students of Rashi. Since that time new waves of anti-Jewish sentiment had
complicated the scene, so that it became doubly difficult for Christian students to learn Hebrew. Johann Reuchlin, a professor of Greek at Basel (ca.
1475), had to go to Italy to study Hebrew. But because of Reuchlin and
other humanists the tide gradually turned, and as a result of their labors the
ground was laid for both textual and exegetical advances.

   Alert readers will be aware that we have come once more to the age of
the printing press, and they will recall what I have already said in connection with the history of the English Bible. The benefits of mass printing
were of course realized in the publication of Bibles in the ancient languages, as well. Gutenberg's two-volume Bible (the Latin Vulgate) had
appeared in 1456, a year after the birth of Johann Reuchlin. By 1488, a
Jewish press at Soncino had improved its Hebrew type enough to produce
the first printed copies of Tanak. Not long thereafter the race was on to see
who would publish the first Greek New Testament; it turned out to be just
that—a race between the Archbishop (later Cardinal) Ximenes of Alcalá
in Spain and the Dutch Humanist Desiderius Erasmus. Though the Archbishop jumped to an early lead, and actually finished his New Testament
in 1514, he intended to publish the complete Bible (a six-volume set) and
had to await completion of the Old Testament to get the official papal ap-

---

[50]Literally "love of words," philology in its broadest sense means the study of literature, but in its narrower, technical sense (as used here) it is the science of language, embracing such specialized fields as comparative linguistics—for example, the study of Hebrew
as one among a "family" of Western Semitic languages.

proval. That may have lost him the race, for by that time Erasmus had hastily put together his Greek text, published in 1516. In fairness to the "loser" it should be pointed out that his work was not only on both testaments but also in *polyglot* —that is, for the Old Testament, Hebrew, Latin, and Greek (LXX) in parallel columns; for the New Testament, Greek and Latin side by side. A magnificent achievement, it came to be known as the Complutensian Polyglot.[51] Yet it was the work of Erasmus, though not so carefully done, which gained scholarly attention and—perhaps because of its handier size—became the favorite Greek text, only slightly revised by Beza to become *Textus Receptus* for centuries to come.

If Humanistic scholarship, aided by the printing press, provided the occasion for emancipation from the Vulgate, Protestantism supplied the cause. The Reformation of the sixteenth century, fueled by long-standing discontent with the Roman Church and sparked by Luther's Ninety-five Theses for debate, set all Europe ablaze. We have already traced its effect on the demand for Bibles in the vernacular of England, and of course the same principle was at work elsewhere. Reformers turned to the authority of the Scriptures to oppose the authority of the Papacy, and just as the Roman hierarchy feared, the Bible in the hands of the laity proved a very dangerous thing. But it was even more so in the hands of scholars like Luther and Calvin, who not only challenged traditional interpretations based on the Latin (for example, the reading "do penance" instead of "repent" in Mark 1:15) but even questioned the canonicity of the Vulgate's "extra" books.[52] Roman Catholics argued that the Bible was the church's book, and only the properly authorized officials of that church could declare its meaning and expound its Truth. The Protestant position, as expressed by Luther, was that *both* church *and* Bible were creations of the Word of God, which was a dynamic that could not be frozen at any one historical period nor equated with the pages of the Book. For Luther it was Christ, the Living Word, to which all Scripture witnessed, and without which no book could be authoritative for the church. In this light even the Epistle of James became questionable, because in Luther's estimation it fell short of declaring the "gospel" of God in Christ.[53]

---

[51]Complutensian derives from *Complutum*, the Latin equivalent of Alcalá.

[52]We refer here to the books designated "Apocrypha" by Luther, because they were not included in the Hebrew canon.

[53]Apparently because of its legalistic tone and (seemingly) un-Pauline view of faith and

In some respects Luther's exegesis still utilized traditional methods, including allegory and typology, but on the whole these procedures were balanced by his insistence on texts in the original languages and his attention to historical context. His debt to Nicholas of Lyra, and indirectly to Rashi, kept him from some of the excesses that had become characteristic of that era. Even more restrained in this regard was the French Reformer John Calvin, who wrote commentaries on almost every book of the Bible. Calvin brought to bear his rich academic, and largely Humanistic, background in his expositions, but always insisted that the true meaning of Scripture depended ultimately on "the inner testimony of the Holy Spirit," the same source of inspiration operating on the reader as on the original author. Like Luther, Calvin was Christocentric in his approach to the Bible, and sometimes in his zeal for the unity of the Old and New Testaments he was inclined to "Christianize" parts of the Old. Yet Calvin, keenly aware of the hermeneutical problem and the dangers of allegorizing, set for Protestants a remarkable example of careful, responsible exegesis. Perhaps more than any theologian of that time, Calvin made clear the necessity of *starting* with the meaning intended by the authors (rather than with the dogma or meaning of the reader) and the need to observe the *context* —chapter, whole book, and so on—in which any given text occurs. Though an ardent advocate of Protestant doctrine, Calvin resisted the temptation to *force* the biblical text to support something it was not meant to support, and he displayed exceptional honesty and humility, refusing to claim that his or any person's interpretation was complete or infallible.[54]

The revolutionary character of Protestant methods of exegesis, set free from the restraints of hierarchical control, was manifest not only in the flood of Bibles in the vernacular—many with highly polemical annotations, as we have seen—but also in the less public, unheralded studies of laypeople who quietly fulfilled the vow of William Tyndale. The ploughman could, indeed, know as much as the scholar about God's Word. Protestants pro-

---

works (cf. James 2:14-26), Luther called James "an epistle of straw." He had little use for the Apocalypse either.

[54]Commenting on the use of Isaiah 6:3 ("Holy, holy, holy . . . ") as a support for the doctrine of the Trinity, Calvin remarked, "I should prefer to employ firmer evidence." See *Opera, Corpus Reformatorum* (Brunsvig, 1863) 36:129, as cited by J. T. McNeill, *The Interpreter's Bible,* 1:125. McNeill (124) also cites Calvin's frank admission that he was unable to fathom the meaning of the Apocalypse of John.

duced commentaries, handbooks, and other aids as well as Bibles. The curiosity about this world, kindled by the renaissance of learning, was matched by a new curiosity about the world of the Bible. And this occurred apart from any partisan or polemical interest—in short, a curiosity about the Bible in itself, as ancient literature, as another object of human investigation. The contents of the Bible were now open to the scrutiny of all, whether believer or infidel, and the stage was set for the opening of the era of modern critical studies.

The Modern Period:
Development of Critical Methods of Interpretation

It would be misleading to suggest that the present status of biblical scholarship is a direct consequence of the Protestant revolt, however much it may owe to the Reformers and their work. But the path of progress was not so simple. For one thing, Protestants did not succeed in escaping the snares of dogmatism; indeed, in some respects they became as authoritarian in their use of the Bible as Roman Catholic theologians had become in their use of Tradition, leading some critics to claim that Protestants had merely exchanged a human Pope for a *paper* one. Moreover, the freedom of interpretation for which the Reformers stood, we now know, was gained at the expense of Christian unity among the Protestants themselves. The proliferation of denominations—Lutheran, Presbyterian, Anglican, Anabaptist—and eventually the further splintering of these testify to one side effect of "the priesthood of all believers."

Above all, whatever gains Humanism and Reformation left behind, they were not immediately appreciated, because of the social and political turmoil that engulfed Europe for the next century and a half. This was the Age of Nationalism, intensified by the Religious Wars (Catholic vs. Protestant), and the real fruits of biblical scholarship would be delayed until the period known as the Enlightenment or the Age of Reason.[55]

Meanwhile, to mention only one more factor in the rise of modern biblical studies, we must take notice of the tremendous strides in the natural sciences during the sixteenth and seventeenth centuries. The Ptolemaic

---

[55]Scholars use the labels, aware of their inherent deficiencies, to mean roughly the seventeenth and eighteenth centuries in Europe. The American colonies, too, felt the impact of this outlook, prominently so among such "founding fathers" as Benjamin Franklin and Thomas Jefferson.

(earth-centered) worldview gave way before the discoveries of Bruno, Kepler, Galileo, and Newton, and circumnavigation of the earth dealt a fatal blow to the biblical cosmology of a flat earth afloat on the cosmic deep. If Humanistic learning had engendered an intellectual independence of Christian doctrine, the new sciences of geology and biology (especially after Charles Darwin's work)[56] fostered an increasing antipathy for religious dogma in general and a skepticism about the Bible in particular. While the ensuing conflict between "religion" and "science" produced more heat than light, running to extremes of acrimony on both sides, it did raise inevitable questions about the nature and authority of Scripture, questions to which I mean to return in the next chapter.

For the present my concern is to isolate those currents of biblical scholarship that emerged out of the seemingly chaotic conditions I have just described, for they provide us for our own day the basic methods and tools of biblical hermeneutics. It is significant that in those tumultuous times, when so many long-cherished Christian presuppositions came under attack, and when Catholic and Protestant theologians alike tended to retreat into new dogmatic trenches, it was largely the work of the independent, nonpartisan scholars that filled the vacuum and rescued from oblivion the hard-won gains of earlier Bible scholars. Rationalists and political philosophers, Thomas Hobbes (1588-1679) and John Locke (1632-1704), while rejecting much of the miraculous or supernatural content of the Bible, were nonetheless serious students of it and, in somewhat different ways, attempted to demonstrate the "reasonableness" of its ethical teachings.[57] At least such scholarship kept alive an interest in the Bible as "literature," and at most it promoted among the more orthodox a quest for meaning that could face the problems raised by science and reason.

The Enlightenment encouraged the academic investigation of religions other than Christianity and Judaism. Under the popular banner of "toleration"—placarded, for example, by Voltaire—the Rationalists tended to look for the "common denominator" behind *all* organized religions, and

------

[56]Charles Darwin's famous *Origin of Species,* providing empirical evidence for a naturalistic or evolutionary theory of human origins, did not appear until 1859, but long before that the fossil remains of animal life embedded in the rock had led biologists to reject the biblical idea of a literal six-day creation.

[57]See, for example Hobbes's *Leviathan* (1651) and Locke's *The Reasonableness of Christianity as Delivered in the Scriptures* (1695).

to view with suspicion (and sometimes contempt) those beliefs or practices that made any one faith distinctive. Over against "revealed religion" they set "natural religion," and alongside the Bible they put the Upanishads, Vedas, the Quran, and any other sacred books of the world religions. In the long run, despite the limitations of this approach, there was to be a considerable gain for biblical scholarship in laying the foundations of comparative study of religious literature and eventually of the discipline we know as the History of Religions. Seeing the ancient Hebrews, for example, in the context of the larger Semitic world, and their religion in the light of contemporary and more primitive religions, began to bear fruit in a deeper understanding (ironically enough) of what was most distinctive about Israel's faith. By the same token, the meaning of Christianity began to emerge more sharply than ever, when viewed within its Graeco-Roman milieu and compared to the cults with which it had to compete. In short, a vast new perspective for the historical interpretation of the Bible came into being, utilizing the investigative techniques employed by the secular historians and applying them to the sacred texts as to any other documents. While, in one sense, losing its privileged and protected status as "the church's book," the Bible became for historical criticism a highly significant source in the pursuit of human learning, perhaps gaining in the process a new respect for what the Bible is in itself.

One specific effect of this approach was to appreciate change, movement, development within the Bible. Earlier interpretation was predominantly "timeless"—lacking in a sense of movement, of one thing leading to another, or one idea giving place to another. Under constraint to dogmatic consistency, traditional interpreters found it unthinkable that two parts of Scripture might disagree as to the character of God or his ways with the world. But with the new historical understanding it became possible to find growth and development even in Israel's concept of Yahweh and the covenant; it became possible, therefore, to account in a very natural way for otherwise baffling or embarrassing "inconsistencies"—for example, the movement from a patriarchal polytheism (or henotheism) to the ethical monotheism of postexilic Judaism. The same principle enabled interpreters to deal with the ethically bothersome spots, such as Joshua's annihilation of whole cities (men, women, and children), not by resorting to fanciful allegory nor by trying to Christianize what is obviously less than Christian, but by simply recognizing the temporal *and moral* distance between what Joshua took to be God's will and what Jesus did. This led, to be sure, to a drastic revision of the concept of revelation itself. But for many thinking people it offered a welcome alternative to older notions, that tended to make of God an arbitrary, irrational, and changeable tyrant. At least, with the revised concept, it could be said that God accommodated his Word to humankind's ability to hear it, or that it was not *God's will* that changed but *human understanding* of it.

Meanwhile research in the *literature* of the Bible, unencumbered by traditional (ecclesiastical) presuppositions, began to focus on such matters as genre and style, time of composition, and authorship. Whereas medieval churchmen had dismissed such questions as irrelevant, even impertinent—since, after all, the same God was Author of it all—the new approach boldly investigated the several books in their individual peculiarities, regarding the Bible as the variegated anthology it is, and bringing about a new awareness of the role of its many human writers. Under the careful scrutiny of scholars trained in philology and literary analysis, some of the old questions of Rashi, Calvin, and others were now taken with new seriousness: did Moses really compose the whole Pentateuch (as long-standing tradition said), and—if so—how is it that he described his own death in Deuteronomy 34? Or why are there conflicting stories of Saul's rise to power in Israel, and of David's introduction to the king? Old questions about the New Testament also occupied the scholars: how were the differences among the four Gospels to be explained? And where was Paul when he wrote his epistles? But the way these and similar questions were answered reflected a far different mind-set and motivation from those of earlier times.

Before, if seriously entertained at all, the question about the authorship of the Pentateuch (for instance) would have been "answered" by simply citing certain accepted authorities—"the Fathers"—and reaffirming the conviction, deduced from the doctrine of divine inspiration of Scripture, that of course God had revealed to Moses in advance the circumstances of his death. Now, in the light of the new critical approach, the argument proceeds inductively rather than deductively, drawing conclusions from the analysis of the literature itself instead of from Church dogmatics. And literary analysis of the Pentateuch, at least by late seventeenth century, suggested that the material was probably not the work of a single author but was composite and finished after Moses' death. A major advance in this kind of analysis came in the eighteenth century as a result of studies by the French court physician, Jean Astruc, who distinguished in Genesis at least two sources, based on the alternation between *'elohim* and *Yahweh* in reference to God. His work was not widely publicized, but a few years later it was incorporated with additional data in J. G. Eichhorn's *Einleitung ins Alte Testament* (1770-1773), and within the next century German scholarship refined what came to be known as the "documentary hypothesis" and extended it to embrace the whole Pentateuch or Hexateuch.[58]

It will be helpful to recall here some of the main considerations that led the literary critics to distinguish and trace their hypothetical sources. As in other scientific investigations, so in the critical analysis of literature, confronted by certain phenomena one must set forth that hypothesis which best accounts for them in the simplest, most plausible way. The phenomena observed in this case included such things as repeated stories—technically called "doublets"—like those of Abraham (Gen. 12:10-20; 20:1-18) and his deception about Sarah;[59] various alternative names, not only for God, but also for the holy mount (Sinai and Horeb), for the inhabitants of the Promised Land (Canaanites, Amorites), and others; anachronisms, abrupt transitions, and apparent discrepancies. To account for these observable peculiarities the scholars, prompted by the work of Astruc and Eichhorn, soon came to a general consensus that underlying the present text were much older sources (first thought of as "documents"), arising from various times and places and brought together many centuries later than the events of which they tell. Thus, as mentioned before, they identified as the "groundwork" of the Pentateuch what we have called the Yahwist Epic (J) from Solomonic times, partly paralleled by the Elohist (E) ca. 850 BCE, and combined shortly thereafter by a redactor (JE). Then, ca. 650 the Deuteronomic "edition" (adding mainly the book of Deuteronomy) of the earlier work appeared, followed finally by the Priestly editors who retouched

---

[58]Among the many scholars who contributed to the hypothesis were Karl Graf and Julius Wellhausen, so that in time it was called the Graf-Wellhausen theory. In the early days it was generally supposed that JEDP referred to existing *documents* (later lost), but more recent studies (by Scandinavian scholars, especially) have been content to think of such sources as "traditions" without prejudice as to whether they were written or oral.

[59]Though the setting is different in the two passages, it is essentially the same story, reported with varying emphasis by two different (Northern and Southern?) sources; actually, there is a third occurrence of the story in Genesis 26, this time told about Isaac and Rebekah.

the whole cluster of material and added their own "introduction" (Gen. 1:1–2:4a).[60]

Much the same analytical procedure came to be applied to other parts of the Bible as well. The book of Isaiah had long ago raised questions about its literary integrity (unity), because it contained a lengthy section (Isa. 36:1-39:8) which obviously duplicated 2 Kings 18:13-20:19, and much of its second half (from chapter 40 on) referred to persons and events of centuries later than the time of Isaiah (eighth century BCE). New investigations, including detailed study of the vocabulary and style of the book, indicated that Isaiah, like the Pentateuch, was a composite work, really a collection of material spanning perhaps two centuries. Only the first thirty-five chapters held the authentic oracles of Isaiah of Jerusalem, and chapters forty through fifty-five were judged to be the work of a poet-prophet of the Exile, eventually designated Deutero-Isaiah. The rest of the book is often assigned to a third author, of a still later date, though not perhaps with the same confidence and unanimity as for 2 Isaiah. But on linguistic, historical, and theological grounds it seems fairly certain that the prophet Isaiah was not the author of the whole book, and that those moving passages (Isa. 40-55) that speak of coming release at the instigation of Cyrus, of the "new exodus" under the one, universal God, and of Israel's mission to be "a light to the nations"—belong to the anonymous prophet of the mid-sixth century.

In the New Testament the literary critics also found evidence that even some of Paul's epistles, as they now stand, might be combinations of more than one original source: such, for instance, are Romans and (most probably) 2 Corinthians.[61] Attention to the Synoptic Gospels began to provide an alternative to the traditional notion that Matthew was the earliest, abridged by Mark and enlarged by Luke—an idea that goes back to Augustine. Careful study of the three now pointed to the priority of Mark and to the use of Mark by the other two. And detailed comparison of Matthew

---

[60]For a very constructive treatment of these sources and their "kerygmatic" (faith-proclaiming) value, see Walter Brueggemann and Hans Walter Wolff, *The Vitality of the Old Testament Traditions* (Atlanta: John Knox Press, 1975).

[61]Romans 16, with its long list of people to be greeted, plus mention of "dissensions and difficulties" not otherwise noted in 1-15, seems to belong to another writing of Paul, perhaps accidentally attached to Romans at a later time. In 2 Corinthians there is an abrupt change of tone between chapters 9 and 10, suggesting that two originally separate letters have been combined—with possibly a fragment of another in 6:14—7:1.

and Luke disclosed about 250-300 verses, not traceable to Mark, but common to the two, and in such similar language that they must have come from the same source; this (again, hypothetical) source the German scholars branded "Q," for *Quelle* ("source"). Though the Gospel of John had long been recognized for its uniqueness, fresh investigations suggested that it, too, might have incorporated certain earlier sources, outside the Synoptic tradition: John's distinctive treatment of the miracles, for example, pointed to his use of a "Sign Source"—the basis, perhaps for his list of seven *semeia* (signs)—no more, no less (John 2:1-11, 4:46-54, 5:1-18, 6:1-14, 6:16-24, 9:1-41, 11:1-53). At the same time John's distinctive Christology attracted the attention of the historians of religion and it became fashionable to look for evidence in John of various influences—Gnostic, Mandean, or otherwise Hellenistic—as a way of accounting for its peculiarities.

It is not necessary to spell out in detail the various lines of inquiry emerging in those early days of biblical criticism. What has just been said about the gospels is enough to indicate the direction and the mood that typified the new approach, and to explain certain aspects of the next stage of development: the so-called "Quest for the Historical Jesus." At the risk of oversimplifying a complex interweaving of theological and historical interests, two movements of thought and inquiry seem to contribute directly to that (largely nineteenth-century) field of research: first, stemming from the literary criticism, there was a growing consensus that, since Mark was the earliest gospel, and "base" for the others, Mark should have priority as a historically reliable source for recovering "the real" Jesus, behind the "theological accretions" that Paul and others had thrown around him. Alongside this, and partly prompting it, was the new theological current identified with Friedrich Schleiermacher (1768-1834), in which a rationalistic skepticism about the Bible merged with a romantic optimism about the person of Jesus. In this view, Christ was to be preferred to Christianity, and making common cause with the students of Mark scholars were persuaded that their new methods of inquiry could "peel back" the layers of churchly legendizing until they found the simple, unadorned (and rationally "believable") Jesus of history.

Underlying both movements, and part of the intellectual "spirit of the Age," was a basic confidence in the *historical method* of inquiry. History during this period sought to be recognized as "scientific"—dealing objectively with its data (*bruta facta*), testing the reliability of its sources, and accepting as "true" only those things that managed to pass the rigid criteria of the historical reason. One of the criteria, of course, was that of conformity to natural laws of cause and effect, and anything that could not be explained thereby—for example, the reported miracles of the Bible— was inadmissible as historical fact. It should be noted that this limitation was inherent in the methodology and was not necessarily a contemptuous dismissal of God or theistic religion. It reflects rather a radically different concept of religion itself, of the way God works in and through the "historical," of the manifestation (in Schleiermacher's terms) of "the Infinite in the finite." But the discipline of the historical method was adopted in those days even by theologians of a more orthodox stance, not with a view to reducing the role of faith or of minimizing the importance of Christ, but precisely for the purpose (as they saw it) of salvaging the pristine purity of "original" Christianity from the accumulated (and disposable) baggage of the intervening centuries. Extravagant as this may seem to us now, many "questers" for the historical Jesus were bent on a rescue mission, intent on defending what they regarded as ultimate and irreducible, against the widespread attacks of Christianity's "cultured despisers."[62]

To attempt any thorough review or critique of the "old quest" (as it is sometimes called) would go far beyond our aims here. It is enough now to acknowledge its contributions to the ongoing work of New Testament studies, and to speak of one or two countermovements that effectively challenged both its methods and its presuppositions. The course of scholarship in biblical criticism, as in many other fields of investigation, has its digressions and its "wrong-way" streets. Progress is rarely traced in straight lines, more often in zig-zags; we learn from our predecessors' mistakes as well as from their successes. Perhaps the Quest for the Historical Jesus may yet prove, by that reckoning, a valuable lesson. At least in retrospect later generations learned something of value about both the meaning of *history* and the nature of the New Testament *gospels*.

It was the monumental work of Albert Schweitzer (1875-1965) that, more than any other single factor, called into question the value of certain nineteenth-century biographies of Jesus, and thus raised serious doubts about the validity of the entire Quest. His book, *Von Reimarus Zu Wrede*

---

[62]A phrase borrowed from Schleiermacher's famous *On Religion: Speeches to Its Cultured Despisers;* see the translation of John Oman (New York: Harper and Brothers, 1958).

(English title: *The Quest of the Historical Jesus*),[63] was a masterful critique of many scholarly attempts to reconstruct "the life of Jesus." In effect, Schweitzer showed, they were all—whether Rationalist, Romantic, Idealist, or "Imaginative"—guilty of *modernizing* Jesus, of portraying him according to the bias of the biographer. Historical reconstruction turned out to be little more than the historian's own reflected image, or—at best—another instance of biblical eisegesis, in which the biographer "finds" the kind of Jesus that he has already decided the texts contain. Even yet, this book serves as a classic reminder of that side of the hermeneutical problem to which I have earlier referred—the reader and his own worldview. And how difficult it is to avoid that perennial tendency to force the gospels to yield "meaning" dictated by our time and place!

Meanwhile another line of investigation had raised questions about the nature of the gospels and, indirectly, about the validity of their use as historical sources. Already, by 1900, research by Hermann Gunkel and others on the book of Genesis and the Psalms had focused on the role of the faithful community in giving shape to particular units of tradition found to be embedded in the books as we now have them. Borrowing terminology used in criticism of other ancient literature these scholars analyzed Genesis and isolated instances of *saga, legend,* and *myth.* They found that like much of the folklore of Mesopotamia, parts of Genesis seemed to take shape in the process of oral transmission, long before being gathered and "edited" by the Yahwist or Elohist. Sagas and legends often were used to account for the *origin* of things—place names, personal names, religious rituals, even ethnic or tribal characteristics—and such stories were called *etiologies.*[64] Similarly, in the Psalms, a classification scheme emerged, based largely on the *form* of the song, which in turn reflected its function (whether as Hymn, Lament, Thanksgiving, or something else) in the worship of Israel. As this kind of analysis was refined and applied to other parts of Scripture, it came to be known as *Formgeschichte* or Form Criticism, and it was this discipline that provided New Testament scholars materials for their strongest objections to the "old quest."

---

[63]Albert Schweitzer, *The Quest of the Historical Jesus,* trans. W. Montgomery, from the first German edition of 1906 (New York: MacMillan, 1962).

[64]Etiology (sometimes "aetiology") comes from αἴτιος, Greek for "cause"; cf. the introduction to Hermann Gunkel's *Genesis,* translated as *The Legends of Genesis* (New York: Schocken Books, 1964).

One of the basic presuppositions of that Quest was that Mark, as the earliest of the gospels, should be the least "theological" and therefore the most "historical" of sources for the "historical Jesus." Form critics found cause to challenge this at two vital points: first, they discovered that, even though in some ways the Markan Christology was relatively primitive, the Gospel of Mark was nonetheless "theological" in its basic orientation and purpose. Scholars now recognized that Mark, just as much as the later John, was grounded in the faith that Jesus was the Christ, the Son of God, and was in fact written to propagate that faith, *not* to provide later historians with anecdotal material for a "biography" of a Galilean carpenter turned teacher. None of the gospels, it was now argued, was designed to make Jesus understandable in terms of a secular causal nexus, and all alike therefore defied modern attempts to "peel away" the layers of theological accretion and find "the historical Jesus." In the second place, it was shown that even Mark was the product of earlier formative forces at work in the faithful community—collectively referred to by the Form Critics as *Sitz im Leben* (the "situation in the life" of the Church). Such forces included (1) preaching or proclamation of the "good news" of Christ; (2) defense of the gospel or controversy (for example, church vs. synagogue); (3) catechesis or teaching, instruction of new converts; and (4) worship or liturgical usage of material. As in the case of certain Old Testament material, so in the gospels small units or *pericopae,* individual stories and sayings, seemed to have taken their distinctive *forms* according to the particular way they were used in the period of oral transmission. So it became clear that whatever could be known of "the historical Jesus" had been mediated to us from the outset by those who adapted it to suit their needs and purposes, and the gospels' order of events could scarcely be taken as a chronologically accurate order for biographical reconstruction.[65]

Scholarly reaction to Form Criticism and its findings has varied from predominantly positive affirmation to almost adamant rejection. Form Critics themselves are not unanimous about definitions of the forms—for example, whether a saying should be classified as "pronouncement story"

---

[65]Thus the work of the evangelists (gospel writers) was seen as collecting and arranging, somewhat arbitrarily, the numerous pericopae (narrative units) that had accumulated through the years, thereby accounting for variations in setting among the gospels for certain sayings—for example, Jesus' teaching on prayer (compare Matt. 6:7-15 and Luke 11:1-4); cf. Edgar V. McKnight, *What Is Form Criticism?* (Philadelphia: Fortress Press, 1969), in the very valuable series, Guides to Biblical Scholarship, ed. Dan O. Via, Jr. et al.

or as "exhortation."[66] Nor did they always agree among themselves as to the correlation between "form" and "function," a weakness of methodology which sometimes led to unwarranted or, at least, highly questionable evaluations of the material under investigation. And yet, despite such admitted weaknesses, the approach has proved fruitful in study of the gospels, if only for calling attention to their *kerygmatic* character.[67] Written "from faith to faith," the gospels proclaim "the good news of God" and all share in some respect the avowed objective of John (20:31): "these are written that you may believe. . . ."

Although the old confidence in Mark's historical accuracy and in the modern scholar's ability to write a "life of Jesus" was duly shaken, students of the gospels, as if to compensate, gained a new confidence in attempts to trace the development of the *kerygma* or apostolic preaching.[68] If one could not with assurance know exactly what Jesus did and said, at least the prospect of knowing what the earliest Christians believed and proclaimed *about* him was hopeful. So in the early twentieth century, along with a general shift of mood among secular historians, came a revival among biblical scholars of the interest in "biblical theology" in general, and in New Testament theology in particular. It was more than just a change of emphasis; there seemed to be a rather profound difference in the kinds of questions being addressed to the gospel material. Instead of asking (with much of nineteenth-century historiography) "what really happened?"—in the case of a reported miracle, for example—and trying to supply a perfectly rational explanation, the question became "what did Mark (or the

---

[66]Classification of the pericopae, traceable to Martin Dibelius and Rudolf Bultmann, usually includes (1) the Passion Narrative (story of Jesus' arrest, trial, and execution); (2) paradigms or pronouncement stories (of isolated events leading to a concluding lesson); (3) legends or "tales" (of isolated events told for "human interest"); (4) myths or stories involving a divine-human encounter; (5) miracle stories; and (6) hortatory sayings or admonitions (usually very brief).

[67]*Kerygma* was the Greek word for "something announced, proclaimed" (as by a κῆρυξ, "messenger"), adopted by modern scholars to refer to the essential claims made by early Christians about Jesus—that he was the Christ, foretold by the prophets, who suffered crucifixion as atonement for sin, was raised by God and now offers salvation to those baptized in his name. In the gospels, as J. M. Robinson said (*A New Quest of the Historical Jesus* [London: SCM Press, 1959] 37), "History survived only as kerygma."

[68]C. H. Dodd set the tone with his *The Apostolic Preaching and Its Development* (London: Hodder and Stoughton, 1936), showing how pregospel kergyma might be represented in certain speeches in Acts and in the letters of Paul.

early church) *mean* by reporting that miracle?'' Or ''what *is* (not was) the significance of this or that understanding of Christ for human existence here and now?''[69]

In this connection the contributions of Rudolf Bultmann must be given special notice, since he not only blazed new trails in the application of Form Criticism to the gospels but also brought his critical insights to bear on the modern hermeneutical problem. Bultmann (1884-1976) has been called ''the most influential New Testament scholar of our time,''[70] a claim that even those who disagree with his conclusions would hardly dispute. While the results of critical analysis of the gospels left little material for a ''historical Jesus,'' Bultmann said, discriminating study of the teachings might still yield a glimpse of his characteristic message—enough of an encouragement that some of his outstanding students are today leaders in the so-called ''new quest.''[71] But for Bultmann the viability or value of the Christian faith did not depend on any such reconstruction, and in fact, he argued, attempts to ground faith on ''historical proof'' flew directly in the face of a truly Christian faith. In Christ and his cross God called humanity away from all false security and worldly values to radical trust and obedience to God alone. Bultmann, in many of his writings, gave to his interpretation of the Christian *kerygma* a definitely Existentialist flavor, emphasizing the function of the gospel as confronting us with the ultimate *decision* between the Kingdom of God or the kingdoms of this world.

Bultmann was convinced that for twentieth-century readers the real and abiding Word of God in the New Testament was obscured, if not utterly obliterated, by its first-century wrappings, its mythical language and worldview. Therefore, he suggested, to determine by exegesis its meaning for our time requires conscious and systematic ''demythologizing''—removal of those antiquated, culturally conditioned wrappings, so that God's

---

[69]Beyond the purview of our survey, but closely allied to this movement, was the theological current associated with Karl Barth, Emil Brunner, and others in Europe (as well as Richard and Reinhold Niebuhr in the United States), sometimes collectively regarded as ''Neoorthodoxy.''

[70]So writes Howard C. Kee, *Jesus in History* (New York: Harcourt, Brace and World, 1970) 24.

[71]For example, Ernst Käsemann (often credited with initiating the ''new quest'')—see his famous reunion lecture, ''The Problem of the Historical Jesus,'' in *Essays on New Testament Themes* (Naperville IL: Alec R. Allenson, 1964); cf. Günther Bornkamm, *Jesus of Nazareth*, trans. Irene and Fraser McLuskey (New York: Harper and Row, 1960).

summons can be heard and authentic faith may be possible. What he meant was, of course, not literally stripping pages from the Bible, but rather an *interpretation* (drawing on Existentialism) that would enable the reader to internalize the mythical and thus to enter into genuine dialogue with the God who meets us in the Bible. To Bultmann both a Fundamentalist defensiveness about the historicity of the gospels *and* a Liberal reductionism missed the point and even served to replace faith in the Living Word with an idolatrous devotion to the written Word, on the one hand, or a fruitless dependence on human reason, on the other. His method, of course, seemed to many a case of "a remedy worse than the disease," and even yet scholars wonder whether the way indicated by his hermeneutic was not a modern form of ancient Docetism. The debate on this and other points of Bultmann's impressive teaching goes on to this day.[72]

The fruits of German scholarship, especially in the period between the World Wars, set an agenda, it seems, for the rest of this century. Nor was it only on the New Testament the Germans worked; building on the earlier work of Wellhausen and Gunkel, scholars such as Gerhard von Rad examined the early traditions of ancient Israel with a view to showing how conscious theological reflection had shaped them, remaking simple tribal stories into affirmations of faith. Thus Old Testament study, like that of the New, began to emphasize the kerygmatic *message* that the earlier, more analytic investigations had ignored or set to one side. In line with a widespread concern for synthesis, for seeing the whole picture, Old Testament scholars produced a number of remarkable "theologies"—a trend that spilled over into Britain and to America. And since mid-century there has been an increasingly centripetal movement of scholarship—that is, away from self-contained and sharply defined specialities toward greater exchange and cross-disciplinary collaboration. While specialization continued to flourish (and still does), we have seen in recent decades a refreshing willingness for specialists to talk to each other, indeed to acknowledge the need to learn from each other. So the History of Religion school profited from the Semiticist (and vice versa), and the archaeologist assisted both; Talmudic scholars have enriched the Christian interpretation of the New

---

[72]For an example of the scholarly dialogue sparked by Bultmann, see H. W. Bartsch, *Kerygma and Myth*, trans. Reginald H. Fuller (New York: Harper and Row, 1961); also Carl E. Braaten and R. A. Harrisville, *The Historical Jesus and the Kerygmatic Christ* (Nashville: Abingdon Press, 1964).

Testament, and the theologians from both sides have inspired the biblical critics to raise new and better questions.[73]

We must be content with two examples of the most recent concerns among the many varied fronts now open to biblical students. One will serve to illustrate the modern shift toward the larger picture, as opposed to former "microscopic" analyses of details, and the other will exemplify the trend toward interdisciplinary collaboration as well as the way that the latest discoveries and techniques of our century have revolutionized our thinking about the Bible.

The first, which has come to be known as Redaction Criticism, grew out of the findings of Form Criticism and is, in many respects, dependent on them. But here the focus changes from the bits and pieces of oral tradition to the gospel as a whole, and especially to the contributions of the editor (German: *Redaktor* —hence *Redaktionsgeschichte*). Among the form critics the authors of the gospels were little more than the gatherers and compilers of pericopae, stringing their pearls together in more or less random order, but adding nothing of substance on their own. The new departure of Redaction Criticism was to look for and find evidence of a more active and creative role for the gospel writers. In some respects the work of Wilhelm Wrede (1859-1906) had pointed the way and provided a model for this kind of inquiry, when he suggested that the several references to Jesus' demanding "secrecy" of those he healed or exorcised were in fact the invention of Mark, reflecting *his* Christology, not the authentic words of Jesus.[74] Mark's "messianic secret"—Wrede argued—was his way of dealing with the tension between certain kerygmatic claims of the post-resurrection church and traditions about his actual career prior to the cross. If it was only by the resurrection from the dead (cf. Romans 1:4) that Jesus was revealed as Messiah, then Mark felt compelled to "explain" how Jesus kept his Messiahship secret in the time beforehand. In this and other ways Mark and all the gospel writers proved themselves more than passive collectors of tradition; they were rather to be seen and appreciated as mold-

---

[73]We cannot forget that it was Karl Barth's *Epistle to the Romans* (1918) that first broke ground for this latter-day development, bringing to bear on biblical exegesis the concerns of the pastor and theologian—Barth's magnum opus is his *Church Dogmatics* in four volumes (1936-1969).

[74]Wilhelm Wrede, *Das Messiasgeheimnis in den Evangelien* [*The Messianic Secret in the Gospels*] (Göttingen: Vandenhoeck und Ruprecht, 1901); cf. the comments of Norman Perrin, *What Is Redaction Criticism?* (Philadelphia: Fortress Press, 1969) 7-13.

ers of that tradition, even as theologians in their own right. And in recent decades it has become almost commonplace to treat each gospel independently, rather than harmonistically, seeking to find what is most distinctive about each, and asking about the motives, peculiar concerns, and emphases that express themselves in it. Although the older questions of authorship (who was Mark? who was Matthew? and so on) have now subsided, there is perhaps a compensating interest today in the fascinating individuality of Matthew, Mark, and Luke, if not as identifiable historical persons, then (more importantly) as real preachers and propagators of the faith.[75]

The second example of recent developments is not so easy to define or to label, because it is a convergence of multiple scholarly interests rather than a single specialty, like a hub with many spokes. I refer to the vast and still growing field of biblical archaeology and its closely related ally, comparative literature. For many observers nothing better epitomizes the twentieth-century contribution to biblical scholarship than the remarkable work by countless teams of diggers, representing scores of nationalities, hundreds of institutions (universities, foundations, and other agencies), and involving Jew and Christian, Catholic and Protestant, conservative and liberal, often side by side. It has enlisted scholars of both Old and New Testament, and has operated on the combined expertise of a variety of disciplines both within and outside the strictly "biblical" fields. A typical archaeological expedition might bring together surveyors, architectural experts, geologists, paleographers, photographers, and possibly others, as conditions dictate, besides the host of laborers wielding shovels, buckets, and camel-hair brushes. Here is a very visible demonstration of modern partnership between religion and science and a collaboration of "brain" and "brawn" as well.

But this is to speak of the situation at present, and to appreciate fully the state of the art today we need to look back (if only briefly) and recall the earliest stages—little more than a century ago. Archaeology as a *scientific* enterprise is relatively new. Of course people have often, through the centuries, expressed their curiosity about relics and holy places, and

---

[75]As foremost examples and exponents of Redaction Criticism: G. Bornkamm, G. Barth, and H. J. Held, *Tradition and Interpretation in Matthew* (Philadelphia: Westminster Press, 1963); Hans Conzelmann, *The Theology of St. Luke* (New York: Harper and Row, 1961); W. Marxsen, *Mark the Evangelist* (Nashville: Abingdon Press, 1969).

certain ancients tried their hand at recovering the ruins of the past. But too often these attempts were prompted by motives more mercenary than academic, and valuable excavation sites were plundered by careless—even if well-meaning—diggers.

To see how far matters have advanced in our time, we need only recall how uncertain was our knowledge of Palestinian geography before 1850, when American professor Edward Robinson made his firsthand survey and practically rewrote the map of Palestine. Before that date very few places mentioned in Scripture could be located with confidence, because over the centuries cities had been destroyed, abandoned, and gradually covered over by the loess and sands of time, or they had changed their names according to a succession of different conquerors—Greek, Nabatean, Roman, Turkish. Robinson found the problem in his day complicated by local lore, often based on pious traditions about the identity of certain "holy places" but having little factual foundation. Even Robinson could not undo all the mistakes of previous geographers and cartographers, but it is to his everlasting credit that he personally investigated hundreds of supposed biblical sites, correcting many false locations, and thus set a scientific course for mapping "lands of the Bible" ever since.

Another pioneer whose work dramatically changed the course of archaeology was the British Egyptologist, Sir W. M. Flinders Petrie (1853-1942). It was Petrie who managed to bring order out of the chaos attending most excavations before 1890, when he began exploring in Palestine. He insisted on thorough and detailed records, from the initial ground survey to the very last report, on every phase of any expedition. He taught his teams to excavate methodically, taking pains to preserve every least artifact uncovered, as potentially valuable evidence. Above all, Petrie developed a basic methodology for determining the relative date of objects found; this involved essentially two things: (1) the technique of stratigraphy, and (2) ceramic typology. Stratigraphy denotes the process of reading the various *layers* (strata) in a tell, or excavation site.[76] The ruined remains of an ancient city might disclose many strata, corresponding to the number of times it was built, destroyed, and rebuilt over the centuries. As a rule, of course, the deeper one digs into the tell, the earlier the level of occupation one finds, but to get beyond this approximate and relative chronological sequence

---

[76]Tell (or *tel*) is a Semitic word for "hill" or "mound," usually with a flattened top, built over the ages by succeeding occupations.

there are objects embedded in the dirt or debris that may be dated more precisely. This is where the ceramic typology comes in. Petrie observed that the lowly but ever-present potsherd[77] offered one of the surest clues of all for dating the surrounding stratum, because the form and style of clay pottery changed from age to age in a remarkably regular pattern, and thereby provided a fairly exact frame of reference for chronological classification. Other artifacts—for example, coins, tools, ornaments, weapons and such— may also serve to date the stratum in which they are found, but the more abundant potsherds became and remain yet "the essential alphabet" for reading the age of the strata.[78]

This photograph of an archaeological excavation at Yafo (Jaffa) in Israel shows clearly defined strata—levels of human occupation and destruction—down to Iron Age II (950-586 BCE). Very ancient sites often disclose twenty or more distinct levels of occupation. (Photo by Milton P. Brown)

---

[77]A potsherd (or "shard" for short) is a fragment of a clay vessel; rarely are whole pots or dishes recovered except in tombs, but these pieces—especially parts of the lip, base, and handle—prove very durable and (to the eye of the expert) highly valuable clues in assigning dates to the strata where they are found.

[78]The expression is used by James B. Pritchard in his very helpful book, *Archaeology and the Old Testament* (Princeton: Princeton University Press, 1958) 9.

Building on the foundations laid by Robinson and Petrie, subsequent generations of explorers and diggers have advanced our knowledge of the lands and people of the Bible in more ways than I have space to list. Credit for such achievements, to be fair, must go not only to the scholars and teams who actually went and dug in the ground but also to many generous sponsors—corporate and individual donors—who invested their wealth in those expensive campaigns. The only return on such investment is the consciousness of having a share in a risky, but exciting enterprise, on the cutting edge of historical inquiry.

But how has all this helped us to understand the Bible? Though I cannot begin to list all the ways, let me try to state in summary fashion the general, overall impact of biblical archaeology, and then cite a few particular examples by way of illustration. First, in general, the findings of the archaeologists have pushed back the horizons of the historical scene on which the drama of the Bible was enacted. Bringing to the light the earliest habitations of the people of Israel inevitably meant revealing the ethnic and geographic roots of their ancestors, tracing the migrations of Arameans and

An excavation in progress at Shechem, scene of Joshua's covenant renewal ceremony (Joshua 24). Many people and many kinds of skills are involved in a successful "dig" like this one. (Photo by Milton P. Brown)

Amorites, Hittites and Hyksos, and others who interacted with them—in short, widening the scope of the inquiry to include virtually the whole "Fertile Crescent," from the Nile Delta to the Persian Gulf.[79] And in the process many inscriptions and documents of Israel's neighbors have turned up, some of which contain remarkably parallel stories, hymns, or other affinities with biblical literature, raising questions about the cultural context or source of much of our Old Testament. To say the least, comparative studies made it abundantly clear that biblical Israelites were often influenced by, and indebted to, their neighbors, and that even their very distinctive faith in Yahweh could no longer be understood or properly appreciated apart from its historical-cultural environment. Moreover, the alliance between the archaeologist in the field and the linguist in his study has practically rewritten the lexical and grammatical textbooks on "Biblical Hebrew" in the past half-century, making possible as never before a resolution of certain textual tangles and many exegetical problems.

A few specific examples will help to explicate these claims. Archaeology has been a valuable aid in establishing biblical chronology. Rarely did the writers of antiquity take pains to date the events that they recorded, and when they did (as in Samuel and Kings) it was by reference to "the fourth year of King Hezekiah" or the like—of value to us only if we know precisely when that king began to reign, relative to some firm point corresponding to our own scheme (before or during the Common Era). By providing such checkpoints, various inscriptions and documents have removed much of the guesswork, not only in the period of the kings but even for the time of the judges and, to some extent, that of Moses and the Exodus. The stele of an Egyptian Pharaoh, erected about 1230 BCE, tells of an Egyptian victory over "the people of Israel"—evidence that there was such a national entity by that date. Further, the "store cities" of Pithom and Raames (Exod. 1:11) seem to correspond to those said to be built by slave labor in the Nineteenth Dynasty, pointing to Ramses II as the prob-

---

[79]"Fertile Crescent" is commonly used to refer to that arc of relatively arable land embracing ancient Canaan northward into Syria and eastward to Mesopotamia, skirting the northern edge of the Arabian Desert, and southeastward to the Gulf. This was the route of main roads between the two great river civilizations of antiquity, making it vividly clear why the land occupied by Israel-Judah was so often an object of conquest and the source of international dispute.

able Pharaoh of the Exodus.[80] The Amarna Letters, early fourteenth-century correspondence from Palestinian vassals to the Pharaoh, together with the findings of Nelson Glueck in Transjordania enable scholars to fix upper and lower limits for the period of Israel's "entry" into Canaan.[81] And in the time of the monarchy various records from Assyria and Babylonia provide dozens of valuable cross-references for establishing the dates, for example, of the revolt of Jehu (2 Kings 9) and Nebuchadrezzar's invasion of Judah.

Though the problem of chronology for the New Testament was never so great as in the Old Testament, one troublesome area—dating events in the career of Paul—has been illuminated by the discovery at Delphi of an inscription in Greek naming L. Junius Gallio as Proconsul of Achaia. In the Acts of the Apostles 18:12-17 is the story of Paul's hearing before Gallio at Corinth, but without any indication of date. Because of its reference to the Emperor Claudius the Delphi inscription makes it fairly certain that Gallio served in Corinth from 51 to 52 CE, thus establishing one fixed point in Paul's career, around which earlier and later events can be relatively ordered.[82] If Paul's letters to the Thessalonians were written from Corinth, as seems likely, they can with some confidence be dated in the year 50-51 CE.

Archaeology has clarified many previously obscure matters—ancient customs, laws, myth and ritual. Findings have been especially fruitful for the Patriarchal Age (ca. 1800-1500 BCE) or what the experts call the Middle Bronze Age, precisely the period where biblical history was always most uncertain. From Mari, an ancient Amorite kingdom on the upper Euphrates, more than 20,000 clay tablets—mostly diplomatic correspon-

---

[80]A more complete statement of the case for a thirteenth-century exodus is in B. W. Anderson, *Understanding the Old Testament* (Englewood Cliffs NJ: Prentice-Hall, 1975) 41-45, which depends largely on archaeologists W. F. Albright and G. Ernest Wright.

[81]The Amarna Letters disclose the anxiety of Egypt in its shaky hold on certain cities in Canaan, the intrigue and possible insubordination of certain vassals there, plus mention of 'Apiru—possibly a term cognate with "Hebrew"—causing trouble in the land. Glueck's work in the territory of ancient Edom and Moab showed that these nations would have presented real resistance to an Israelite passage (Num. 20) only after 1250 BCE. It now seems likely that not all the "twelve tribes" left Egypt with Moses or entered Canaan en masse; cf. Martin Noth, *History of Israel*, rev. ed. (London: Adam and Charles Black; New York: Harper & Brothers, 1960).

[82]A thorough analysis of the inscription is given by Adolf Deissmann, *Paul: a Study in Social and Religious History* (New York: Harper and Brothers 1957) 261-86.

dence and business records of the eighteenth century BCE—provide evidence of the ethnic and linguistic ties between the Amorites and people of Abraham.[83] At Nuzi, in the land of the Hurrians (probably to be identified with the biblical Horites), were found records bearing directly on Genesis stories, such as that of Abram and Hagar (Gen. 16) or that of Jacob and his wives (Gen. 29-30). Because Abram's wife Sarai was childless, she gave her handmaid Hagar to Abram to bear him children. This, it seems, was precisely what Hurrian law required of barren wives; in fact, it turns out that the husband, in such cases, was actually forbidden to expel the concubine or her child, in the event the first wife did eventually have a child. If such laws governed Abram's conduct, it would explain his reluctance to expel Hagar and Ishmael after the birth of Isaac (cf. Gen. 21:8-11). Again, in the story of Jacob and his agreement with Laban, it turns out that the latter acted strictly according to Hurrian custom in first giving his daughter Leah, then the younger Rachel, in marriage. Also, the once-puzzling episode of Laban's *teraphim* ("household gods" in Gen. 31:34 RSV) becomes clearer in the light of the Nuzi texts, where they are symbols of clan leadership and property rights; Rachel's theft of these figurines was apparently her way of "insuring" her husband's title to his goods and his independence of the wily Laban. In view of these and other close affinities with the cultural and social conditions of upper Mesopotamia, the delineation of patriarchal faith has become far sharper than was ever thought possible. While there is much that still reflects the legendizing of monarchical times, we have learned lately to respect the considerable layer of authentic historical data in Genesis, and to appreciate its contribution toward a far more realistic portrait of Israel's ancestors.

The numerous codes of law that have been unearthed also cast light on both the general background of the Hebrews and specific laws in Exodus. The picture that emerges from Mesopotamia in the early second millennium is one of intense interaction among city-states, growing domination of Amoritic people, and the pervasive influence of their law and order. One of the strongest Amoritic states, eventually controlling most of Mesopotamia, was Babylon. Its famous ruler, Hammurabi, systematized (and pos-

---

[83]The Mari Texts contain a number of personal and/or place names cognate with some in Genesis—for example, Nahor, Ish-mael, and Levi—plus references to prophecy with formulae much like the "thus saith . . . " of the Bible. The language of Mari was a form of Northwest Semitic, of the same family as Hebrew.

sibly revised) the vast legal tradition as he received it (eighteenth century?),[84] and left much of it inscribed on a black diorite stele in cuneiform, which was recovered from Susa in 1902. Once its contents became known, comparison with the biblical codes of law was inevitable. In both form and substance many of Hammurabi's laws were found to be remarkably similar to laws in the Covenant Code (Exod. 21:1-23:13) in particular. Common to both sets was the basic principle of *lex talionis* (law of retaliation)—"an eye for an eye . . . " (Exod. 21:24)—as well as such procedural rules as demanding an oath "before the gods" in cases of disputed testimony.[85] While major differences also appeared—for example, a more sophisticated society in Babylonia, greater latitude for tempering justice with mercy in Hebrew laws—the overwhelming degree of similarity ruled out mere coincidence, and scholars acknowledged Israel's debt here, not perhaps by way of direct borrowing or conscious imitation of Babylon, but more likely by way of the Canaanites, who had already absorbed the common stock of Semitic law, then passed it on to the Israelite settlers.

The myth and ritual of its neighbors also left an impression on the early Israelites, an impression that we can now recognize in various parts of the Old Testament, thanks to discoveries of Babylonian, Canaanite, and Egyptian documents. To cite just a few examples, texts of the ancient Epic of Gilgamesh—possibly Sumerian in origin—include a story of a world-engulfing flood, complete with "ark" and birds released to search for land, so similar to the story of Noah (Gen. 6-9) that both must be traceable to a common stock of pre-Israelite lore; again, the differences are more pronounced than the agreements, and comparison serves to demonstrate the peculiar genius of Israel for turning such stories into vehicles of her highly ethical religion. Likewise, the Babylonian *Enuma Elish* contains an account of the creation of "the heavens and the earth" by the god Marduk, victor over the "monster of primeval chaos," Tiamat. In Genesis 1, it seems, there are echoes of such a mythical account—for example, in the

---

[84]Scholars still have some disagreement over the dates of Hammurabi, but a strong consensus puts him at his peak around 1700 BCE. It is no longer considered likely that he is the Amraphel of Genesis 14:9, although "Shinar" was the usual Hebrew term for Babylon.

[85]In Babylonia this involved swearing before a sacred idol to affirm the truth (cf. "the whole truth, and nothing but . . . ") of one's testimony, the clear implication being that lying in the presence of deity was sure to bring swift retribution. Cf. Exodus 22:8-9, where parties to a dispute were to "come before God."

reference to "the deep" (Heb. *tehom*, cognate with *ti'amat*) and the concept of primeval chaos represented by it. But, here too, Israelite monotheism has removed all but the slightest trace of the older, polytheistic myth, and completely recast its plot to serve religious purposes of an entirely different kind. In Babylonia the story of creation apparently figured prominently in the annual New Year celebration, a time when Marduk was said to be reenthroned, setting "the destinies" of his people for another year. Study of this festival and certain hymns that may have been used in the enthronment ritual has suggested to some scholars that Israel, too, once celebrated the New Year with a similar ritual enthronement of Yahweh, pointing to Psalms 93 and 95-99 (all dealing with the Lord as King) as evidence of the practice. Whether or not the parallels support that contention, careful study of the Hebrew Psalter in the light of Babylonian and Canaanite texts shows unmistakable signs of the influence of Near Eastern mythology on some of its hymns.[86]

Of course, Israel's response to such influence might be violent opposition as well as acceptance and adaptation, as the struggle against Baalism so clearly shows. The Elijah Cycle in 1 Kings and the books of Hosea and Jeremiah testify to the long-standing contest between two cults *and* two cultures, represented by Yahweh and the *ba'alim*. But the powerful attraction of Canaanite religion and the strenuous opposition of the Hebrew prophets have been richly illuminated since the discovery in 1929 of numerous clay tablets at Ras Shamra.[87] Among these were texts containing the Canaanite story of El (or Father Shunem), his consort Asherah, their son Ba'al ("rider of the clouds") and daughter Anath. For the first time scholars could piece together the basic mythology of the cult of Ba'al, not only clarifying specific references to it in the Bible but also enriching our understanding of the whole cultural complex in which Israel began its life in "the Promised Land."

---

[86]The primitive motif of creation through conflict seems to cast a long shadow, lingering behind the language of Psalm 73:13-15, Psalm 89; 9-10, and possibily in Psalm 29:10.

[87]Ras Shamra is the modern name for the site on the coast of Syria; the excavations uncovered the cemetery, then the ruins of the ancient city called Ugarit. J. B. Pritchard (*Archaeology and the Old Testament,* 106-26) recounts the story of the deciphering of the Ugaritic tablets and summarizes their mythological contents. For a more complete translation see Pritchard's *Ancient Near Eastern Texts Relating to the Old Testament* (Princeton: Princeton University Press, 1955).

Finally, archaeology and its allied disciplines have served to supplement, and sometimes to correct, information or impressions derived from the Bible. In some way, it seems, virtually every period of biblical history has been illuminated in the sense of adding pertinent data about kings, political conditions, and the like. It may indeed be said that the results of modern archaeology have *generally* confirmed and supported the essential reliability of the Bible's *historical* statements. Yet, to avoid misunderstanding, it must also be said that no reputable archaeologist would claim that his purpose was either to "prove" or "disprove" the Bible. As a scientist he will not predetermine his conclusions, and this means leaving open the possibility that findings may at times call into question certain "facts" as reported in the Bible. Moreover, as in other areas of interpretation, the findings of today may be challenged by those of tomorrow and, in any case, are subject to reevaluation at all times. Above all, it is imperative to remember the nature of the biblical literature, and to keep in mind that purely *historical* accuracy (in *our* sense) was seldom if ever its purpose. Foremost for biblical writers was what *God* was doing and saying to his people through those "mighty acts"—events of history interpreted by faith—and there is no doubt that the facts and figures that seem so important to us were only incidental to them.

One case in point is the reign of Omri as king of Israel. In the Bible (1 Kings 16:23-28) he gets only six verses, mostly words blaming him for the "evil" he did—explained only by a vague reference to "idols." But according to the Moabite Stone, a stele of Mesha, king of Moab, Omri had subjugated Moab; Assyrian documents referring to descendants of Omri years later as "the house of Omri" offer a much fuller account of that king's importance; and by contrast such extrabiblical sources underscore for us the very specialized motives of the biblical sources. In the view of our Deuteronomic Historian all of Omri's accomplishments were overshadowed by the outcome of his treaty with Phoenicia—the religious apostasy encouraged by the marriage of his son to Jezebel.[88]

To illustrate how archeological excavation has called into question certain historical statements of the Bible, one instance will suffice: the notorious instance of Ai, the Canaanite stronghold said to be attacked by

---

[88]Omri apparently sealed a treaty with Phoenicia, as was customary, by taking the Tyrian princess to be Ahab's wife, thus unwittingly inviting her to campaign for recognition of her native religion in Israel, the consequences of which the Elijah Cycle vividly portrays.

Joshua's men in Joshua 7 and 8. Excavations there (now called et-Tell) show that the city was destroyed around 2200 BCE (at least nine centuries before Joshua) and not rebuilt, except for a few domestic dwellings around 1000 BCE. Chances are, as W. F. Albright contended, that the Deuteronomic writer or his source had confused Ai with *Bethel,* a mile and a half to the west, which was (according to archaeologists) destroyed around 1250.[89]

Of all the expeditions that could be cited for filling gaps in our knowledge of biblical background, perhaps none is more famous now than the widely publicized work at Qumran, following the unexpected discovery of the so-called Dead Sea Scrolls. This, incidentally, also illustrates how important the fortuitous, accidental, wholly unpremeditated find can be in this field. The story of how the young goatherd happened on the cave and its contents, or how the scrolls came to scholarly attention in the midst of Arab-Israeli hostilities, is a fascinating romance, but it cannot be repeated here.[90] Let me confine the description to a few of the many ways the scrolls and the excavations at Qumran have supplemented and enhanced study of the Bible.

Mention was made earlier, in connection with textual transmission, of the tremendous value of the Dead Sea Scrolls in supplying witnesses to the Hebrew text—for example, of Isaiah—almost a thousand years earlier than previously existing (Masoretic) texts. Beside their textual value should be mentioned their contribution to the study of Palestinian paleography and to linguistics. But, more importantly for hermeneutics, the scrolls from Qumran have provided a wealth of interpretive light for students of intertestamental Judaism and, indirectly, for students of the New Testament as well. The documents are of three kinds: (a) copies of biblical books already known to us (canonical or otherwise); (b) biblical texts with *pesher*—a running commentary on the text; and (c) strictly sectarian writings, de-

---

[89]W. F. Albright, ''Israelite Conquest of Canaan in Light of Archaeology,'' *Bulletin of the American Schools of Oriental Research* 74 (1939): 11-23. For other possible explanations, cf. G. Ernest Wright, *Biblical Archaeology* (Philadelphia: Westminster Press, 1957).

[90]Many books on the scrolls tell the story—for example, Geza Vermes, *The Dead Sea Scrolls: Qumran in Perspective* (Cleveland: Collins Press, 1978); for a transcript of the goatherd's own version of his discovery, see William H. Brownlee, ''Muhammad Ed-Deeb's Own Story of His Scroll Discovery,'' in *Journal of Near Eastern Studies* 16 (October 1957): 236-39.

scribing or alluding to matters of faith and practice within the (apparently) Essene community.

From the *pesher*-type texts—for example, the Habakkuk Commentary—we gain a fascinating view of Jewish exegesis in the first two centuries before Christ, anticipating in some sense both the rabbinic methodology and the Christian use of Scripture, as found in Matthew and the letters of Paul. Parallels in terminology between the Gospel of John—for example, in the use of such opposing pairs as "light" and "darkness"—and some of the sectarian documents of Qumran have challenged New Testament scholars to reopen the old question of the provenance of that gospel and its date of origin. At many other points, as well, the Christian vocabulary has tended to find greater affinity of meaning in the sectarian scrolls than in the writings of "mainstream" (Pharisaic) Judaism.[91]

Above all, the scrolls and the results of excavation at the site of the community complex have added a whole new chapter to our knowledge of Judaism at the opening of the common era. Although the so-called "silent centuries" were never exactly silent, direct testimony to the religious life among Palestinian Jews was, before 1948, very limited and fragmentary; with the discovery of Qumran and its scrolls older impressions of Judaism (as a monolithic structure, dominated by Pharisees and Sadducees) quickly gave way to a new picture of things—ascetic Jews, retreating from their "worldly" compatriots, estranged from the Temple cultus, and prepared to await the final destruction of wickedness and the End of this Age. Here was evidence, from actual participants, of that eccentric mode of Jewish piety of which Philo and Josephus had given only hints and allusions, demanding a thorough reappraisal of our previous sources *and* of our former conception of the cradle of Christianity. The highly eschatological orientation of that community, in particular, like the finding of a long-lost piece of a jigsaw puzzle, helped to bring the picture of Judaism into better focus *and* to account for the impact on it of the Nazarene who rose up to proclaim the coming of the Kingdom of God.

---

[91]In other words, many phrases and idioms found in the scrolls enable us to reconstruct more confidently the Aramaic "original" underlying many Greek phrases, heretofore obscure—"spirit of truth," "sons of light," Paul's use of "righteousness" and "flesh," perhaps Matthew's "poor in spirit." Cf. R. E. Brown, "The Qumran Scrolls and the Johannine Gospel and Epistles," *Catholic Biblical Quarterly* 17 (1955): 403-19, 559-75; Krister Stendahl, *The School of St. Matthew and Its Use of the Old Testament* (Philadelphia: Fortress Press, 1958).

We can prolong this survey no longer. To add further examples of recent discoveries and their contributions to interpretation of the Bible would serve only to underscore what must by now be clear enough: the drama of the people of God has been highlighted as never before, filling with new color the historic and cultural background of biblical times, and making the ancient actors and their actions vividly real and three-dimensional. Truly remarkable is the bridge archaeology and its allies have built across the cultural gap that separates us from the world of the Bible; the ''traffic'' now flowing over that bridge is bound to bring about improved understanding of that distant world and, in so doing, bring about greater penetration into the meaning of the drama there enacted.

Conclusion

Our long survey of various kinds of interpretative efforts should have made clear the dynamic, ever-changing character of the human quest for meaning in the Bible. Just as the Bible itself had a history—growing gradually through the ages—so has its interpretation. In a sense, it could be said, the hermeneutical task I have traced over the past nineteen centuries partakes of the same spiritual dynamic that initially produced the books— a kind of continuing divine-human encounter, where every succeeding age has been compelled to respond to the Word, and each in its own peculiar way. It should not surprise us that the form of our questions today is not exactly the same as that of the ancients, nor even as that of our grandparents. What we have seen here of the varying moods, motives and methods of past interpreters ought to tell us how necessary it is for each new generation to search for that meaning appropriate to its own time and place. Heirs to the Scriptures of the Old and New Testaments are also heirs to that long succession of scholars and teachers we have surveyed, but if ''new occasions teach new duties,'' those who are serious about their own quest will be open to still newer insights and fresh meaning for this our own day and age.

It is in light of this rich heritage, and in view of the challenge it poses, that we move on now to consider some of the implications of what has been said for understanding the Bible's authority.

For Further Reading

Examples of early Christian hermeneutics:

Matthew 5	**Galatians 3**
Luke 24	**Hebrews** (all, but especially 1-7)
John 9	

On Rabbinic literature, Jewish hermeneutics:

Barrett, C. K. *The New Testament Background: Selected Documents.* New York: Harper and Row, 1961. Pages 139-72, esp. 139-52.

Cohen, Abraham. *Everyman's Talmud.* New York: Schocken Books, 1975. Especially the introduction.

On history of an interpretation, methodology, and so on:

Barr, James. *The Bible in the Modern World.* London/New York: SCM Press and Harper and Row, 1973.

_____ . *Old and New in Interpretation.* London/New York: SCM Press and Harper and Row, 1966.

Blackman, E. C. *Biblical Interpretation.* Philadelphia: Westminster Press, 1957.

Brown, R. E. *The Critical Meaning of the Bible.* New York: Paulist Press, 1981.

Grant, R. M. *A Short History of the Interpretation of the Bible.* Second edition revised with David Tracy. Philadelphia: Fortress Press, 1984.

Hayes, John H., and Carl R. Holladay. *Biblical Exegesis: A Beginner's Handbook.* Atlanta: John Knox Press, 1982.

"History of the Interpretation of the Bible: I. Ancient Period," by R. M. Grant; "II. Medieval and Reformation Period," by J. T. McNeill; "III. Modern Period," by Samuel Terrien. In *The Interpreter's Bible.* Volume 1. Nashville: Abingdon Press, 1951. Pages 106-41.

Kaiser, Otto, and W. G. Kümmel. *Exegetical Method.* New York: Seabury Press, 1981.

Knox, John. *Criticism and Faith.* New York/Nashville: Abingdon-Cokesbury Press, 1952.

Smart, J. D. *The Interpretation of Scripture.* Philadelphia: Westminster Press, 1961.

Stacey, David. *Interpreting the Bible.* New York: Seabury Press, 1979.

See also the series, "Guides to Biblical Scholarship," edited by Gene M. Tucker and Dan O. Via, Jr. published by Fortress Press, Philadelphia.

Chapter 6

How the Bible
Can Be "Word of God"

The Question of Authority

Readers who have endured thus far will have found along the way many points at which questions were—or could have been—-raised about the implications of this or that statement for our understanding of the Bible's inspiration and/or authority. At some of those points, in fact, I promised that we would eventually return to such questions, a promise I now will keep. Discussion of this matter has been postponed for at least two reasons: (1) its importance is such that it demands a more complete treatment than it could have received if injected or woven into the matter of previous chapters; (2) it benefits from following, rather than preceding, all that has been said of the Bible's origins, growth, transmission, and so on. One can appreciate more fully the force of the question only in the light of such basic information as the earlier chapters contain.

On the other hand, it should be pointed out that at no time in the foregoing discussion has the dimension of the divine or transcendent been simply dismissed or forgotten. It was rather assumed from the start—the underlying fact to which the whole of the Bible testifies and on which the hermeneutical efforts of all the ages rest is the faith of the Covenant People in their God and, later, in his Christ. Without that faith, without that conviction that God had made a covenant with Israel and maintained this covenant through his Word (whether spoken by his prophets or written in ''the books''), there would have been no Bible at all. So what I do now is not so much to raise an entirely new question as to make explicit and emphatic what has all along been assumed and implicit, and in doing so I look at some of the contemporary issues involved in taking the Bible as God's Word to us.

Once again let me start with familiar, traditional terminology and suggest ways of sharpening the definition or clarifying the usage of such terms. Familiarity with language sometimes proves deceptive, hiding an underlying diversity of meaning. Even the much-used phrase ''the inspiration of the Bible'' can mean different things to different people. Based on the Latin for ''in-breathed,'' the term is applied to the Bible in the sense that God ''breathed into'' these books his own Holy Spirit (*spiritus sanctus*). But, while there is widespread agreement within both Jewish and Christian communities *that* God *some*how inspired their Scriptures, there is no unanimity in either camp over *how* and *with what effect*. Christians, for example, disagree among themselves as to whether inspiration refers primarily to *persons*—the men and women whom God inspired—or primarily to the *words* they spoke or recorded in writing. Even more disputed is the question of *effect*, for some would insist that if God inspired human agents to speak *his Word*, what they uttered was wholly divine and therefore without error of any kind, while others would argue that those who spoke for God were *not* rendered somehow infallible and that inspiration *need not* imply inerrancy in every detail of their utterance.[1]

Much the same variation appears among those who use the phrase ''Word of God'' in reference to the Bible. A thoroughly biblical phrase, its provenance is primarily the prophetic tradition in which such formulas as ''thus says the Lord . . . '' and ''the word of the Lord came to . . . '' recur, suggesting direct and immediate, sometimes even ecstatic, communication. It is easy to see how the experience of the old prophets of Yahweh became a paradigm for understanding the authority of other writings, and in time ''the Word of God'' could embrace the Torah (and Moses could be called a ''prophet'' in both ''D'' and ''P''), and later the Writings as

---

[1]Within and between the two positions here mentioned are, of course, many variations and subtle distinctions, which comprise the subject matter of countless articles and books; see, for example, *Biblical Authority*, ed. Jack Rogers (Waco TX: Word Books, 1977); Paul J. Achtemeier, *The Inspiration of Scripture* (Philadelphia: Westminster Press, 1980); and others listed ''for further reading'' at the end of this chapter.

well. It may indeed be the ancient equivalent of our term canon, or the nearest thing to it in the Bible itself. In any case, the essential idea, inherited by the earliest Christians, was given classic expression in the Epistle to the Hebrews (1:1-2).

> In many and various ways God spoke of old to our fathers by the prophets; but in these last days he has spoken to us by a Son, whom he appointed the heir of all things, through whom also he created the world.

In Jesus, God's Word "became flesh and dwelled among men."[2] And finally, by the same kind of extension as Jews made in regard to Tanak, Christians began to apply "the Word of God" to the apostolic message *about* Christ (cf. Luke 1:2; 2 Cor. 4:2; 1 Thess. 1:6, 2:13) and eventually to the whole of Christian Scriptures.

But the divergence of opinion comes not so much from the somewhat flexible use of the phrase in antiquity, but rather from the later tendency to harden and fix the meaning of it for the apologetic and theological purposes of the church. As with the vocabulary of "inspiration," once people asked *how* the Bible could be Word of God, or what that implied for interpretation of it, there were bound to be different answers. Thus for some the phrase meant that the Bible was an actual "transcript" of God's words, specially dictated to passive human writers, in which case every part was equally divine, not some part more or some less.[3] For others it was enough to affirm that the Bible as a whole was—or, better, *contains*—God's Word, the supreme revelation of his Will for mankind, without insisting that every single word or syllable came directly from God.

In view of the historical development of such terms, at many points parallel to the growth of the canon itself, it seems fair to say they arose within the cultic community as verbalization of the notion already implicit in canonization—that is, that *these* books (and no others) define who that community is and what it must do, because they speak for God. In short, both sets of terms have the same essential force: to validate the *authority* of the Bible as ultimately that of God himself. And seen in this light it be-

---

[2]John 1:14, where the "Word" (Greek λόγος), said to be active in creation, no doubt alluding to God's "let there be" in Genesis 1, embraces the idea of divine reason/thought/purpose, as well as the outward expression of it (in words, or in a Person).

[3]The position is often referred to as "plenary inspiration"—that is, "full" as opposed to partial—a view that usually goes hand in hand with the insistence on verbal inerrancy, but on this point Fundamentalists may still differ among themselves.

comes clear that, whatever we may think about *how* (or by what mode) God spoke to the ancients the crucially important affirmation of the church is twofold—*that* God so *spoke,* and that he still *speaks* through the Bible.

Before I try to expand on this, however, another implication of the earlier discussion of canon needs to be emphasized here, because it serves in large measure to set the parameters of the present discussion. Just as cult and canon belong together, and there is no understanding the one without the other, so it makes sense to ask about the authority of the Bible today *only* within the context of the community for whom it is Scripture. This is not to say that "outsiders" can make no contribution to the inquiry, but it is rather that the problem of determining the significance of the Bible for contemporary life is primarily the problem of those who have already accepted the canon as a given. Or, in other words, it is precisely those who identify in one way or another with "biblical faith" and thus place themselves inside the historic cultic community who inherit the burden of the sacred tradition and the necessity of declaring who they are and what they must do. While one may find it true that the Bible has exerted an authoritative influence far beyond the walls of church and synagogue (as in American "civil religion"), this should not deny that the task of demonstrating the value or relevance of the Bible lies with the community of believers and is not to be alienated or resigned to others. Also, outsiders are not likely to take very seriously claims about the Bible's authority that have not been commended to them by exemplary thought, word, and deed on the part of "insiders."

Given this community of faith, then, with its devotion to this particular selection of books,[4] we wish to know what the nature and scope of its authority is, where the problems are, and how we may cope with them *in our time.* The emphasis on "our time" is important, for it calls attention to another "given" in our discussion: not only *this Bible,* but *this kind* of *interpretive milieu* in which we now live and move. It is not enough to take seriously the canon; we must take seriously *our world*—our present spot on the continuum of time and space—as well. This is not only to acknowledge the historical and cultural distance which separates the writers and the

---

[4]The principle would seem to hold, whether we apply it to synagogue or church, to Roman Catholic or Protestant canons. For the remainder of this discussion, as it will become clear, I will take a point of view within the Protestant Christian tradition and thus I will speak of the Scriptures of the Old (*sans* Apocrypha) and New Testaments.

interpreters of the Bible today, but it is also to recognize especially the developments in the hermeneutics of the past century. These developments have radically altered the way we understand the Bible, not only in exegesis of specific passages but in terms of its overall significance as well. So I approach the matter of its authority in the full light of all those inquiries and disciplines, questions and answers, to which the preceding chapters were devoted. And there is no turning back the clock, pretending that nothing has changed, or taking refuge in the solutions of ages past.

One illustration of what I have in mind (a false refuge) will serve to indicate the danger of this kind of anachronistic thought. In the seventeenth century, when Catholic-Protestant controversy was in full swing, and Reformers challenged the accuracy and authority of the Latin Vulgate, Westminster divines spoke of God's "immediate" inspiration of the autographs and argued for the relative purity of the original languages over against all translations. In view of their ignorance of what we know as textual criticism (a science developed only since their time), we should be able to excuse their exaggeration as a case of misguided zeal. But it becomes something more serious for people today, who ought to know better about the state of the text than the Westminster divines but who still try to defend the doctrine of verbal inerrancy by appealing to "perfect" autographs—MSS that no longer exist! Even if such a flawless Bible ever existed, it can scarcely help us now; indeed, the argument turns against its own purpose in conceding that what we *now* have is other than "perfect."[5]

At this point it may help to divide the question and look at various aspects of authority, because there is a real danger of confusion in lumping them all together. As the illustration just cited warns us, the question of biblical authority is far larger than that of textual *authenticity*—though the latter may be understood as one aspect of the former. Obviously it is important to establish, for example, which of the various text types best represents what the original writers wrote, and it is legitimate to speak of this or that text (or a particular reading) as having greater "authority" than another. In much the same sense we may claim for the original Hebrew and Greek superior "authority" relative to modern translations, when it comes

---

[5]The relevant section in the *Westminster Confession of Faith*, completed in 1646, is I. 8. This Confession became part of the "constitution" of Reformed and Presbyterian Churches, and is still a part of the Standards (Book of Confessions) that most American Presbyterians endorse; cf. Achtemeier, *The Inspiration of Scripture*, 50-57.

to doing exegesis. But if we raise the question of the authenticity of Ephesians, to ask whether in fact Paul was its author, does the weight of the question change or not? For some it does, because it now seems to involve the authority of the epistle itself, and not just the state of the text. In fact, as it has sometimes been argued in defense of Paul's authorship, to deny that Paul wrote Ephesians is to contradict what the text clearly states as well as what centuries of Christian tradition have maintained.

To settle the scholarly dispute is not my purpose here; it is rather to show that the different aspects of the question tend to vary in their significance, somewhat depending on the presuppositions one holds. In the case of Ephesians—whatever the ultimate verdict on its authenticity—recent studies in the area of pseudonymous literature, its widespread use, and its acceptance in the ancient world would seem to render suspect these presuppositions: (1) that it was a reprehensible or deceitful practice; (2) that Christians would never use it. And a close look at the history of the formation of the New Testament should put to rest the notion that the value or authority of a given book depended (or depends) on knowing who its author was.[6] Thus the anxiety over questions of authenticity is misplaced, and the more serious danger lies in the prejudicial effect of arguments that are based on mistaken presuppositions rather than the grammatical and literary evidence.[7]

Christians of the second and third centuries often applied the term "apostolic" to certain teachings and to the books which contained them, and this was largely their way of affirming the authority of these books in the sense that they faithfully represented the original apostolic preaching and teaching; they provided for later generations the most reliable link with those past events that were the fountainhead of the Faith. As we have seen, however, even in that early period "apostolic" could not be restricted to mean "actually written by an apostle." Not only was the title itself flexible—capable of meaning other than the twelve disciples of Jesus—but its primary significance was the recognition of what Papias called "the living voice" (though he preferred the oral transmission) within the gospel or

---

[6]Kurt Aland ("The Problem of Anonymity and Pseudonymity in Christian Literature of the First Two Centuries," *Journal of Theological Studies,* new series 12 [April 1961]) traces the Christian practice to a "charismatic" element, speaking for the Lord, or in the name of a revered apostle.

[7]Cf. C. L. Mitton, *The Epistle to the Ephesians* (Oxford: Clarendon, 1951) 25-29.

epistle, no matter who the author might be. What counted for people of that formative time was the assurance, born of repeated exposure to the *content* of the book, that it was true to the apostolic witness and thus to Christ himself. They were not literary or historical critics, nor were they much concerned with the kind of questions that occupy scholars today.

But it is precisely this distance, this difference between their time and ours, which is ignored or dismissed by those who object to source analysis in the Bible on the grounds that Jesus and/or the writers of the New Testament contradict the modern conclusions. It is argued that because Jesus quotes from various parts of the Torah, saying "*Moses* said . . ." and the like,[8] any scholarly investigation that denies that Moses wrote the whole Pentateuch must be wrong. Likewise in the case of Isaiah, there can be no question of the book's literary integrity and authorship by the eighth-century prophet, unless we reject the explicit testimony of the New Testament to Isaiah's authorship of all parts.[9] Unfortunately, such arguments carry weight with many Christian people because of the insinuation that to question such testimony is to deny the authority of Scripture and even the Lordship of Christ. This is to confuse the issue and to compound the problem.

The basic fallacy again lies in the presupposition that Christian faith in Jesus entails belief in his omniscience. But nowhere is such a belief said to be required; on the contrary, to attribute to Jesus power to know all things seems more characteristic of the Gnostic apocryphal gospels than of the canonical gospels, and theologically it effectively denies the real humanity of the Christ. And whatever else the doctrine of the Incarnation may mean, it surely implies the same historical finitude for Jesus as for anyone else, including the limitation of his knowledge of science or language and literature. Thus to quote Jesus (or the apostles) as an authority on the authorship of the Pentateuch or the book of Isaiah is almost as absurd as taking him to be an infallible physicist, settling for all time the relationship of earth to sun!

---

[8]For example, Jesus cites "Moses" as author of Leviticus 14 (Priestly laws) and of Deuteronomy 24 ("D" source) and of Exodus (JEP); cf. Matt. 8:4; Mark 10:3; and Mark 12:26 respectively. By the same kind of traditional shorthand Jesus referred to various psalms as what "David said," without regard for the question of actual authorship.

[9]Recall here the critical distinction between Isaiah's oracles (mostly in chapter 1-24) and those of an anonymous prophet of the Exile (Isa. 40-55) now called "Deutero-Isaiah." Parts of Deutero- (and even Trito-?) Isaiah are quoted in Matthew, Luke, Acts, and Romans as, simply, "Isaiah."

The consequence of all this, of course, is that the Lordship of Christ and his authority for the Christian have little or nothing to do with Jesus' statements about the sun or about agriculture—matters incidental and peripheral to the point of his message. He is Lord, not by virtue of his superior knowledge of human arts and science, but by virtue of "taking the form of a servant. . . . And being found in human form he humbled himself and became obedient unto death."[10] He is Lord because, as Scripture and Christian theology alike declare, God raised him from the dead and exalted him.

Here, it seems, we are getting very close to the heart of the matter, and corresponding to the distinction just made regarding Jesus as Lord there is likewise a distinction to be made regarding the Bible as a whole. Just as the Christian's faith in Jesus Christ need not depend on the accuracy of his historically conditioned remarks about Moses or the mustard seed,[11] so the reader of the Bible need not be distracted from the central message and real authority of it by the discovery of peripheral inaccuracies. We have, in short, to acknowledge that its writers never intended to write textbooks on biology or geology, nor to write journalistic accounts of ancient history as such, but they did write to witness to their faith in God and by their testimony transmit that faith and propagate it. It is not as sober, objective history, nor as "great literature" (however great it may indeed be), that the Bible came to be, was preserved, and yet remains "the world's best-seller." It was rather because in and through the testimony of its various and sundry books, in and through its very human words, people encountered the very God of which the writers wrote. As one modern scholar has put it, "The real authority of the Bible is its ability to bring about this encounter," and this is "the authority that counts."[12] Or, to quote another of my mentors:

> The great saints who have found in the Bible the very Word of God, who have been rebuked, humbled, enlightened, cheered, and changed by the Bible, because they have found Christ there, and have found life in him—

---

[10]Philippians 2:7-8, but see the whole creedal poem, 2:6-11; cf. 1 Corinthians 15:1-4 and Romans 1:4.

[11]It has often been noted that the statement about the mustard seed being "the smallest of all the seeds on earth" (Mark 4:31) is not scientifically correct.

[12]Leander E. Keck, *Taking the Bible Seriously* (Nashville: Abingdon Press, 1962) 126, in his valuable chapter, "The Authority That Counts."

these people have not been bothered about the habits of rabbits or whether the bat is a bird.[13]

This is to admit that there are different kinds of "truth," different categories of "fact," in the Scriptures. For instance, attempts to write a "biography" of Jesus came to grief largely because of the kerygmatic nature of the sources, the gospels. Yes, one might sift out a few "historical facts" for such a biography—where and (roughly) when Jesus lived and died, and how he was executed—with some degree of confidence. These were public facts, subject to verification by reference to contemporary records, but such *bruta facta* hardly constitute "gospel" (good news), until they are interpreted in the light of the Easter faith and thus made *revelatory* of a kind of truth altogether different: that Jesus died *for the sins of mankind* and was raised *for their salvation*. Likewise, in virtually every part of the Bible, it is the *value* placed on particular facts or events ("mighty acts of God") that makes them kerygmatic and offers them to succeeding ages as good news. But it is precisely at *this* level of truth, and not among the countless *bruta facta* as such, that many Christians claim to hear the Word of God mediated to them in the Bible. To confuse these different levels, or to equate the *Word* with the human *words* (as in verbal or plenary inspiration), is to reduce the Bible to a kind of monotone oracle and ultimately to trivialize its authority for our day.

This is not to demean all those parts of the Bible that seem to carry no obvious or immediately recognizable "revelatory" value for our time, much less to dismiss them from the canon. One must sympathize with the concern of plenary inspiration—if not with its premises—that "Liberals" tend to *minimize* the importance of some parts of the Bible and, in effect, have a "canon within the Canon." There is truth in the accusation, of course, but to be fair, the tendency is not exclusively that of the "Liberal" nor that of modern times. Martin Luther, as we have noted, would have excised from the canon the Epistle of James, if it had been left to him, insisting that testimony to Jesus Christ be the touchstone of what was truly canonical (regardless of tradition). And for a great segment of Eastern Christendom in the early centuries we may recall that the Apocalypse of John was rejected, and even yet for their heirs it has no place in the lec-

---

[13]Kenneth J. Foreman, "What Is the Bible?" in *Introduction to the Bible*, ed. B. H. Kelly (Richmond: John Knox Press, 1959) 27.

tionary or preaching in their churches. Beyond that it is not inappropriate to remark how Judaism always has given to *Torah* the central place in Tanak, implicitly if not explicitly relegating the rest to a subordinate role. And even within many conservative Christian churches, where lip service is paid to plenary inspiration, actual practice in preaching and teaching would suggest the same tendency. The isolation of certain doctrines as "fundamentals" of the Faith virtually insures it, encouraging (as it does) an appeal to the selected "proof texts" and a tacit dismissal of others. All of which prompts me to ask; practically speaking, can we avoid this tendency? And, theoretically speaking, why should we?

The die was cast for Christians, when they first accepted Paul's dictum, "Christ is the end (*telos*) of the law" (Rom. 10:4) and began to reinterpret Tanak and Jewish tradition in the light of their faith in Jesus as Messiah. It was inevitable that certain elements, like the dietary rules and ritual cleansings, should be abandoned, because they were considered abrogated by the "new covenant" in Christ's blood. And before the New Testament was complete, Christians had "baptized" Tanak as its "*old* covenant," but left no doubt in doing so that its *authority* for them was primarily as preparation for the gospel, as the prophetic promise that had now been fulfilled in Jesus. So the momentum was there very early for a canon within the canon, in the sense that most Christians ever since have read the Old Testament in the light of the New—not vice versa—and thus, in effect, subordinate the one to the other. And even within the New Testament there has been a historic tendency for Roman Catholics to prefer "the Gospel" to "the Epistle," at least in the classical liturgy of the Mass, whereas traditionally Protestants of the Reformed family of churches have emphasized the Pauline Epistles (where, for example, "justification by faith" is prominent). Most conspicuously, there are the sectarian groups who tend to fasten upon one strand of biblical heritage, such as the apocalyptic, and virtually ignore all the rest. A review of their published sermon topics week after week would suggest that their functional canon was indeed very limited—little more than portions of Ezekiel, Daniel and the Book of Revelation.

Perhaps needless to say, what has been true of whole churches and movements is also true of individual readers of the Bible: each of us tends to favor some parts over others, and—whether consciously or not—we thus reflect our personal evaluation of *those* parts, either as somehow more satisfying devotionally, or as more meaningful theologically and ethically, or whatever. But whatever the reasons for this partiality, it is only natural and not something for which we should feel guilty. Unfortunately, certain "back-to-the-Bible" promotions in the churches, well meaning though they may be, have exaggerated the importance of reading the Bible "from cover to cover," as though that in itself were a virtue. Ministers who preach regularly from the texts of the lectionary probably benefit personally from the discipline of study this entails, but it often results in some strained exegesis and somewhat desperate measures to make the appointed text "speak" to the needs of the congregation. In this age of widespread "biblical illiteracy" one may well applaud any efforts to educate people to read the Bible, but surely this can be done without insisting that every book, much less every chapter of it, demands the same attention or offers the same prospect of edification as any other. So to insist, in effect, puts us in the position of that man in the often cited story, who made a daily habit of seeking "divine guidance" from the Bible by randomly opening the book and putting his finger on a verse—whatever it happened to be, that would be his command for the day. The system served him well for a time, but one day he opened his Bible and chanced upon the place (in Matt. 27) where it was said of Judas, "and he went and hanged himself." Not happy with that, the unfortunate seeker tried again, only to land this time on Luke 10:37, where Jesus said, "Go and do likewise."

Such is the danger, it would seem, of treating the Bible as if it were a kind of literary Ouija board or magical answer book. But such is the logical consequence of supposing it to be monolithic either in terms of its literary content or in terms of its relevance for our times. To read the Bible intelligently and with the greatest prospect of hearing in it a Word of God our reading *must* take account of its diversity both in literary genre and historical setting and be directed accordingly in our quest for meaning today. Hence the importance of the prolegomena set forth in the first two or three chapters of this book. What modern scholars have to say about the origin and purpose of the ancient books, far from being the optional "extras" or excess baggage of serious Bible study, can and does provide essential information, enabling us to see and appreciate the rich variety of that holy anthology and the many dimensions of its meaning. Used properly, it can in fact liberate us from all kinds of bondage, whether to dogmatic presuppositions such as those that compel us to allegorize everything, or to wooden literalism such as that which compels us to reduce the sublime to the ridiculous.

The point could be illustrated from almost any section of the Canon; I here restrict my selections to two: one from the Law, the other from the Prophets. On the basis of the Fundamentalist view, presupposing that Moses wrote Genesis (and the rest of Torah) at the dictation of God, it is logical—if not necessary—to argue that the Creation story[14] contains the divinely revealed record of the actual, step-by-step process by which this earth and life upon it came into being. One is thus bound to conclude that our world was literally created in the space of seven days, and (to be entirely consistent) the "days" can hardly mean anything other than twenty-four-hour periods.[15] In this view Genesis gives *the* explanation of the origin of the universe, clearing the field of all others, obliging all who "believe in the Bible" to reject out of hand any scientific hypotheses that would call into question the "truth" of the biblical account. It was this way of thinking that lay behind the dramatic Scopes Trial of 1925—often called the "Monkey Trial" because of the question of biological evolution involved[16]—and that underlies even yet the recent attempts to give "Creationism" equal time with evolution in the public schools.

On the other hand, the modern critical approach to the Creation stor*ies* begins with certain assumptions, too, but very different from those of the Fundamentalist. One is that methodologically it is better to start with the data—linguistic, stylistic, historical, and so on—that lies before us in the text, and ask what it tells us about the sources or authors of the books, rather than to let a theory of inspiration decide the question in advance. Another is that, regardless of authorship or mode of inspiration, what we have in Genesis is an instance of ancient Semitic literature, subject to the same kind of literary and historical analysis as any other piece of human writing. And

---

[14]Note the singular, "story," for it is problematic to admit, in this view, that there is more than one Creation Story, so that one is driven to various machinations to show that the Eden story (Gen. 2-3) is really a continuation of that in ch. 1, or some kind of supplement to it.

[15]It has often been supposed that the "day" in Genesis 1 could mean "a thousand years" (after Ps. 90:4; 2 Pet. 3:8) or some indefinite span of time, thus permitting a curious compromise of literalism, sometimes even suggesting a parallel to modern scientific theories of evolution. But there is no solid ground for such strained exegesis in this passage.

[16]*Tennessee v. Scopes,* tried at Dayton, Tennessee. Scopes was a young science teacher and football coach who was found in violation of a state law against teaching the theory of evolution in public schools. The trial brought the famous lawyers Clarence Darrow and William Jennings Bryan into confrontation, attracting nationwide attention.

what analysis tells us in this case is that at least two different sources (editors) have produced Genesis 1-3, that they were probably separated in time by three or four centuries, and that each had its own, historically conditioned point of view and theological purpose.[17] Moreover—and here the liberating value of this approach becomes most apparent—we are thus prompted to raise the level of question about Genesis 1-3 and its meaning for us, because we now view it in the category of ancient cosmological myth and no longer in that of literal history or "prescientific" science. No longer hamstrung by petty bickering over such questions as where Cain got his wife, or where "Eden" was, we may focus on the more profound and timeless question raised by Genesis, as to the transcendent Ground of all being and the ambiguous, dependent character of the human creature called *Adam*, "Man." Taking our cue from the theological intent of such stories, we are emancipated from the shackles of their primitive cosmology and find their value not in divine information about a process "then" but in a divine invitation "now"—a Word of God that comes *through* the words of ancient men and *to* us here and now, holding before us both the demand and the promise of the *imago dei*.[18]

I used just now (as once or twice before) the term "myth" to refer to the Creation stories, and this calls for further explanation, especially in view of certain unfortunate connotations that cling to the word as used colloquially today. In popular usage it often connotes "fictitious" as opposed to "true" or "actual fact." Thus it is understandable that readers, unless initiated into its technical uses in Anthropology or Comparative Religion, most likely take references to myth in the Bible as derogatory, and perhaps as an outright rejection of the "truth" of the story. But it is a pity if we let the common usage of "myth" stand in the way of new insight, and fail to see the value of the term in its technical sense, as employed by biblical scholars today.[19] What is meant by "myth" is that kind of story, some-

---

[17]Recall that by modern analysis Genesis 1:1-2:4a belongs to the Priestly source (ca. 500 BCE) and Gen. 2:4b-3:24 to the Yahwist (tenth century BCE).

[18]*Imago dei* is Latin for "image of God" (Gen. 1:27), a term expressing the divine *likeness* in the human creature, implying both highest dignity and loftiest responsibility; cf. the very trenchant comments on this passage by B. D. Napier, *Song of the Vineyard* (New York: Harper and Brothers, 1962).

[19]*Taking the Bible Seriously*, 112-14, is especially helpful; cf. also the essay by Avery Dulles, "Symbol, Myth, and the Biblical Revelation," in *New Theology* 4, ed. Martin E. Marty and Dean Peerman (New York: Macmillan, 1967) 39-68.

times dramatized in cultic rites, that objectifies the deepest convictions about the God-man relationship, usually in terms of primeval beginnings or (as in the case of apocalyptic myth) the End-time. In this sense it is beside the point to ask about its truth as an *event in time and space,* for its truth lies at a deeper level of meaning and speaks to us of "what is" rather than "what was." Its *authority* is that of a confession of *faith,* not that of a journalist's account of observable and datable facts. Moreover, to find mythic elements in the Scriptures should pose no great obstacle to the affirmation of their inspiration—unless one means to exclude all metaphorical stories in the Bible—including the parables of Jesus—simply because they were not necessarily factually "true." By what law, indeed, do we suppose that fiction cannot be just as "inspired of God" as historical fact?

The other illustration we take from the Prophets: the story of Jonah. Because the book of Jonah appears as a part of "the twelve minor prophets," two very natural assumptions were ordinarily made about it: first, that (like the other eleven) its name refers to the historical prophet and author of the book; second, its words describe (as do narrative sections of the other books) what actually happened to the prophet whose name it bears— that is, it contains historical events, factually reported. Such has been the predominant and traditional understanding of Jonah over many centuries, and again it is little wonder that conservative readers tend to object to suggestions that (1) the eighth-century Jonah was not its author, only its "hero"; or (2) the story was not to be taken as literally true, but rather as allegorically true. Fundamentalists, in fact, have seen in such suggestions from critical scholars "another modernist attack" on the "truth" of the Bible, and even more sadly, various Christian circles have so insisted on the literal, historical interpretation of Jonah as to make it in some instances a test case for determining whether ministerial candidates are "orthodox" enough for ordination. In this view the meaning of the book of Jonah is bound up with acceptance of every detail—yes, even Jonah's ride in the belly of the great fish—as a historical fact, and many heated arguments have turned on the issue of what kind of fish that must have been, and how a man could breathe in such conditions for three days and three nights! Its value is thus seen to rest in its "object lesson" on disobedience—see what happens to a human being who runs away from God's command—or else in the miracle of Jonah's rescue from disaster.

These values are not to be despised, and yet how much *more* the book can mean, when set free from bondage to pedestrian literalism! Aside from the *sacrificium mentis* it imposes on the reader, the tragedy of a narrowly literalistic position is that it defeats its own avowed purpose; it dishonors the very truth that it seeks to defend, because in its preoccupation with proving this or that event "really happened" it often misses altogether the one overriding point, the ever so much more profound lesson, which allegorical or metaphorical stories like Jonah were meant to give. As marvelous as God's rescue of Jonah may be, far more amazing still is the miracle of Israel's resurrection from the death of exile in Babylonia, which the story symbolizes, and the wondrous enlargement of vision and of mission that the book as a whole promotes. Set within its proper historical and theological setting, and cut free from traditional misconceptions about its literary genre, the real uniqueness and distinctive purpose of the little book are allowed to stand forth, and Jonahs of our own time are challenged to have done with their wilting "gourd vines" and become sensitive to the whole cities of human souls "who know not their right hand from their left."

How can the Bible be "Word of God" to this generation in this our own place and time? I put the question in this form on purpose, and the key word is "can," because it is not my intention to prescribe but only to recommend and to suggest what is possible, given the nature of the sacred Scriptures and the character of the contemporary world. In one sense, if the authority of the Bible is ultimately that of God himself, using these books to mediate his Word to us, it would be foolish and presumptuous for any single interpreter to prescribe or to pontificate for others precisely what that Word is. "God moves in mysterious ways," and who can say in advance just how (or *where* in the Bible) God will speak to readers today? One clear implication of this is that the believing reader of the Bible should be *open* to the possibility at all times, therefore reading receptively (prayerfully?) and expectantly. Reading the Bible this way can, of course, be risky, because there is the possibility that the Word that we hear, like that which the ancients heard, will be a Word of summons, inviting the reader to active participation in the story he is reading. It may, again, be a Word of rebuke and judgment, convicting us of sin and guilt, whether personal or corporate. Or it could be that in what we hear is the assurance of pardon, the Word of forgiveness, which in itself carries life-changing potential and the call to a new future. In any case, as the "Letter to the Seven Churches"

(Rev. 2-3) urges, "he who has an ear, let him hear what the Spirit says to the churches."[20]

What I have come to, then, is essentially what John Calvin long ago said:

> For as God alone is a fit witness to himself in his Word, so also the Word will not find acceptance in men's hearts before it is sealed by the inward testimony of the Spirit. . . . Scripture indeed is self authenticated.[21]

While scholarly books, commentaries, and other aids to exegesis may be of great value, even indispensable, as means of discovering the original message (or messages) of the Bible, they cannot guarantee that we shall invariably hear that message as God's Word *to us*. Only the Spirit of the God who inspired the message can make it authoritative for us in our day, so that the ancient message becomes more than interesting facts about Israel or the early church, becomes indeed a confrontation with God himself. When that happens—and it does still happen—then the Word is no longer an ancient message *about* God but is a contemporary Word *from* God, involving us totally (not just intellectually) in God's purposes for this world. When that happens, then and only then can we talk of proof or guarantee of the Bible's authority, and that not in terms of neat, logical arguments in defense of a theory of inspiration, but rather as a fact of one's own experience.

---

[20]Revelation 2:7, 11, and so on—part of a recurring refrain.

[21]John Calvin, *Institutes of the Christian Religion*, I. 7.4.

For Further Reading

Achtemeier, Paul J. *The Inspiration of Scripture: Problems and Proposals.* Philadelphia: Westminster Press, 1980.

Barbour, R. S. "The Bible—Word of God?" In *Biblical Studies: Essays in Honor of William Barclay.* J. R. McKay and J. F. Miller, eds. Philadelphia: Westminster Press, 1976. Pages 28-42.

Barr, James. *The Scope and Authority of the Bible.* Philadelphia: Westminster Press, 1980.

Gilkey, Langdon. "Scripture, History, and the Quest for Meaning." In *Humanizing America's Iconic Book.* Society of Biblical Literature, Centennial Addresses, 1980. K. H. Richards, ed. Chico CA: Scholars Press, 1982.

Keck, Leander E. *Taking the Bible Seriously.* Nashville: Abingdon Press, 1962.

Neil, William. *The Rediscovery of the Bible.* New York: Harper and Brothers, 1954.

Swaim, J. Carter. *Right and Wrong Ways to Use the Bible.* Philadelphia: Westminster Press, 1953.

Additional help with "Myth" in the Bible:

Dulles, Avery. "Symbol, Myth, and the Biblical Revelation." In *New Theology* 4. Martin E. Marty and Dean Peerman, eds. New York: Macmillan, 1967. Pages 39-68.

Eliade, Mircea. *Myths, Dreams and Mysteries.* Trans. Philip Mairet. New York: Harper, 1967.

Loew, Cornelius. *Myth, Sacred History, and Philosophy.* New York: Harcourt, Brace, and World, 1967.

Throckmorton, B. H. *The New Testament and Mythology.* London: Darton, Longman and Todd, 1960; reprint: Philadelphia: Westminster Press, 1959.

Subject Index

Aaron, 40
Abraham (Abram), 158, 165, 166, 201
Acts of the Apostles, 50, 54, 80, 102
Ahaz, 31
Alexandria, 169, 170, 175
Alexandrian text, 103
Alexandrinus, Codex, 135
allegory, allegorizing, 160, 165, 166, 169, 174, 180
Allen, William, 127
amanuensis (scribe), 50
Amarna Letters, 200n
American Standard Version, 138
Amos, 28, 29
Antioch (of Syria), 170, 175
Antiochus IV (Epiphanes), 49, 75
apocalyptic(-ism), 48, 49, 67, 218
Apocrypha (Old Testament), 47, 48, 66, 67, 77, 88, 179
Apocrypha (New Testament), 85n
apostle(s), 50, 82, 214
Apostolic Fathers, 80, 112, 151
apostolic period, 50
Aquila of Pontus, 109
Aquinas, Thomas, 177
Arabic, 111, 177n
Aramaic, 72n, 206n
archaeology, 153, 195-207
Aristeas, Letter to, 9, 108
Assyria(n), 27-32, 69, 70, 200
Astruc, Jean, 184
Athanasius, 88, 90
Augustine of Hippo, 172
authority of Scripture, 209-24

Ba'al, Ba'alism, 26, 203
Babylonia(n), 36, 71, 200, 201, 203

Barabbas, 113
Barnabas, Epistle of, 85, 166
Baruch, 35
Bathsheba, 18, 19
Bede, the Venerable, 118
Bernard of Clairvaux, 173, 174
Bishops' Bible, 126-28
Bultmann, Rudolf, 192
Byzantine text, 103, 112

Caedman, 118
Calvin, John, 121, 125, 126, 180, 184, 224
canon, canonical, 1n, 2, 63, 66-90, 172, 211, 212, 217
Catholic (General) Epistles, 51, 57, 102, 110
Chaldean(s), 33-35
Challoner, Bishop Richard, 133
Christology, 89, 164, 187, 190, 194
Chronicler, 44, 45, 49, 72
Chronicles (1 or 2), 12n, 18n, 39, 44, 49
chronology of biblical literature, 60, 199, 200
Clement of Alexandria, 85
Clement, First Epistle of, 80, 81, 85
codex, 104
Colossians, 51
Complutensian Polyglot, 178, 179
Coptic, 87n, 111; *see also* Nag Nammadi
Corinthians (1 or 2), 51, 80, 186
cosmology, ancient, 150-52, 182, 221
Council of Constance, 121
Council of Nicea, 88, 171n
Council of Trent, 66, 67
Coverdale, Miles, 123, 124, 126, 140
creation story, 20-23, 202, 203, 220
Creationism, 220